# THE TRAMPLED GRASS

Tributary States and Self-reliance
in the Indian Ocean Zone
of Peace

*George W. Shepherd, Jr.*

New York
Westport, Connecticut
London

**Library of Congress Cataloging-in-Publication Data**

Shepherd, George W.
  The trampled grass.

  Bibliography: p.
  Includes index.
  1. Africa, Eastern–Foreign relations.  2. Africa,
Eastern—Dependency on foreign countries.  3. Africa,
Eastern—Politics and government—1960– .
4. Africa, Southern—Foreign relations.  5. Africa,
Southern—Politics and government.  6. Indian Ocean
Region—Dependency on foreign countries.  7. Nuclear-
weapon-free zones—Indian Ocean Region.  I. Title.
DT365.8.S54  1987b      327′.09182′4      87-9302
ISBN 0-275-92608-7 (pbk. : alk. paper)

Copyright © 1987 by George W. Shepherd, Jr.

All rights reserved. No portion of this book may be reproduced, by any process or technique, without the express written consent of Greenwood Press, Inc. For information address Greenwood Press, 88 Post Road West, Westport, Connecticut 06881.

A hardcover edition of *The Trampled Grass* is available from Greenwood Press (Contributions in Political Science; 169; ISBN 0-313-25772-8).

Library of Congress Catalog Card Number: 87-9302
ISBN: 0-275-92608-7

First published 1987

Paperback edition 1987

Praeger Publishers, 1 Madison Avenue, New York, NY 10010
A division of Greenwood Press, Inc.

Printed in the United States of America

The paper used in this book complies with the Permanent Paper Standard issued by the National Information Standards Organization (Z39.48–1984).

10  9  8  7  6  5  4  3  2  1

# Contents

| | |
|---|---|
| *Preface* | *vii* |
| *Abbreviations* | *ix* |
| 1. Origins of Dominance: Power, Tribute, and Liberation | 1 |
|    *The Dominance of the Core Superpowers* | 3 |
|    *Tribute and War* | 6 |
|    *Self-reliance and Liberation* | 13 |
|    *The People's Right to Peace* | 16 |
| 2. Subimperialism and South Africa: Controlling Resources and Liberation on the Cape Route | 21 |
|    *The White Power Protection System* | 23 |
|    *The Failure of "Constructive Engagement" and Change* | 32 |
|    *Namibia: Plunder and War* | 42 |
|    *Sanctions against South African Racism* | 53 |
| 3. War on the Horn among Tributary States: Intervention from Above and Revolution from Below | 67 |
|    *U.S.-Soviet Rivalry and the Ethiopian Revolution* | 68 |
|    *The Somali and Eritrean Pawns in the Great Game* | 77 |
|    *The Second Scramble for the Nile: The Afro-Arab Sudan* | 83 |
|    *Civilian Rule and Reconciliation* | 86 |
|    *Conclusion* | 89 |
| 4. The Struggle for Self-reliant Development against Dominance: The Kenya Comprador Class Rule and Tanzania's Self-reliant Transition | 93 |

|  |  |
|---|---|
| *Kenya and the* Matajiri *Compradors* | 95 |
| *Tanzania's Transition to Self-reliance* | 104 |

5. Collective Self-reliance: The Indian Ocean Zone of Peace — 119
    *Collective Self-reliance as Development* — 119
    *The Indian Ocean Zone of Peace* — 128
    *South-South Regional Cooperation* — 131

6. Liberation from Dominance — 141
    *Nondominance* — 141
    *Demilitarization and Arms Control in the Indian Ocean Zone of Peace* — 144
    *People's Rights: The End of Dominance* — 153

*Bibliography* — *159*

*Index* — *171*

# Preface

This book was conceived of as an attempt to form an adequate explanation of the failures of former colonial peoples, who nevertheless continue full of hope in their search for a better life. Their search has been the greatest human rights enterprise of the twentieth century, yet it is far from completed.

Failures have been obvious when judged in terms of the world conceived of by the original nationalist leaders, from Nkrumah to Nehru and Sukarno and Mao. But if there is an explanation for these failures, then there is a basis for revitalization and for a new projection of freedom.

The title of this book is derived from an African proverb that gives some initial insight into the nature of the conflict. It will be appreciated by those who know Africa firsthand that once the bull elephants have trampled the grass, it can be burned to generate new life. The people then build again.

One caution: "tribute" is used here to characterize a world system of relations between superpowers and new states. It is an allegory for the position of weak states in a world dominated by powerful concentrations of industrial capital and superpower rivalry. War, famine, and exploitation follow the course of the arms race and the struggle for dominance in which the Third World is more often the victim than the victor.

Whether the countries of the Third World can escape their tributary status under the superpowers through self-reliance is a subject of great controversy. This book analyzes self-reliance as it has been presented by a number of African intellectuals and leaders. The issues are hotly debated. Readers will have to decide for themselves who is correct.

My research, travels, and personal experiences cover a lifetime. But the primary research was made possible by two extensive tours of Africa and the Indian Ocean in 1979 and again in 1981 and 1986. The generous and hospitable people from all walks of life who provided information, views, and insights are too numerous to note. Universities where I visited and lectured—from Cape Town to Nairobi, New Delhi to Perth—were particularly helpful. Government officials were extensively interviewed. State Department and USIA officials were of great assistance, despite differences in views which they patiently endured. Soviet officials and academics were also interviewed.

Research sources are noted in the bibliography and are far too extensive to outline here, but two sources should be particularly mentioned, since they have consented to the use of extensive information originally collected for them. One is *Africa Today* which has published several of my related articles on South Africa and the Horn, and the other is the Carnegie Endowment for International Peace and its Indo-American Indian Ocean Task Force, headed by Selig Harrison and V. Subrahmanyan. All previously published material has been extensively rewritten. Earlier versions of chapters on South Africa, the Horn, Namibia, and the Indian Ocean Zone of Peace were presented as papers at conferences on the Indian Ocean at Perth, Australia, in 1979, and Dalhousie, New Brunswick, Canada, in 1982. The 1983 Africa Human Rights Development conference in Buffalo, New York, the 1984 Indo-American Indian Ocean Task Force conference in New Delhi, and the 1985 African Studies Association meeting in New Orleans were occasions for other presentations.

The discussion and comments of students in seminars have been important contributions. Several research assistants, especially Dr. Mustapha Pasha, have assisted with materials but are not responsible for my conclusions. Shirley Shepherd's editing has given clarity and brevity to several drafts.

# Abbreviations

| | |
|---|---|
| ACOA | American Committee on Africa |
| ACP | Africa, Caribbean, and Pacific |
| AID | Agency for International Development (U.S.) |
| ANC | African National Congress (South Africa) |
| ANZUS | Australia, New Zealand, and United States |
| ARMSCOR | Armaments Development and Production Corporation (South Africa) |
| ASEAN | Association of South-East Asian Nations |
| CENTCOM | Central Command (U.S.) |
| CIA | Central Intelligence Agency (U.S.) |
| COMECON | Council for Mutual Economic Assistance |
| COSATU | Congress of South African Trade Unions |
| DTA | Democratic Turnhalle Alliance (Namibia) |
| ECOWAS | Economic Community of West African States |
| EEC | European Economic Community |
| ELF | Eritrean Liberation Front (Ethiopia) |
| EPLF | Eritrean People's Liberation Front (Ethiopia) |
| EPRP | Ethiopian People's Revolutionary Party |
| FLN | National Liberation Front (Algeria) |
| FRELIMO | Front for the Liberation of Mozambique |
| GAWU | General and Allied Workers Union (South Africa) |
| GCC | Gulf Council of Cooperation |
| HNP | Herstigte National Party (South Africa) |
| ILO | International Labor Organization |
| IMF | International Monetary Fund |
| IOZP | Indian Ocean Zone of Peace |

| | |
|---|---|
| KANU | Kenya African National Union |
| KAU | Kenya African Union |
| MAAG | Military Assistance Advisory Group (U.S.) |
| MEISON | All-Ethiopian Socialist Movement |
| MNR | Mozambique National Resistance |
| MPLA | Popular Movement for the Liberation of Angola |
| NALT | Naval Arms Limitation Talks |
| NATO | North Atlantic Treaty Organization |
| NDC | National Development Corporation (Tanzania) |
| NIC | newly industrialized country |
| NIEO | New International Economic Order |
| NNF | Namibia National Front |
| NRM | National Resistance Movement (Uganda) |
| NUP | National Unionist Party (Sudan) |
| NWFZ | nuclear-weapon-free zone |
| OAU | Organization of African Unity |
| OECD | Organization for Economic Cooperation and Development |
| OPEC | Organization of Petroleum Exporting Countries |
| PAC | Pan-Africanist Congress |
| PLAN | People's Liberation Army of Namibia |
| SABA | South African Black Alliance |
| SACTU | South African Congress of Trade Unions |
| SADCC | Southern African Development Coordination Conference |
| SADF | South African Defense Force |
| SALT | Strategic Arms Limitation Talks |
| SLBM | submarine-launched ballistic missile |
| SLCM | sea-launched cruise missile |
| SPLA | Sudanese People's Liberation Army |
| SPLM | Sudanese People's Liberation Movement |
| SWAPO | South-West Africa People's Organization |
| TIB | Tanzania Industrial Bank |
| U.A.R. | United Arab Republic |
| UDF | United Democratic Front (South Africa) |
| UDI | unilateral declaration of independence |
| UNITA | National Union for the Total Independence of Angola |
| UWSA | Federation of United Workers of South Africa |
| WSLF | Western Somalia Liberation Front |
| ZANU | Zimbabwe African National Union |
| ZAPU | Zimbabwe African People's Union |

*THE TRAMPLED GRASS*

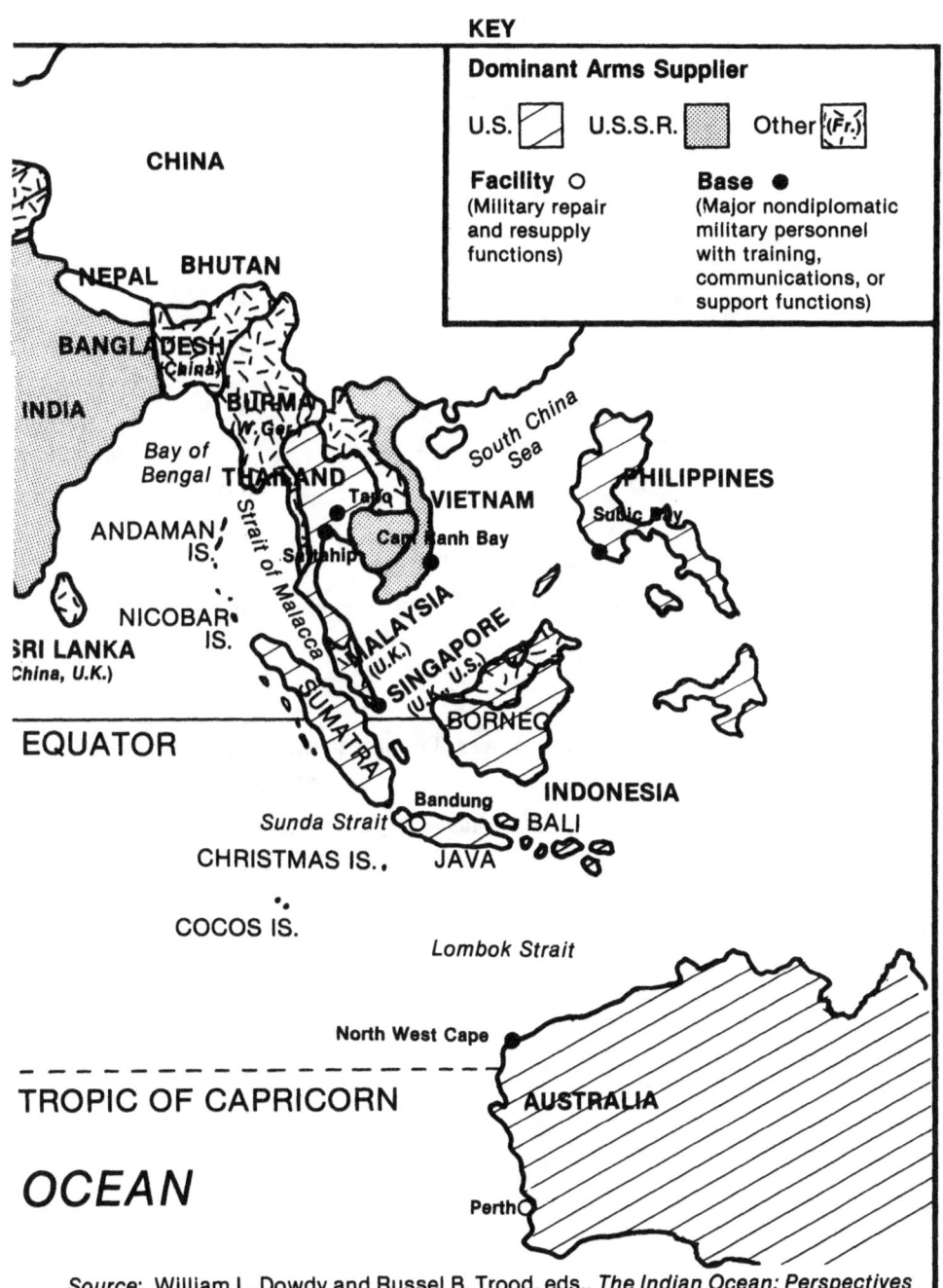

Source: William L. Dowdy and Russel B. Trood, eds., *The Indian Ocean: Perspectives on a Strategic Arena* (Durham, N.C.: Duke University Press, 1985); U.S. Arms Control and Disarmament Agency, *World Military Expenditures and Arms Transfers* (Washington, D.C.: ACDA, 1985); Center for Defense Information (Washington, D.C.); International Institute for Strategic Studies (London); Stockholm International Peace Research Institute (Uppsala); *New York Times*.

To the Soweto students—a new generation

> Courage brothers. Despair is only for the defeated.
>
> —Oswald Mbuyesni Mtshali,
> "Sounds of a Cowhide Drum"

# 1

# Origins of Dominance: Power, Tribute, and Liberation

> When two bull elephants fight, the grass gets trampled.
>
> —Swahili proverb

The achievement of independence by over half of the world's people has been widely hailed as the greatest advance in human freedom in this century. The end of imperialism, it is claimed, was the beginning of a new era for the human race. As Rupert Emerson expressed it: "A great era of human history has come to a close ... the era of Western domination over the rest of Mankind."[1]

However, conflict has spread through these areas of newly established independent states, leaving millions of victims in its wake. The superpowers have entered the arena to protect their interests and to compete for the loyalty of these new states. The conflicts have threatened to escalate from local religious wars to a major international war. Political fanaticism of the right and left has spread, bringing down existing governments, disrupting trade, and introducing new patterns that affect the entire world economy. Leaders who brought independence have been overthrown; military and iron-handed regimes have replaced them in the name of stability; conflict has grown and with it, deep antagonism between the old world and the new.

Is there any explanation for this chaos and failure of human expectations?

This book assumes that the answers can be derived from the idea that the old system of dominance has taken on new forms that are poorly understood. The mistake of most observers is that they assume that Western domination has, in fact, withdrawn or been defeated in favor of national self-determination. Closer to reality is the view that the world system of Western dominance has at best been fractured but its major structures remain intact. "I see no possibility of liberation for Latin America in this century," stated the liberation theologian Jose Comblin.[2] The capitalist system of imperialism in the Western world which began about the time Columbus set sail for the "new Indies" has remained intact, L. S. Stavrianos argues, and, if anything, has grown in power.[3]

New ways of describing the expansion of human freedom through new states cannot erase the reality of the continuation of the exploitation of the weak by the strong and the domination of the world system by those who have power. Yet, does this new dominance pattern mean that the mountain of struggle for human freedom in the Third World "has labored and brought forth only a mouse," and that the majority are worse off than before?[4]

A limited optimism was expressed by the elderly and prominent Chinese social scientist Huan Ziang: "I think the world is now better than it was when I was born. That was a very bad world. So many countries have independence; the suffering of the people although still very great, is a little less, compared with former times. But there has been one very big change. The people are now more politically conscious."[5]

If decolonization and political consciousness have brought even limited advances in human freedom, how is freedom defined and what are the trends? These are major questions of our era that can only be answered by establishing a theoretical perspective that raises them. William Appleman Williams put it well: "In order to think seriously about empire as a way of life, we must choose a strategy of enquiry that is appropriate to the subject."[6]

The liberal and largely Western decolonization concepts we have used are no longer adequate to explain the growing conflicts between Third World countries and former imperial powers. New weak states repress opportunity for human rights development in part because of the character of the global system into which they have emerged. How we have looked at independence in the twentieth century needs to be reconsidered.

Nation-state power has been considered the primary means of creating and perpetuating the benefits of social organization on behalf of Westernized man. Despite a limited advance in human rights in the new states, the major benefits of the international power system have continued to flow from the South to the North. Fundamental inequality over the past 150 years has widened, between a human quality of life for what dependence theorists have called the Westernized "core," and the misery of the "Third World periphery." Deepening absolute poverty has widened the quality of life gap and increased the violations of human rights.[7]

There is almost as much illusion among Third World intellectuals as in the First World about the nature of world power and the demise of dominance. New forms of sovereignty and the heady atmosphere of international conferences and recognition are deceptive symbols of power. The old forms of dominance are there, but are easily hidden by the new opportunities open to the assimilated elites. Their own vested interests perpetuate these illusions, since they are frequently associated through education and employment with the dominant powers.

In the tributary analysis, this often corrupt and privileged coalition of elites is considered a transnational political class, willing to collaborate in order to obtain the protection of external powers and the weapons with which to maintain their increasingly militarized regimes. Their transnational class interest has broken down the sharp dichotomies of race and colonialism and provided the basis for continuing the so-called development objectives of the dominant powers. René Dumont in *False Start in Africa* initially identified this problem. He argues that a small elite in the new African states—corrupt, inept bureaucrats, nouveau riche bourgeoisie, and intellectual Westernized syncophants—have hijacked the revolution. Aided by ambitious military officers and even tribal leaders and clergy, they have seized the system of power and privilege.[8] They have widened the gaps of poverty and intensified ancient tribal, racial, and national enmities. Working on behalf of their own privileges, they have perpetuated the domination of the Westernized core. Leaders courageous enough to oppose them, of whom Gandhi, Bhutto, Mboya, and Biko might be mentioned, have frequently found imprisonment and martyrdom to be their reward. The military coup has often been employed as a means for making adjustments between rival elites within this political class.

## THE DOMINANCE OF THE CORE SUPERPOWERS

Dumont's insight is limited, however, because he fails to link the responsibility for this failure to the world system as much as to the Third World elites and the individuals who serve dominance.[9] The system of power is rooted in the continuance of northern domination and privilege. The European colonial powers' "scramble for Africa" in the nineteenth century has been replaced by two new core superpowers whose interests and capabilities are very similar to their colonial predecessors. However, their power is much greater as they control core power regions (East and West). Their means are more sophisticated and indirect: working through "independent" states in the regions of the Third World. This new tributary system of dependent states who associate themselves closely with a core power region and obtain protection in return for trade resources and military alliance has replaced colonialism. In short, indirect rule has achieved a new level of control in the world system that Lord Lugard would never have dreamed possible.

Rivalry between the two core superpowers, the United States and the Soviet Union, for the allegiance of the tributary states has become the center of the post–World War II crisis between the North and the South. Following the Korean War, the focus of rivalry shifted to new crisis centers in the Middle East, Central America, and the Indian Ocean region. Superpower rivalry has been central to the crises of Vietnam and the Persian Gulf, the conflicts between Israel and the Arab states, the irredentism and national wars of the Horn of Africa, the unsettled enmity between Muslims and Hindus, and the racial struggle for control over the rich and strategic region of southern Africa. All of these have provided new arenas for the rivalry between the two superpowers to preserve vital resources, trade, and strategic position.

In a study for the World Council of Churches, Marek Thee stated: "Historically, socio-politically, and technologically, the great powers represent a higher class in the nation-state system. They have mastered the use of force, devising a vast gamut of methods from militarily supported, political/diplomatic pressures to outright military intervention."[10]

Regional conflicts involving religion and boundaries have become important variables in the new state crises, and they have frequently become the means for indirect intervention by the core superpowers. The two centers of power view the rivalries of the new states as an opportunity to extend their interests, through access to trade and resources, as well as their global security struggle. And, in turn, the small states exploit this superpower rivalry for arms and aid. This later "scramble" is different from the earlier one because it uses indirect rather than direct establishment of political-military control. It encompasses Latin America, Africa, the Middle East, and Asia, with particular emphasis in the Middle Eastern, South Asian, and African regions bordering on the Indian Ocean. These regional conflicts have moved to the center of the world crisis and have had a global impact. The conventional view in international politics and area studies that considers antagonisms such as Somalia's irredentist war against Ethiopia without noting the global linkages has missed the importance of the new power relationship. The old rivalries have escalated and become the tributary wars of the superpowers. The new states, as they have emerged, have been caught in the hegemony of core power interests and superpower rivalry. This perception is contested by regionalists who fail to see the forest for the trees. The importance of new state leadership in policy making cannot be denied. The leaders are not puppets and have moral responsibility for their actions. But they are held by the major currents of the global system and can only modify their course without changing basic direction. Third World leaders can and do declare war, and tributary people make huge sacrifices, but the outcome is determined by economic and military forces they only remotely influence.

The core powers have supplied the means for Arabs and Israelis to fight three wars, for Somalia to attack Ethiopia, and for Iraq and Iran to wage a major war. Pakistan and India have fought each other four times with heavy weapons provided by the dominant powers. Because the outbreak, as well as the outcome, of these conflicts cannot be explained simply on a regional level, the concept of the tributary state, more accurately than the weak state or "dependent or interdependent" state, captures the interrelationship of dominant power and tributary responsibility for regional warfare in the Third World.

This relationship of dominance and tribute is also seen in the repression and internal inequities resulting from superpower support for the tributary class. While the dominant powers are not entirely responsible for the repression of dictators like Idi Amin and the corruption of the Shah of Iran, the support provided the tributary state in loans and investments, as well as in military supplies and training, is crucial. It perpetuates a tributary ruler's repressive regime, with its violations of human rights, long after it would have been overthrown by internal opposition.[11]

Thus, a tributary state is not a puppet state, but in return for providing "facilities" to one of the superpowers its political class is subsidized, protected from internal and external enemies, and even tolerated in its excesses of persecution of internal minorities or of external aggression. However, when such policies reach a point of threatening directly the interests of the patron power, the reins of restraint are pulled sharply. Provided it is made clear that the withdrawal of superpower protection will be the price for noncompliance, an acceptable accommodation or regime change takes place. This drastic step is very seldom taken, not because of moral insensitivity but because the superpower does not want to lose its strategic "facilities." The Third World illusion that a Third World state can control this relationship, especially after the weaker partner has become a liability, has contributed to the overthrow of many tributary regimes.

The consequences of this superpower confrontation for Third World peoples and states is not generally fully recognized. Not only have they paid the price of continuing economic exploitation, but they have also become the front-line combatants in a violent rivalry between the superpowers that has frequently led to regional wars and internal upheavals. Casualties and loss of life have been enormous. In addition, resources have been drained or remained undeveloped. While the tributary elites have grown rich, the expected redistribution of wealth has failed to materialize. The diversion of resources to the purchase of arms, either as a part of the wider arms race or for use in internal repression or wars against each other, has been disastrous. The casualties have already been greater than in all of World War II.[12] The refugees from these conflicts have been numbered in the hundreds of millions, and the consequences of these conflicts have reached crisis levels, overwhelming the humanitarian agencies of the world with the escalating human need.

One of the objectives of the superpowers in this indirect system of rivalry is to escape the price of ultimate war themselves. Thus, the tributary system has enabled the major powers to stand outside dangerous direct confrontation. In the era of nuclear weapons, the suicidal consequences of atomic war have exerted great pressure on the superpowers to resort to maneuvering through the "expendable" Third World states.

These dangers and inequities have created a new freedom movement against internal repression. And Third World reaction to the wars and exploitation of tributary states has contributed to the emergence of a rival elite to the tributary class. "Dialectically, human rights are both victims of militarization and provide an effective tool to counter it."[13]

Reactions have varied from cultural, religious, and military to active popular revolution. A pattern of revolt has arisen, rooted in a deep cultural awareness and similar to that of the earlier Afro-Arab and Asian nationalism, but also giving rise to a new class consciousness and struggle against the tributary class for self-reliance. The Afghans, Iranians, and Namibians have resorted to populist resistance and armed struggle to oppose the new and old intrusions of the superpowers and their camp followers. Though it has led to protracted conflict, the struggle for self-reliance as a means for obtaining the peoples' right to development and peace has become a rallying point for a progressive class against tribute and dominance. They have begun the revolt in some cases only to be repressed, and they have then turned to armed struggle, as in South Africa, Afghanistan, and El Salvador. In other states, like Tanzania, Iran, and Nicaragua, an initial breakout from dominance has been achieved, but the long struggle toward self-reliant development has only begun.

## TRIBUTE AND WAR

The tributary state analysis is a product of the general quest for a new theory about the nature of state relations in a global system which can no longer be viewed simply from the standpoint of the values and interests of Western dominance and the myths of state independence.[14]

One of the major contributions of dependency theory has been to revive the study of development using a new paradigm that requires new value criteria and concepts of social change.[15] Tributary analysis, while using dependency and underdevelopment concepts, is influenced by the multicausal explanation of power relationships between states. A single factor, primary explanation of historical change is too simplistic. As Johan Galtung has maintained, imperialism is much too complicated a phenomenon to be constrained within the single-cause framework.[16]

> It may well be that at the present juncture in world history in looking at international relations at large, an economic point of view would be the most fruitful in explaining what is going on.
> However, it is felt that there is a need for a broader theory of imperialism that also can come to grips with other phenomena, some of them contemporary, some of them from the past, some of them to come in a possibly very near future.[17]

The tributary explanation of nation-state behavior in the structure of the world system views power as comprised of a mixture of consent and coercion. If economic interests are predominant at certain times in the formation of classes and group dynamics, they play a subordinate role to other forces such as security or ethnicity in different circumstances and stages of change. The neglect of production forces and their role in class formation in contemporary Western social science does not justify an exclusive preoccupation with them. The tributary analysis recognizes the importance of the security or protection drive of social groups under certain conditions. The herd instinct of self-preservation can be regarded as a basic source of nationality. The territorial (geographic and ethnic) imperatives associated with this group consciousness are a fundamental part of human behavior. Therefore, the drive to preserve the group against perceived external enemies is a basic source of ethnic, national consciousness. The class struggle for the control of the means of production is another way groups collectivize to protect themselves. Thus, ethnicity and nationalism as well as class are different forms of the organization of power and production to protect and advance the interests of the groups involved. National and ethnic expressions of this are cultural, though they also have a class dimension which may or may not be determinative. The classic case where it has not been determinative is the settler states of Africa, where the white working class has identified with the core power interest and against the African working class. The predominance of class, race, or nationalism varies according to historical conditions, as Galtung has argued. The tributary theory is not a single-explanation thesis, and it does not aim simply at the identification of the security drive, both defensive and offensive. It seeks to explain why the policies of the new states, as projected by their ruling classes and elites, are usually subordinated to the dominant interests of external hegemonic powers.

The dependency analysis has made a major contribution in its focus on the underlying reality of the international capitalist system which structures the relationship between the core powers and the periphery.[18] However, the nation-state system is not simply or basically an economic relationship. Economically and politically, the contemporary world is divided into state capitalist and state socialist systems, rather than comprising a single international capitalist system. Since the end of World War II, two dominant core political/economic systems have been competing for the Third World: the Soviet–COMECON (Council for Mutual Economic Assistance) system, and the U.S.–OECD (Organization for Economic Cooperation and Development) system, to which Japan has been admitted.

The basic conflict between East and West in Europe is reinforced by the security considerations of the Warsaw Pact and the North Atlantic Treaty Organization (NATO). These cold war centers of power appear to be fracturing and withdrawing like giant glaciers, and new axes of power are emerging to challenge them. Fred Halliday has argued that "Cold War II" must be distinguished from "Cold War I" as essentially an East-West rivalry for control of the South:

> The onset of the Second Cold War owed little to conflict in Europe. The Berlin issue was dormant while Cold War I began in Europe and then shifted to the Far East. The events that precipitated Cold War II lay in the third world, in, for example the Arc of Crisis, the region running from Afghanistan through Iran and the Arab world to the Horn of Africa.[19]

The colonial system has been replaced by tributary states of the core powers in a Cold War II rivalry.

This East-West pyramidal power system is evident, not only in the arms race, but in core relations with the periphery. The repression of Mossadegh who was a Westernized Iranian nationalist, by the United States and Great Britain during the 1950s inevitably led to the overthrow of Western interests in 1978–1979. Thus, this security drive is frequently counterproductive to the actual economic interests of the core power. The objective of each superpower, the preservation of core power supremacy, is highly nationalistic and even "Bonapartist." Within each superpower, this power projection easily becomes confused with the universal, since both superpowers have ultimate pride and conceive of themselves as incorporating the world's interests in their own national interest.[20]

Thus, the U.S. world view is that international order and its own capitalist system ultimately depend upon American virtue and power. The Soviet Union has its own version of this in terms of socialist security and human liberation, which depends upon the defense of "the motherland of socialism." Neither of these class-based visions is true, in either the short or long run, as Harold Laski foresaw.[21] But the concentration of power creates illusions of grandeur and destiny among those who rule the state power systems, and they often fail to see the ways in which they have lost control to new, emergent centers.

Thomas Hobbes, in his *Leviathan*, described how the strong have provided protection for the weak in return for benefits which have usually disproportionately favored the protector. Weaker groups have traditionally been willing to pay for protection in various forms of tribute, from "gold and beautiful maidens" to resources and contingents of armed men, ready to fight for the protector of the empire.

With the expansion of the industrial empires of eighteenth-century Europe, economic rewards were used to incorporate the Asian and African mercantile class. Later, when the system began to decline in the twentieth century, as Harold Laski argued, industrial states resorted to war to maintain the central capitalist system that had subjected the weaker societies.[22] Thus, colonialism was weakened by two world wars that resulted in the rise of a new center of power: the U.S.S.R. It was the cost of these struggles, in addition to the conflicts with the nationalists, that led to the rapid decolonization process in Asia, Africa, and the Middle East. However, the resilience of postwar international capitalism, under American dominance, enabled Europe to maintain a continuing relationship of unequal exchange, despite independence and the challenge presented by Soviet socialism.

Force has always been maximized by dominant powers at the point of decline of empire. Following the first scramble for Africa, increased force was necessary to maintain Western colonial power. This resulted in an arms race and contributed to the outbreak of World War I. A continuation of this rivalry in the 1930s with Japan, Italy, and Germany precipitated World War II. The postwar world has been dominated by the cold war, which since the 1970s has primarily become a struggle between the U.S. and Soviet systems for control of the emergent states of the Third World. Initially, they came into conflict through tributaries, such as Iran and Iraq, and Somalia and Ethiopia. However, strong indications that this indirect rivalry was failing to provide the security and control the superpowers sought led both to resort to a direct buildup of naval and land forces around the Indian Ocean in the 1980s. Although the superpowers will deploy their own forces only as a last resort, World War III may result from a continuation of this Cold War II confrontation of the tributary system.

Because the West perceives that the Soviet threat has expanded into previously exclusive Western spheres of influence in the Third World, in both an economic and a strategic sense, security considerations have increasingly motivated U.S. policy. In the past, force has been used by the United States indirectly through subimperial tributaries like Iran and South Africa. Following the defection of Iran and the declaration of the Carter Doctrine, which claimed that America's interests were vital in the Persian Gulf, the most extensive deployment of U.S. armed forces since the Vietnam War has taken place in the Indian Ocean under what is known as U.S. CENTCOM (Central Command).

The Soviet Union, as a superpower, does not stand outside this world system of dominance. Despite the fact that the Soviets have a different approach to the Third World and are obviously not utilizing the same economic techniques to exploit new states, they have built into COMECON dependent and tributary relationships.[23] However, the basis for their expansion is the search for increased military security for "socialist states," especially within what they consider to be their national security theaters. The protection of the U.S.S.R. is a primary concern of the leaders of COMECON, and this frequently requires the utilization of smaller states to provide buffer zones and bases for the continuance of the rivalry with the United States. The increase in Soviet military capacity in the 1970s has been exaggerated by the Reagan administration; but the Soviets have held up their end of the arms race, especially in the sale and supply of weapons abroad, where they are number one in the world. Thus, the origin of the arms race lies with the leaders of both sides who scramble for dominance. Some regional theorists have argued that the Soviet Union is cautious in its use of force and awaits its historic opportunities rather than rashly pushing ahead. But this is a question of strategy. The extent of Soviet military expansion has been highly exaggerated for political purposes by the Reagan globalists.[24] Yet, the penetration of Soviet military forces into Africa and West Asia, particularly in Ethiopia and Afghanistan which they consider to be within their security zone, is characteristic of dominance. Furthermore, the Soviets have shown an increasing readiness to supply the protection tributaries expect both in arms shipments and direct support. The Chinese, who were closely aligned with the Soviet Union until the late 1950s, have described this phenomenon as "social imperialism." Through experience, they came to believe that the Soviets also sought ideological conformity and subordination. Soviet external relations, as will be demonstrated, are based upon the search for a secure hegemony.

Therefore in tangible terms, tribute is payment of value extracted from a weaker state by a stronger one in return for protection of the existing political-economic system from its perceived internal and external foes. This may be provided in the form of transfer payments for services, in trade, and in military exchange. The transfer of value is identified in terms of excess profits, unfavorable terms of trade, the sale of arms, and military concessions such as facilities and bases for the dominant power on the territory of the tributary.[25] The terms of trade are generally unfavorable to the tributary state, and this situation is aggravated by the cost of arms sales which increases the debt structure. While the superpower pays for the use of bases or facilities, the cost is generally nominal and in no way offsets the enormous indebtedness of these tributary economies who borrow to consume what they do not produce. They are saved from bankruptcy only through increased aid and loans from the banks and agencies of the core powers, which furthers their dependence and tributary weakness.[26]

Thus, both profit and protection are at the root of the relationship between the superpowers and the new states. They are independent variables that have become essential pillars of the nation-state world system. The superpower provides the force by which the system is established to provide production and profits. Production, in turn, finances the state and its force. The power of the state is central to the operation of the system, and the repressive rule of the tributary states is carried out by classes and elites who reflect this basic drive for protection and profits.

The lessons are innumerable and worldwide. We now see a transnational political class emerging to control the operation of the nation-state and international tributary system. The international ruling class links the tributary periphery with the center. There are similarities, therefore, among members of the ruling class in both the Soviet and American states despite the differences of ideology. Both states are ruled by a political class, based upon profit and protection motives, albeit with different objectives. Members of the ruling class in their dominant power systems share ethnocentric values of Western superiority and even racial arrogance as well as economic privileges. The power of the organization man within the bureaucracy and parties is enormous, and extended by modern electronic technology. Increasing militarization of governments, despite civilian traditions, is also a common trend. Northern dominant power links with Third World tributary leaders are based upon a reflection of the same values and interests of comfortable consumption, and in each system, increased militarization maintains stability against growing protest. The scramble for dominance by Washington and Moscow has created praetorian tributaries that wage internecine war from Asia to Africa and Latin America. Merek Thee has stated this well:

A vicious circle is setting in. The establishment of military-related economies and the perpetuation of the North-South dominance/dependence relationship feed the process of international militarization, stimulating its repressive/destitution function around the globe.... This produces opposition and rebellion, which in turn are met by increased repression and further militarization . . . and the struggle for liberty and freedom acquires the quality of a material confrontation with militarism.[27]

Without this political-military class linkage between the dominant powers and the tributary states, the system would not work, because core control of tributary decisions would lack a transmission system. This political class is based upon transnational power and similar consumption standards, cultural values, and ideology. The indirect rule of British colonialism was a predecessor of the system, but it is far more sophisticated today. The ruling class is educated in the culture and interests of the dominant power and is then employed in the corporations and bureaucracies established for the new Third World countries. There is no particular conspiracy to do it this way; it has simply emerged naturally as a result of the mutual interests of the new class and the centers of core power.

With this political class as the medium, dominance relationships have developed on both sides of the cold war through client, comprador and subimperial stages. The patterns are marked by the extent of economic penetration by the dominant power and of security dependence by the tributary. Class changes respond to these external influences. It is important that any comparative analysis take into account the constantly changing factors that define this relationship. Internal factors of economic and political change are as important here as the shifting interests of the superpowers in their rivalry with each other. Therefore, there is a cold war axis to the North-South struggle which is continuously turning economic issues into political-military conflicts between and within Third World states.

In an empirical manner, the pattern of economic and military tributary development can be studied from the underdevelopment of economies, the amount of arms transferred, the debt structure, and the loss of profits through unfavorable terms of trade and surplus extraction in favor of the core powers.

Third World tributaries do not all fit in the same way into these patterns. They are not neat categories into which all systems find a place, nor is there a necessary progression from one pattern to the next for all tributaries, though there are indications of such a pattern for several. Thus, there are limited predictable directions in the dominance relationship.

The first pattern is that of the client state, in which there are high levels of economic penetration and low levels of arms sales on the part of the U.S.–OECD system. Tributaries at this stage are Western oriented, ruled by single-party, ethno-class systems and dominated by an ethnically based comprador class. Their economies are increasingly "underdeveloped" by unequal trade and multinational resource exploitation. Western arms sales and military facilities are small. Military contacts with the East European countries are purely nominal "nonalignment." Repression of opposition remains at a relatively low level, as the ruling ethnic group has achieved a brief populist base of support provided by the struggle against colonialism (such as in Kenya), despite the growing disparities of income.

As the client system matures, some states may shift to greater superpower dominance and a more "developed" tributary state. This second pattern is marked by an internal change to a highly repressive single-party system or military regime, led by the comprador bourgeoisie who have gained wealth and power. The ruling class firmly establishes control of the state with the help of the dominant power relationship (as has been demonstrated in Pakistan and the Sudan), assimilates some rival ethnic groups and alienates others. There is an increase in economic aid and penetration by multinational corporations. A growing marginalization of the working class occurs, while privileges for the ruling groups increase. The economy is marked by a deterioration in the terms of trade, increased financial indebtedness, inflation, and maldistribution resulting from corruption and parallel black market systems. Several shifts from the U.S.–OECD system to the Soviet–COMECON system, and vice versa, often take place in this unstable dependent relationship, the result of the internal struggle for power and the changing character of superpower interests. Egypt and Ethiopia are two primary examples of this pattern. The comprador class usually goes through a phase of repressing the opposition and then establishes a military regime which more efficiently enforces the interests of the compradors. Such a pattern can be traced in the militarization of the governments of Indonesia, Pakistan, Nigeria, and Ethiopia.

The third pattern that emerges is that of the subimperial state under the leadership of a fully developed tributary class. Such a state is identified by a superpower as a major regional strategic support base for its imperial interests, and it receives enormous amounts of military and economic aid. Much of this is paid for, but considerable quantities are written off as a strategic expense. The tributary ruling-class regime of such a state is based on a powerful military system fostered by the superpower. The government is allowed to use training and weapons from its patron for repressive and often unpopular policies, such as devaluation enforced by the gun.[28] Through increased wealth and arms trade, the ruling class grows powerful and militarized. While economically semiautonomous, the subimperial state is more militarily dependent on its protector than that of the compradors, and it is ruled by an aggressive "martial class," difficult at times to restrain.

Pakistan, South Africa, and Israel have all become subimperial tributaries, ruled by militarized regimes with nominally elected leaders, in close alignment with basic U.S. regional interests. The regional role of multinational corporations in terms of trade and investment expansion, as well as security support, was especially important in prerevolutionary Iran. External finance and corporations built an industrial infrastructure in apartheid South Africa. Vietnam and, to a much lesser extent, Cuba have become important strategic centers of Soviet influence within their regions, providing bases from which to counterattack the global reach of U.S. military operations. These subimperial regimes are praetorian and expansionist, and have been provided with the means to build the most sophisticated weaponry "for their own defense," and the necessary supplies in time of conflict.

Although semiautonomous, with a wide latitude of discretion, the tributary ruling class nevertheless owes allegiance to its protector power, as this type of regime cannot survive for long without huge military and economic subsidies. The litmus test is that the subimperial state would be overthrown by either internal revolution or global intrusion if protection were to be withdrawn. Neither Cuba nor Israel could long survive without the enormous military and economic subsidies they receive annually from their patron powers.[29] They are therefore dependent upon the subimperial system. During times of superpower detente, their existence is precarious, and they therefore promote an atmosphere of conflict and arms race. This is not true of tributaries in the first two stages, who are less militarily dependent. Kenya's government would be shaky if U.S. protection were withdrawn but it might survive, while it is doubtful that Zia ul Haq of Pakistan could withstand the Soviet presence in Afghanistan with only Chinese and French backing. South Africa has been shaken by the threat of withdrawal of U.S. protection. And Israel's "democratic" government has no alternative to U.S. heavy subsidies if it is to survive. These countries have highly nationalistic class rulers, who depend upon U.S. backing for aggressive external relations and repressive policies at home. Such policies may appear to be contrary to the protector's objectives, but on major issues the rulers of subimperial states usually support the patron power's interests in resource access and security.[30] Thus, diplomats will create the illusion of differences between the United States and South Africa in speeches denouncing racism and minor sanctions may even be adopted; but the bottom line is that the United States protects South Africa against Soviet expansion in southern Africa and the Indian Ocean and seeks reform only to control the rise of radical movements. Other Western powers, for the most part, accept this attempt to maintain dominance.

## SELF-RELIANCE AND LIBERATION

The subimperial tributary system, however, contains within itself the seeds of revolt against dominance.[31] War, underdevelopment, genocidal repression, racism, economic collapse, famine, and bankruptcy create the conditions under which opposition to the tributary system becomes widespread. Thus, the conflicts aggravated by the rivalry between the two hegemonic core powers have produced revolutionary forces for change. Such upheavals took place in Ethiopia in 1974–1977, and in Iran in 1978–1979. Similar self-reliant revolutions are underway in South Africa, Afghanistan, Nicaragua, and the Philippines. Their outcome will be as much determined by external intervention as by the character of internal political factors.

Self-reliance is the alternative to remaining within the tributary protection system. It is a strategy of development that emerges from the revolution against dominance. Most proponents speak of it as a stage in the development of independent socialism and control by the people over their own lives. It leads to the essential break with dependence upon the core powers, which may require moderate and nonviolent means or a revolutionary overthrow of existing class rule and linkages. Self-reliance should be distinguished from autarky which is an isolationist and extreme reaction. (Cambodia became self-destructive under the Khmer Rouge terror, which was ended by the Vietnamese invasion.) Self-reliant options evolve gradually over time. Rather than making a sudden total break, this popular revolution proceeds by stages of liberation struggle to independent development. If an attempt is made to leap over any of these, failure is the result, or a return to dependence. In several cases, from Egypt to Ethiopia, the breakout merely resulted in a switch from one superpower to the other.

Careful attention has to be given to the steps of change. A new class consciousness must first emerge, with strong intellectual and political support. The revolutionaries become a class "in the process of formation" who oppose the tributary class. These dissenters emerge from the educational, political, and administrative bureaucracy. Professionals, church leaders, small shopkeepers, cooperative and farm leaders, as well as workers, form the core of the new consciousness. Amilcar Cabral called them "progressive petit bourgeoisie," and he believed they were the hope of Africa because of their dedication to the rediscovery of their cultural heritage and to the realization of a socialist and independent future. The dynamic for Cabral was a combination of cultural and productive change in which new values triggered new material forces. This dualism of class and culture in revolutionary analysis enabled him to grasp reality and mould forces of change in a way that was exceptional for his time.

> The more one realizes that the chief goal of the liberation movement goes beyond the achievement of political independence to the superior level of complete liberation of the production forces and the construction of economic, social, and cultural progress of the people, the more evident is the necessity of undertaking a selective analysis of the values of the culture within the framework of the struggle for liberation.[32]

Cabral's self-reliant socialism tapped the deep root of African consciousness as well as the emerging class awareness that has characterized the more successful Marxist Third World revolutions against dependence and dominance. This culture-class concept preserved the spiritual force of African identity while maintaining the reality of material necessities. In a similar way, black consciousness, as expressed in African liberation theology, has released the pent-up forces of class struggle in South Africa and Latin America. Even some forms of Islamic revolution have used the same base, though with less success as the religious bureaucracy has coopted all capacity for change. The rehabilitation of Confucian values in Marxist China is another example. In South Africa, the black liberation theologian Allan Boesak connected with deep insight the Christian universal vision of a new society with the new liberated African man, who could be black, brown, or white:

The gospel of Jesus Christ, to repeat the words of M.M. Thomas, should not be identified with any one culture. Inasmuch as Black Power serves the new humanity through liberation and the wholeness of life out of which flow justice, peace, and reconciliation and community, Black Power is God's work and an authentic Christian witness to God's presence in the world today.[33]

This is the irresistible new humanity that is overthrowing Western dominance and the apartheid apostasy in South Africa, despite the repression.

The independent socialist alternative that the self-reliance struggle builds in the Third World has several principles. The first is the restructuring of consumption in favor of basic human needs, such as food, but without imitating Western standards. This means equity through redistribution first.[34] Production for use rather than export and the profit of the comprador bureaucracy has become another central principle.[35] External aid and trade are tied to these objectives of equity and redistribution.[36] Therefore, the role of multinational corporations and international finance is to be controlled by the people for their own objectives rather than those defined by the World Bank or the Agency for International Development (AID).[37] Further, the rejection of military dependence through the arms race is a major principle.[38] The development of collective systems of regional defense around real security needs rather than the dominance objectives of the superpowers is recognized as the alternative to being forced back into the tributary system.

Pressures from the world dominance structure against such independent development are enormous. But there are also increasingly powerful links of brotherhood and solidarity from nongovernmental movements which provide hope that a new approach is in the process of being born.

Fouad Ajami has stressed that "no concept of human rights is really sufficient unless it includes the freedom to survive without constant threats of mass annihilation and freedom from racial discrimination."[39] The military is the least likely vehicle for self-reliant change. Unless the military delinkage is first taken, a self-reliance change is undermined by the interventionary force available to the tributary class. Mobuto in Zaire, facing the Shaba rebellion, and the Amin regime in Afghanistan, in late 1979, both invited intervention to save their tributary systems. Thus, the first indicator of a self-reliance revolution is the termination of the tributary link with a superpower that provides assistance primarily for its own security. The creation of an alternative, collective self-reliance system may then follow.

In a world dominated by two rival hegemonic powers, independence for small states with weak economies is very limited. As a consequence, their capacity for human rights enhancement remains low. But as power is diversified, as a result of core power conflicts, through centers of collective self-reliance, the relative power relationship becomes more equitable. Under these circumstances, small independent states will be able to provide more of the basic human needs of their citizens. The global system will also be able to move toward greater relative balance using regional interdependence as the basis for a new world order. Self-reliance grows in the interstices of power and conflict.

We are a long way from such balance and equity. Independence has not been the panacea the nationalists proposed. As noted, the world system has caught most new states in a tributary relationship. However, a new political consciousness which opposes this unequal and unjust system has emerged in both the core powers and the countries of the Third World. Some see this as a transnational class change and others view the new consciousness as the stirring of a new political elite who can bring change within establishment structures, like the progressive wing of the Catholic church which has reentered politics on behalf of the poor, issuing radical appeals for change rather than charity.[40] Gustavo Gutierrez saw this as "a permanent cultural revolution":

Today the seriousness and scope of the process which we call liberation is such that Christian faith and the Church are being radically challenged.... The goal is not only better living conditions, a radical change of structures, a social revolution, it is much more the continuous creation, never ending, of a new way to be a man, a permanent cultural revolution.[41]

## THE PEOPLE'S RIGHT TO PEACE

Thus, out of conflict and change there is a new world order emerging, for which the nationalist and liberation movements of the twentieth century have been important catalysts. While we will not see the end of dominance in this century, the next era may well be a better world for the "wretched of the earth," if only because the power of the privileged few has been seriously challenged by those who, faced with extinction, have found the spirit to resist and demand the people's right to peace.

This right to peace, as several church and United Nations statements have outlined, can be seen as "a collective claim to the right to life."[42] A UNESCO General Conference resolution stated: "Peace cannot consist solely in the absence of armed conflict; but implies principally a process of progress, justice, and mutual respect among people." One of the strongest statements about the centrality of peace in the Catholic church is found in the National Conference of Catholic Bishops' Pastoral Letter on War and Peace (1983), which maintained that the religious vision has much to contribute because it "has an objective basis and is capable of progressive realization."[43] Thus, the people's right to peace everywhere cannot be ignored by states in the pursuit of their security or national interests. The right has a moral and objective basis as well as a collective legal ground for implementation. The superpowers cannot circumscribe it because, while they profess to act for peace, their policies often lead to war and aggression.

Lately, we have tended to ignore the reality of a higher law; but the recognition of a common peril is restoring this awareness of international human rights. The tributary theory of the state reveals the violation of human rights; and liberation by collective self-reliance provides a vision of international behavior based on the basic human necessities of development, justice, and peace.

It should not be surprising that this new theoretical framework leads to many conclusions that are at sharp variance with the established wisdom of world politics on the right and the left. The test of its validity is whether this analysis is any closer to the reality of state behavior and provides a better explanation of how those interested in greater peace and justice should proceed in trying to improve the human condition. In our age, unless we understand the changing forms of imperialism and their consequences, we will not have a world in which we can continue to search for greater social justice. "We, as a culture, have run out of imperial games to play," William Appleman Williams has warned us. "Assume the worst. Empire as a way of life will lead to nuclear death."[44] We are therefore forced to find an alternative in order to survive.

## NOTES

1. Rupert Emerson, *From Empire to Nation: The Rise of Self-Assertion of Asian and African Peoples* (Cambridge: Harvard University Press, 1960), p. 5.

2. Jose Comblin, quoted in Penny Lernoux, *Cry of the People* (New York: Penguin, 1982), p. 409.

3. L. S. Stavrianos, *Global Rift, The Third World Comes of Age* (New York: William Morrow and Co./Quill, 1981), p. 37.

4. Xan Smiley concluded the majority have slipped backward in "Misunderstanding Africa," *Atlantic Monthly*, September 1982.

5. Huan Xiang, interview by Altaf Gauhar, "The Bird in Hand," *South* (London), no. 31 (May 1983).

6. William Appleman Williams, *Empire as a Way of Life* (New York: Oxford University Press, 1980), p. 4.

7. Human rights are defined in terms of economic and social needs as well as civil liberties. Various versions of the widening gap in standards of living are discussed in Michael Harrington, *The Vast Majority: A Journey to the World's Poor* (New York, Simon and Schuster, 1977):

Who are the wretched of the earth? . . . They are the overwhelming bulk of the 70 per cent of the world's population without safe water. Four hundred and fifty million of them are afflicted by schistosomiasis and filaviasis, the leading causes of blindness. They are the more than two billion human beings—54 per cent of mankind—who live in countries where the per capita Gross National Product in 1973 was under $200. The poorest among them, 30 per cent of the world's population, have 3 per cent of its income. (p. 15)

8. René Dumont, *False Start in Africa* (New York: Praeger, 1969), pp. 78–87.

9. Dumont's more recent book, *Stranglehold on Africa* (London: Andre Deutsch, 1983), is theoretically stronger.

10. Marek Thee, "Militarism and Human Rights: Their Interrelationship, Concepts, Norms and Alternative Action," *Militarism and Human Rights* (Reports and papers of a

workshop commission of the Churches on International Affairs, World Council of Churches, Geneva, 1982), p. 11.

11. Michael Klare and Cynthia Arnson demonstrate this relationship in *Supplying Repression: U.S. Support for Authoritarian Regimes Abroad* (Washington, D.C.: Institute for Policy Studies, 1981).

12. See the reference to studies by Istran Kende on the scope of civilian casualties in World War II conflicts, in Johan Galtung, *The True Worlds: A Transnational Perspective*, (New York: Free Press, 1980).

13. Thee, "Militarism," p. 12.

14. Samir Amin, *Unequal Development, An Essay on the Social Formation of Peripheral Capitalism* (New York: Monthly Review Press, 1976); Claude Ake, *Revolutionary Pressures in Africa* (London: Zed Press, Ltd., 1978).

15. See Andre Gunder Frank, "The Development of Underdevelopment," *Monthly Review* 18, no. 4 (September 1966); Immanuel Wallerstein, *The Modern World, Capitalist Agriculture and the Origins of the European World Economy in the 16th Century* (New York: Academic Press, 1974); William Hansen and Bridgette Shultz, "Dependency Theory, Social Class and Development," *Africa Today* 28, no. 3, (1981); and Patrick McGowan, with Bohdan Kordan, "Imperialism in World System Perspective: Britain, 1870–1914," *International Studies Quarterly*, March 1981.

16. Johan Galtung, "A Structural Theory of Imperialism," *Journal of Peace Research* 2 (1971); Colin Leys, "The 'Overdeveloped' Post-Colonial State: A Re-evaluation," *Review of African Political Economy*, no. 5 (January-April 1976).

17. Galtung, *The True Worlds*, p. 108.

18. See Gunder Frank's first hypothesis, "that in contrast to the development of the world metropolis, which is no one's satellite, the development of the national and other subordinate metropoles is limited by their satellite status," in *Dependence and Underdevelopment*, ed. James D. Cockcroft, Andre Gunder Frank, and Dale L. Johnson (New York: Doubleday, 1972), p. 9.

19. Fred Halliday, *The Making of the Second Cold War* (London: Verso, 1983), p. 21.

20. Reinhold Niebuhr, in *Moral Man and Immoral Society* (New York: Charles Scribner's Sons, 1932), stated "for there is no miracle by which men can achieve a nationality high enough to give them as vivid an understanding of general interest as of their own" (p. 45).

21. Harold Laski, *The State in Theory and Practice* (London: George Allen and Unwin, Ltd., 1949), p. 229.

22. "My argument therefore is the simple one that postulates that the imperialist phase of capitalist development necessarily involves war, and that an effective international order is, a priori, incompatible with it." Ibid., p. 243.

23. Gunder Frank argued the single-empire thesis in his earlier work but later concluded that Soviet imperialism is exploitative in Eastern Europe. *Alternatives* 6 (Summer 1981).

24. Fred Halliday, *Soviet Policy in the Arc of Crisis* (Washington, D.C.: Institute for Policy Studies, 1981), p. 16.

25. Klare and Arnson, *Supplying Repression*.

26. The terms of trade are deceptive with OPEC because the high return for oil gives a favorable picture since 1973; but their economies are often deteriorating on other measures.

27. Thee, "Militarism," p. 17.

28. Even during the Carter years these supplies for repression increased, despite the commitment to human rights. Klare and Arnson, *Supplying Repression*, p. 63.

29. It is estimated that the U.S.S.R. subsidizes Cuba at the cost of $3 billion a year. *New York Times*, December 25, 1981.

30. The classic case of U.S. subimperialism was in Iran in the 1950s. See Iqbal Ahmed, "Iran and the West: A Century of Subjugation," in *Tell the American People: Perspectives on the Iranian Revolution* (Philadelphia: Movement for a New Society, 1980), pp. 14–25. For a different view, see Gary Sick, *All Fall Down: America's Tragic Encounter with Iran* (New York: Random House, 1985).

31. James Karioki, *Tanzania's Human Revolution* (University Park: Pennsylvania State University Press, 1979), p. 21.

32. Amilcar Cabral, *Return to the Source: Selected Speeches of Amilcar Cabral*, ed. Africa Information Service (New York: Monthly Review Press, 1973), p. 52.

33. Allan A. Boesak, *Farewell to Innocence* (Maryknoll, N.Y.: Orbis, 1976), p. 97–98.

34. See Jan Tinbergen, "The Need for Ambitious Innovation of the World Order," and Johan Galtung, "The Politics of Self-Reliance," in Heraldo Munoz, ed., *From Dependency to Development: Strategies to Overcome Underdevelopment and Inequality* (Boulder, Colo.: Westview, 1981).

35. See Okwudiba Nnoli, *Self-Reliance and Foreign Policy in Tanzania* (New York: NOK Publishers, 1978), pp. 205–207.

36. Lance Taylor points out that non–oil-producing Third World countries bought $65 million worth of arms in 1978. Not only does this affect their balance of trade but also "economic studies suggest that each extra dollar spent on arms reduced domestic investment by about 25 cents and agriculture output by 20 cents." Sub-Saharan Africa increased arms imports from 1.3 to 9.3 percent of total imports between 1969 and 1978. "The Costly Arms Trade," *New York Times*, December 22, 1981.

37. Guy Gran, in *Development by People* (New York: Praeger, 1983), outlines steps toward this goal (p. 22). The danger is that this theory remains leadership rhetoric rather than empowering people to action.

38. Johan Galtung suggested a scenario in which "the power machinery itself—the military—turns against its old masters and makes the satisfaction of the needs of the masses its top priority." See *True Worlds*.

39. Fouad Ajami, *Human Rights and World Order* (New York: World Order Model Project [WOMP] Institute of World Order, 1978), p. 37.

40. Judith Vidal Hall, "Crisis of Conscience," *South*, no. 31 (May 1983).

41. Gustavo Gutierrez, *A Theology of Liberation* (Maryknoll, N.Y.: Orbis, 1972), p. 32.

42. Thee, "Militarism," p. 15.

43. "The Challenge of Peace: God's Promise and Our Response," A Pastoral Letter on War and Peace, May 3, 1983. National Conference of Catholic Bishops, publication no. 863 (Washington, D.C.: U.S. Catholic Conference).

44. Williams, *Empire as a Way of Life*, p. 213.

# 2

# Subimperialism and South Africa: Controlling Resources and Liberation on the Cape Route

> If we continue as we are continuing, there is no question at all that we are going to end up in a blood bath.
> —Bishop Desmond Tutu, to the Indiana University Board of Trustees, September 1985

Subimperialism is the final phase of the superpower tributary system and is the primary means of indirect rivalry between the superpowers, who identify and strengthen their regional positions with the help of the ruling classes of these semiindustrial states. These countries are chosen for their strategic position in the zones of security and are supplied with all the modern weapons of warfare. In addition, they are semiindustrialized through core power technology and capital which assists them to play an important economic role within their region for reasons of profit as well as protection. This semiindustrialization has strengthened the comprador class, who, through their praetorian regimes, have repressed dissent at home as well as aggressively extended their influence in the region. The mythology of their democratic or socialist independence and importance to world order is the propaganda of their protectors; yet their political dependence on the good will and support of the core power is, in the last analysis, primary. While the subimperial state may have a contradictory ideology, at times embarrassing to the patron power, their transnational class interests sustain the alliance.

The primary function of the subimperial state is to provide bases from which the superpower can project its power into the region and security zone. This power, part of the global rivalry, also has a regional focus: the overthrow of recalcitrant opponents, for example, or the exploitation of regional resources.

Not all tributary states evolve to this level of subimperial relationship; those that lack the resources and the industrial infrastructure are assigned lesser roles.

The subimperial states are externally aggressive and are frequently the center of regional warfare and counterrevolution. Despite its pariah status, South Africa has increasingly assumed this role in southern Africa and the Indian Ocean region. In the Middle East, the United Arab Republic (U.A.R.) (and later Egypt) and Israel have exemplified this function, and on the Indian subcontinent, Pakistan has been moved into this position. While Iraq and Iran in the Gulf played this role for a time, they have begun to consume each other in aggressive war. Vietnam has become a similar subimperial base in Southeast Asia for the U.S.S.R., occupying Kampuchea (Cambodia) and threatening Thailand.

Those who argue that the superpowers do not have a significant responsibility for these regional powers point out how they have sought without success to restrain or alter the policies of these violent and aggressive states. However, what this view fails to understand is that this is generally the result of secondary moral or political differences of strategy which do not alter the subimperial primary collaboration in the market and security interests of the core power.

Eventually, the subimperial state is wracked by internal revolution and/or external regional conflict. Frequently, the support the tributary ruling-class leadership receives from the patron power is the decisive element preventing internal forces for change from operating gradually because these leaders have been encouraged to resist and repress dissent. Their policies prevent the necessary internal reforms, external adjustments, and cooperation that would ensure their survival as their class and/or racial system of rule changes over time. Those who ultimately pay a heavy price for their failures are the indigenous people and the comprador leaders, not their superpower patrons.

Until 1975, South Africa did not appear to be seriously threatened by security factors, internally or externally. But the intrusion of both U.S. and Soviet influence into southern Africa has created a third and new security zone for the United States in the Indian Ocean. The other two zones, Europe and the Pacific, were established during Cold War I. Southern Africa, like Southeast Asia, has been a product of Cold War II.

In the early 1970s, the United States began a buildup of power in the Indian Ocean to counter alleged Soviet threats to energy and security sources, of which the South African Cape became a major focal point. The Cape Route was viewed critical to preserving the flow of oil and strategic minerals, and maintaining access to the troubled waters of South and Southeast Asia. The establishment of the Diego Garcia base by a U.S. agreement with Great Britain in 1966 was the initial step that expanded into the CENTCOM of the 1980s, now a security region of nineteen countries protected by the United States. While South Africa lies outside of CENTCOM, any major conflict in the Indian Ocean with the Soviet Union would raise the demand for access to South African ports.

Because it possessed the most powerful army on the continent of Africa and was far removed from the conflicts of the Middle East and what appeared to be

Soviet interest at the time, most Western authorities in the 1960s viewed South Africa as a troubled yet secure country.[1] In a period of two decades, all that changed and South Africa has become a major uncertainty in the security of the southern oceans. Today, it is a country subject to a major internal rebellion supported by liberation forces based in neighboring states, and backed by a worldwide sanctions movement which includes the U.S.S.R. and Cuba. Moreover, the protective security mantle provided by the United States has become doubtful. Growing Western dissatisfaction with South African failures to produce any meaningful reform has led to growing economic sanctions and stricter bans on military ties.

As Robert Jaster so aptly stated in discussing the defeat of the South African intervention in Angola against the newly installed MPLA (Popular Movement for the Liberation of Angola) government: "The very situation which South Africa has always most feared, a strong conventional communist military presence of some 20,000 Cuban forces on her border,"[2] backed by a superpower, fundamentally changed her position. The victory of African liberation forces in Mozambique and especially in Zimbabwe further aggravated South African fears of a closing circle of "communist power." This led to an increase in South African intervention and aggressive actions against neighboring African states.

A second major change noted primarily by naval strategists was the advent of the Soviet fleet with nuclear capability in the 1970s in the Indian Ocean.[3] While Soviet submarines and battle cruisers were deployed mainly in the Arabian Sea far to the north, they were capable of approaching South Africa in support of either Cuban or African forces under attack by South Africa. The South African navy, even with limited nuclear capability, would be no match for the Soviet force. The likelihood that the Soviets would undertake this action is very slight at this stage; yet capability is what strategists take into account. Only an equal or superior force can deter such action and only the United States and NATO have such force available. Thus, their nuclear naval forces have been implicitly, if not openly, deployed for the protection of South Africa.

## THE WHITE POWER PROTECTION SYSTEM

For internal political reasons, both the South Africans and the West have denied any formal alliance. The African opponents of the South African regime have preferred to describe their struggle as indigenous; yet the support of the communist powers, as well as other external groups, has been important to African success in southern Africa. Thus, the indirect imperialism of the tributary system has encompassed the major dimensions of this conflict on the Cape of Good Hope.

The South Africans' response to the perceived "threat from the 'Marxist' North" has been to launch a massive internal armaments campaign as well as to import sophisticated technology. They have built modern armed forces and militarized their entire society while subjecting the African population to a degree of repression and confinement to restricted areas of living and employment only paralleled by the Nazis' treatment of the Jews prior to and during World War II. There can be no question about the growing militarization of South Africa affecting both its black and white populations. For the past decade, the annual budget for military purposes has grown exponentially.[4]

The South African Defense Force (SADF) has developed, without question, the best-trained and equipped military force in Africa. Most of their weapons are produced in South Africa through their own national arms industry called ARMSCOR (Armaments Development and Production Corporation).[5] South Africa has been supplied with the sophisticated technology for arms production by Western powers, despite the arms ban called for under the 1963 United Nations resolution. But even with this internal production, South Africa remains highly dependent upon Western licensing agreements and resupply for her guided missiles and advanced aircraft, not to mention nuclear weapons technology.[6] There is disagreement among specialists as to the nature and extent of Western and U.S. commitment to South Africa. Several maintain, for different reasons, that the West has formed an alliance with South Africa. James Roherty sees it as a commitment to defend a security zone that extends from the Cape to the Mozambique channel to Somalia.[7] The Cape Route advocates of the Western navies and political conservatives also fall into this category of those who see an implicit commitment to defend South Africa against "the Soviet threat."[8] In addition, there are those who see evidence of a South African alliance with NATO, which is part of a set of secret military agreements among southern Atlantic ocean powers to defend themselves with the help of the West. This is said to include Argentina, Peru, and Brazil, and to have been the result of a 1976 secret meeting between Henry Kissinger, General Alexander Haig, and Prime Minister Vorster of South Africa in Geneva.[9] Later agreements have been reported as a result of a conference in Buenos Aires in 1981, involving military strategists from the southern Atlantic countries. The statement adopted by a NATO meeting in Williamsburg, Virginia, in 1976, voiced this concern:

If Southern Africa is separated from the West, not only will we be deprived of essential minerals but that would also mean that we have lost a strategic position which is vital to our interests. This would mean a dramatic tipping of the balance, since Europe would be isolated and open to an eventual Soviet domination.[10]

Others disagree and argue that there has been a steady disengagement from earlier military associations between South Africa and the West. They point to the withdrawal from the Simonstown naval base, the closing down of Silver Mine Communications, the United Nations arms ban agreements, and the pressures against nuclear weapons development. Their argument is that the Soviet threat is vastly exaggerated, and therefore the prior, minimal security links with the South Africans were not required.[11]

While the Nixon and Carter administrations loosened these ties, the Reagan administration reversed the process and began the development of a bilateral defense arrangement with South Africa, which by 1982 had the substance of a subimperial alliance. Under NATO, the United States is limited to the concurrence of other Western powers. While Great Britain may agree with U.S. support for South Africa's strategic position, other NATO members like Norway and Holland have explicitly dissented and France was not happy over aspects of the Cuban linkage strategy concerning Namibia. Through bilateral agreements and relations, the United States moved toward the creation of a subimperial system in South Africa. South Africa meets all the basic criteria: a regional semiindustrial power with an extensive multinational corporate presence, an ideologically subservient ruling class, and a military capable of projecting core power military and economic interests in the region and into the Indian Ocean.

The Reagan administration in its so-called "constructive engagement" policy has reversed the efforts of previous administrations to restrict military links. Shortly after taking office, the president authorized the sale to South Africa of militarily useful materials, such as advanced computers like the Cyber 170/750, as well as trucks and aircraft that were previously on a banned list.[12] Even cattle prods for controlling crowds and political prisoners were removed from the ban. Military intelligence information was exchanged. More importantly, channels such as Israel were utilized for the supply of sophisticated weapons and parts to improve the South African navy and air force. The United States, France, and Israel have supplied South Africa with the technology and enriched uranium necessary for nuclear weapons. Of course, officially much pressure has been placed upon the Botha government to sign the Non-Proliferation Treaty, but there are few experts who believe that nuclear capability is limited to peaceful uses.[13] Proposals have been made within the Reagan administration for much wider bilateral agreements; but it is not known whether they have been adopted or not. They include the use of Simonstown, Durban, and Walvis Bay by the U.S. Navy, and overhaul and maintenance agreements, since South Africa has the industrial capacity to make repairs needed in wartime. Replacement of the Shackleton air force, and SADF upgrading have been facilitated through third parties. The South Africans have been very successful in finding arms and technology on the international arms market. Indications are that the United States has helped to improve the SADF through its secret arms supply program.[14]

The U.S. doctrine of "power projection from the Cape" is well suited to the development of these bilateral security arrangements. The phrase was coined by Assistant Secretary of State for Africa Chester Crocker, even before he took office.[15] It remains one of the most ambiguous and dangerous concepts ever defined in U.S.-African diplomacy. While the policy may not have meant a specific embrace of military linkages with South Africa, it certainly left the door open to such agreements, which have traditionally been secret. No American president can admit to a direct alliance with South Africa because of internal political opposition and the opprobrium attached to apartheid in the world. However, the Reagan administration and others before it have justified dissemblement on the basis of the national security interest, as Option 2 of Kissinger's National Security Council Memorandum 39 has shown. The difference is that some restraints have been operative in the past; but the Reagan administration, in pursuing regional dominance, has allied the United States with South Africa.

### Soviet Strategy in Southern Africa

The Soviet-Cuban threat has been vastly overrated by the "globalists" as well as the Afrikaners. While ready to move against a weak side in the rivalry, the U.S.S.R. does not regard southern Africa as a primary security zone. As many specialists have pointed out, the Soviets have little use for the strategic raw materials of southern Africa, nor does the southern Indian Ocean threaten them directly.[16] They are very much opposed to Diego Garcia, which is only 1,000 miles from the subcontinent, but the southern African Cape is thousands of miles distant from the borders of the Soviet Union. Because the Soviets have shallower draft ships, the Suez Canal is more important to them than the Cape Route. Soviet concern arises from the fact that the Western powers have built a surveillance and naval maintenance base in South Africa and have established Diego Garcia since the withdrawal from Simonstown. The Australian naval specialist, Jeffrey Jukes, has maintained that the West does not need Simonstown or other South African facilities and that Diego Garcia is more than sufficient. Cape Route strategy advocates in the West, however, fear that the U.S.S.R. might interdict vital Western shipping around the Cape, but this is a remote possibility, except in a conventional war setting. There are other points for interdiction much closer to Soviet air bases.[17] Since the chances of a U.S.-Soviet naval confrontation remaining at the conventional level is even less probable in the eyes of Russian admirals than American, the Cape, for them, remains a secondary matter.

But South African attempts to equate Soviet policy with African armed insurgency has succeeded, to a degree, in the minds of some conservative Western strategists. They are convinced that the African revolution cannot succeed against South Africa without the direction and support of the Russians.[18] Therefore, they see any threat to the present regime as a Soviet threat and advocate a policy of Soviet deterrence, though it may have the effect of negating African revolution as well. It is this fear of the intertwining of Soviet expansion and African revolution that has created the Gordian knot which has not been untangled in U.S. and Western policy.

The tangle results from a basic misreading of the nature and intent of Soviet policy in this region. Conservative and neoconservative fears were aroused by the events, as they saw them, in the former Portuguese territories. The rise of Marxist regimes in Angola and Mozambique was viewed as the culmination of long-term Russian strategy and the defeat of Western and U.S. interests. The victory of the MPLA in Angola particularly was seen as a triumph of Russian aid and Cuban intervention which defeated the forces backed by the United States. After these events, Henry Kissinger undertook his famous mission to

Rhodesia and South Africa to attempt to strengthen the position of the pro-Western camp. With demands for reforms of racist regimes, coupled with promises of aid, he set the pattern which was followed by the Carter and Reagan administrations, despite their disclaimer of the policies of the former secretary of state.

The prospect that the U.S.S.R. might at some point back up an invasion force of African states with their air power and naval forces greatly concerns conservative Western strategists who are opposed to African forces winning with Soviet aid, as in Angola.[19] However, Soviet strategy in southern Africa is a cautious exploitation of existing economic, political, and military opportunities. They have pursued a policy of expansion of trade through treaty arrangements, protection of "socialist states," support for chosen liberation movements, and exclusion of Chinese influence. Rather than a design for world conquest, this drive can be described as one of opportunism in the dominance rivalry when the occasion arises. They have pursued vigorously the new opportunities in the political, economic, and strategic fields. These objectives are very much the same as those of the United States, as Crawford Young described them: "Soviet, Cuban, or Chinese influence in Africa is no more abnormal than American or Western influence."[20]

The U.S.S.R. was excluded for a long time from southern Africa, and unexpectedly broke through in 1974 with the revolution in Portugal, which gave the Russians an opportunity they were in a strong position to exploit. The unlimited and unwise backing of Portuguese colonialism by U.S. and NATO policies had alienated the African nationalist leadership during the liberation struggle. However, the new Marxist African states proved to be remarkably open to Western influences after independence.[21]

The People's Republic of China has further reduced Soviet influence. The Soviets had been excluded for some years from the Zimbabwe African National Union (ZANU), when it was operating out of Maputo, by Chinese anti-Soviet activity in Mozambique. Their attempt to back an alternative winner with Joshua Nkomo and his Zimbabwe African People's Union (ZAPU), a wing of the Patriotic Front, was a major error they paid for in later strained relations with Zimbabwe. However, Chinese withdrawal from the southern African liberation struggles about 1977 left the Russians as the sole major suppliers of arms and money. And the difficulties Mozambique and Angola have encountered in dealing with the United States have enhanced their position as the major aid source for the first Marxist states in Africa.

As the focus has shifted to South Africa and Namibia, the Soviet Union has emerged as the principal supplier and supporter of the two leading liberation movements, the African National Congress (ANC) and South-West Africa People's Organization (SWAPO).[22] This is not because the leadership is Communist, as alleged in conservative western circles, but because they are organizations that are well positioned through popular support, secret organization, and experienced guerrilla warfare to take over in the developing crises of this region of Africa. Those willing to fight and make enormous sacrifices have proven elsewhere to be able to seize power when others are divided and repudiated by failure.

The Soviets' strategy is therefore fundamentally a program of varied means of support for liberation movements that meet their criteria of "national democracy" and appear to be compatible with their ultimate aims of economic and political collaboration. Their strategies have varied over the years in southern Africa, depending upon the conditions for revolution and their own enormous growth in capabilities.

As many Africans and Asians have discovered, particularly in Egypt, Somalia, Guinea, and Afghanistan, the Soviets have created tributary relationships very much as the United States has done and have maintained or dropped them according to their own changing needs. They have been willing to provide the various forms of assistance necessary for the liberation struggles against the South Africans and Western interests and have shown in the Angolan struggle a readiness to provide considerable materiel and a number of technicians, though they prefer to use Cuban manpower. Whether they will go to a direct intervention policy, committing their own troops in southern Africa, is doubtful. They have only done this in Afghanistan because of its proximity to the U.S.S.R.

The Horn of Africa is part of an extended security zone for them, but not southern Africa. While they identify with the struggle of African people, they lack the Cuban dimension of racial solidarity and share much of the European distrust of African ability. They are, however, quite prepared to pursue the indirect intervention policy of arms sales to independent African states to enable Africans to defend themselves against South Africa. Moscow has supplied and helped train the guerrilla forces of the liberation movements through the Frontline African states and other channels of support. The ANC has long benefited from this aid as well as other sources of external assistance provided by COMECON and Commonwealth countries, such as East Germany and India.

The naval contest is a limited one, though it has an important bearing on South Africa. The two sides have built enormous capability. The expansion of Soviet naval power has given it the capacity to play an important role in southern African events. The South Africans and their allies must take into account the fact that the Soviet fleet can appear suddenly in support of a variety of liberation actions, from insurrection to invasion. They can protect African states to an extent against South African attack or even internal coup d'état attempts. And, most important, they can protect the supply lines to African states and liberation movements.

The fact that Soviet intrusion is ultimately limited in scope does not alter its progressive role in the liberation struggle in the eyes of African nationalists. Some distinction needs to be made between the quality of Soviet economic aid and the utility of military assistance. While there has been some disappointment with COMECON aid among African countries, those liberation movements whose victory in large part was due to Soviet arms have good reason to be grateful and have continued this military link after independence. Thus, Mozambique and Angola have a mixed economic relationship with the rival centers of power, but have moved toward a closer tie in security matters with the Soviets because of increasing South African intrusions.

After the Chinese withdrawal from Africa in the late 1970s, southern African liberation movements had little backing for armed struggle against South Africa except from the U.S.S.R. Thus, while liberation leaders are frequently non-Marxist, they are not anti-Soviet, though there are a few exceptions, like the leaders of the South African Pan-Africanist Congress (PAC). In these circumstances, the Soviet Union has been able to move into the role of champion of the poor and oppressed in southern Africa. In contrast, the policies of the United States and other Western powers, which seek internal reform, have appealed primarily to white liberals and comprador African leaders.

Thus, rather than a design for world conquest, Soviet policy in southern Africa has been a competitive intrusion into a previously exclusive western preserve. The Russians have used Angola and Mozambique as leverage points—but not for invasion. As the principal backers of the leading liberation movements, they are in a strong position to benefit from the counterrevolutionary policies and collapse of white rule under the erosive impact of African revolts in Namibia and South Africa.

## Subimperial Breakdown

The subimperial relationship is powerful though transitory. It begins to break down rapidly under the weight of its costs and failures to adapt to the rising demands of internally repressed groups, such as the blacks in South Africa. Ethno-class and religious sects have similar force in other countries, for example, militant Islam. This situation gives rise to revolution which is aggravated by foreign conflicts and wars resulting from the aggressive and counterrevolutionary activities in the region.

For a time, the close class relationship between leaders of the subimperial state and its patron hides the danger and losses. Policies of collaboration are maintained as the superpower assumes that its hegemonic interests are promoted by continued support of its regional surrogate. But the contradictions become obvious in time, and when the process of disengagement is begun, the revolutionary groups and the forces of self-reliance gain the upper hand. South Africa's pattern is no exception to this process. It is complicated by the ideological battles and the enormous illusions about the strength of white power that exist on all sides. The failure of reform, the growth of the Afrikaner right wing, and the maturing conflict with Western states as well as the Frontline African states, are cracks in subimperialism. This has launched an intensive debate in the West regarding reforms, investments, sanctions, and negotiations with the ANC.

## Profiting from Aparthied

The United States began its tributary relationship with South Africa in the 1960s, when increased investment and trade made it the second largest foreign investor after Great Britain. During this period, 350 of the major 500 U.S. corporations opened subsidiaries in South Africa. They were primarily interested in manufacturing. Ford, Chrysler, and General Motors led the way. Major mining firms, such as AMAX and Union Carbide entered the minerals field. Black trade unions were banned at that time and profit levels were high. Following the Sharpeville massacre, the ANC leadership was decimated and went into exile. A temporary failure of investor confidence was restored with the help of U.S. banks.[23]

Between 1965 and 1975, the level of U.S. investment increased to $2 billion and shortly thereafter, American corporations became the primary importers of South African goods. The investment outlook seemed promising. South African industry was beginning to open the African market throughout southern Africa to Western goods. The O'Dowd thesis of reform through production had carried the day in U.S. and Western economic circles.[24] Sir Harry Oppenheimer, the mining magnate and chief exponent of South African enterprise, was widely feted in the Western financial world.

Then the Soweto riots broke out in 1976, and the prospects for corporate reform took a dismal downward turn, from which they were only temporarily rescued again by the United States. Discovery of the security importance of South Africa for the supply of strategic minerals, and the growing predominance of the Cape Route advocates in American foreign policy, raised South Africa to the full tributary status. This meant security subsidies became available.

Although interest in investment by multinational corporations declined after Soweto, as the political future looked unpromising, the so-called reverse dependence argument became popular. South Africa had become a major source of several strategic minerals: chromium ferroalloys (72 percent), manganese ferroalloys (58 percent), vanadium (72 percent), and platinum (67 percent). Gold and uranium supplies to U.S. and Western industry are also important. Although conflicting studies have been made about the extent of the importance these minerals have for the U.S. and Western economies,[25] the South African government has played up the indispensable role its minerals perform in U.S. and OECD production.

By 1978, South Africa began to feel the impact of the worldwide recession. The price of gold was halved and other minerals were no longer in short supply. Investments declined and South Africa was forced to borrow heavily in the world market. Liberal congressmen concluded that the U.S. economy was not dependent upon South African markets and strategic resources. The comparison of dependence of the U.S. or U.K. economy on South Africa with the importance of Arab Gulf oil supplies is farfetched. While the loss of Gulf oil supplies had an immediate impact on the United States and the West, in terms of shortages and inflation, a U.S. Senate report showed that although the loss of South African minerals might have some inflationary impact, this could be absorbed in three to six years by stockpiles, technological innovation, and alternative sources of supply in Australia, Canada, and even the Soviet Union.[26] World reserves in the 1980s of most of the so-called strategic minerals are ample for several years, without serious effects on prices or availability.

## South African Subimperialism

Despite this decline in importance of South Africa as an investment market and source of strategic minerals, the Reagan administration in the 1980s transformed the country from tributary to subimperial status. This was due to the strategic concerns cited earlier, and recognized fully by the United States, of the importance of the Cape route and South Africa's role in the defense of the Western world against the perceived Soviet and Communist threat.

This perspective fitted well into the new "total" strategy that had been gradually accepted in South Africa, where it had originally been proposed by the military under the leadership of the chief of the defense force, Magnus Malan. His policy, first defined in a 1977 Defense White Paper, called for an unrelenting use of force against South Africa's enemies, internal and external.[27] The strategy, dubbed *swaardmag* ("power of the sword"), opposed compromise with black African neighboring states which had been proposed by P. K. Botha prior to Zimbabwe's independence in 1980. Botha, South Africa's foreign minister, argued that Bishop Abel Muzorewa could be brought to power in Zimbabwe and deals could be struck with Frontline States using South African economic power. But Malan, who later became minister of defense, pushed for the use of military and paramilitary force as the centerpiece of the "total strategy." There would be no compromise with the ANC or its supporters, and a military victory was to be achieved in Namibia. At home, this strategy at first included reforms aimed at winning over a portion of the African and nonwhite population, especially with new wage incentives.[28] But as repression and revolution grew, *swaardmag* became a total strategy.

The Reagan administration has disguised its support for this strategy with concepts such as "constructive engagement" which are intended to achieve change and peace in South Africa; but the effect has been to give sanction to an internal counterrevolutionary program and to aggression abroad.[29]

Recent events have demonstrated that the South African government has interpreted "constructive engagement" to mean support and protection for its racial system.[30] It has, therefore, been increasingly belligerent with its northern neighbors. In 1980, the SADF launched a campaign of destabilization and aggression. This was occasionally deplored by the Reagan administration; but in actuality this anti-Communist "power projection" against the governments of Angola and Mozambique and support for the National Union for the Total Independence of Angola (UNITA) and the Mozambique National Resistance (MNR) found warm support in Washington through secret supply channels to these nonindigenous movements backed by South Africa.

## THE FAILURE OF "CONSTRUCTIVE ENGAGEMENT" AND CHANGE

The basis for "constructive engagement" is the questionable argument of the "O'Dowd thesis," named after a South African economist in the employ of the Anglo-American Corporation. O'Dowd maintained that industrialization would create a demand for black labor that would increase wages and opportunities for blacks and tear down the divisions of the apartheid society. "My contention is that there is nothing in either language or religion and still less, colour, which is an inherent source of conflict between people."[31] A more sophisticated version of this has been developed by American and South African social scientists who contend that the emergence of an African middle class as a result of industrialization would bridge the gulf between the races.[32] This idea became popular in the 1970s with Western corporate leaders and governments and even found favor with some South African leaders. Prime Minister Botha has espoused the ideas of the O'Dowd thesis, though they have become primarily the thesis of the opposition, the Progressive Federal Party.

The Reagan administration's policy is similar to that of earlier administrations who embraced a naïve belief in the reform of apartheid. During the Carter administration, U.S. policy makers adopted the O'Dowd thesis in the form of the Sullivan Principles, aimed at establishing a code of interracial practices for American corporations.[33] It was assumed that these reforms would be adopted by companies and the practice would spread through the industrial system. However, only a few companies showed any interest in the reforms. Many opposed them, especially the South African firms, and only token changes were adopted after ten years of advocacy by both the American and South African governments. The result was the emergence of a small privileged elite of African workers who received higher wages. But the vast majority of the African workers found themselves at the bottom of the apartheid pyramid, providing an increasingly high standard of living for the white minority and suffering the same racial discrimination that had excluded them from the benefits of modern life from the very beginning of industrial society. However, one effect of industrialization was heightened African liberation-consciousness: the exiled movements were able to create a massive underground.[34]

Awareness of the impossibility of this situation had begun to dawn upon the Carter administration but was repressed by the Reagan rehabilitation of apartheid strategy. The American superpower attempted to support the Afrikaners' weakening position by increased military and police assistance and financial investment. Attempts to disassociate itself from internal repression, while supporting the belligerent expansionist policies of Pretoria, fell apart in the Reagan second term.

## The Internal Breakdown

The new political-economic class among South African blacks has taken two directions: one toward assimilation into the white power structure, and the other toward African liberation. Thus, the dynamic of change is, as Cabral described it, the conflict between the assimilationists and the revolutionaries, rather than the O'Dowd thesis which assumed an African comprador class that would cooperate with the white-led economy and control their black population. Ironically, a strong black comprador class would have developed had not apartheid provided the means for racial division of the country into what John Rex has called "two nations." And, instead, the liberation movement spread.

Africans have not been able to own land outside of the reserves (except in restricted areas) or gain access to the major resources of production. They are, therefore, a racial subclass that both opposes and collaborates with the white ruling classes. Ben Mugabane has put it well: "Racial aggression and class exploitation are inextricably intertwined in the modern world."[35] This new subclass has acquired "petite bourgeois" characteristics: small property ownership, professional standing, and education. They are traders, teachers, lawyers, doctors, government bureaucrats, and trade unionists, typical of all African states. During several visits to Johannesburg, the author met many of them. They are exceedingly well educated, with degrees from the United States and the United Kingdom, despite the discrimination at South African universities against them. Their leaders are lawyers and doctors. For example, Nelson Mandela, the imprisoned leader of the ANC was a lawyer and his predecessor, Chief Albert Lithuli, was a teacher in the Congregational Church-related prep school, Adams College.

The new subclass has many ideologies but one task: "the insemination on history" of their cultural identity; as Amilcar Cabral put it, the "development of a national culture, based upon the history and the achievements of the struggle itself."[36] This struggle became an armed struggle, as their peaceful resistance was repressed. Born in nonviolent resistance, the ANC was forced underground and into exile to preserve itself. The progressive branch of the movement of liberation came into conflict with the assimilated and traditional groups who were manipulated by the subimperial rulers. As Cabral observed, these collaborationists are gradually re-Africanized as the liberation struggle develops, "through daily contact with the popular masses in the communion of sacrifice required by the struggle."[37]

In South Africa, the liberation movement has consciously sought the retention of African ethnic and national values within one nation against Western racism and tribalism. The Bantustans are not their African heritage but "a white imperialist imposition." Their black consciousness is an affirmation of national ethnicity more than race. In this respect, class cuts across ethnic differences, moulding a national struggle very similar to the class-culture idea of Cabral. The class struggle is also seen as uniting the races of the two nations against external exploitation and thereby forming one new nation out of the liberation struggle.[38] Race, at this stage, has given way to class solidarity in the struggle for the new united South Africa. This is why the ANC leadership of the liberation movement does not see the problem as primarily a racial struggle but considers nonracial national consciousness as most important. The indigenous African base out of which the liberation struggle has emerged has taken on a national, nonracial direction, which includes all ethnic and racial groups.

### Reform from the Top

The issue of whether fundamental change can be brought to southern Africa by the assimilationists working with a reform-minded white leadership is basic to the conflict. What kind of change is desired and considered fundamental? Those who have accepted positions in the new Bantustan governments, like Chiefs Lucas Mangobe and Gatsha Buthelezi, have been prepared to endure a solution that entails a permanent tributary status.[39] Mangobe, now head of the homeland Bophuthatswana, recognized only by South Africa, told the author in London that he wanted to put as much distance as possible between his people and the whites, and he eagerly accepted separation.

Although he has opposed independence for KwaZulu and other Bantustans on existing terms, Buthelezi has accepted a role in the dual-nation system by becoming a chief minister, despite the fact that the Ciskei Report indicated nominal independence cannot improve the lot of the African.[40] There is no doubt that a tributary elite benefits, as the experience of the Transkei shows; but the position of migratory laborer has, in most respects, worsened, especially as they are compelled by the Group Areas Act to retire to homeland reserves, rubbish heaps for wornout labor with no capacity to support their retirement in old age. Barry Streek refers to the assimilationists as "systems users" who want to change the system. The leading groups are the Labour party, Jukatha, the Reform party, the ruling Dikwan Kwetla party in Qwaqwa and the KaNgwane government, all of whom formed in 1979 the South African Black Alliance (SABA). More recently, a coalition of some 200 black organizations formed the National Forum Committee (NFC). Rejecting the Freedom Charter of the ANC, they adopted the Manifesto of the Azanian People's Organization. On the right of this group, the vigilante "fathers," counterrevolutionaries who fought in the shanty towns with the whites against the "comrades," emerged in the mid–1980s.

### Reformism

When Pieter Botha became prime minister in 1978, he began a push toward "reform," using the slogan "adapt or die," and appointed a cabinet of *verligtes* ("reformers"). However, the impact of reform was mostly smoke and no fire. What was conceded to blacks on the one hand was withdrawn with the other. Labor reform was a key example of this, as was the creation of separate representative Councils in Government for Coloured and Indian minorities in 1984.

Botha initially won support for this step in a referendum by promising to exclude Africans from the extension of the franchise. The proposal split the Coloured community and temporarily united Africans against it. Even moderate blacks and homeland leaders opposed the proposal as too obviously a farce.[41] A later attempt to create an African council for urban dwellers was rejected by assimilationists like Buthelezi.

The reforms in labor control and trade unions were most contradictory. While following the Wiehahn Commission proposals to allow black trade union organization, the government retained the power to refuse to register unions which do not "serve to maintain peace and harmony within the undertaking, industry, or occupation."[42] Union leaders have, in fact, been extensively arrested and banned, especially during the national emergency of 1986. The right to strike in South Africa has never existed. However, illegal strikes have been increasing in numbers and violence, as the trade unions have mushroomed despite repression.[43] Restrictions on the employment of illegal workers and penalties for firms who do so have set back disastrously the position of migratory labor, according to the moderate white group, the Black Sash.[44] Numerous reports indicate that the gap between white and black workers has been growing, in terms of pay scales and supervisory roles.[45] Absolute destitution has also spread in the reserves. Nevertheless, a great deal of propaganda and research has gone into the attempt to show that reforms in opportunity are significant in the "neo-apartheid" structure.[46]

The contention of some corporations and the U.S. State Department that these sham reforms are bringing real change shows the extent to which this superpower and its clients will go, both in Europe and Africa, to develop support for subimperialism. Reformist campaigns on behalf of South Africa were initially highly successful in blunting the antiapartheid demands on Western powers, the United States, and the United Nations.[47] But the notion that significant reform has or can take place in apartheid is "sheer fantasy," according to many white liberal South Africans.[48] A careful assessment of the research done on various aspects of Botha's *verligte* policies led *The Economist* to conclude perceptively in 1980 that "he has been stymied by the right wing resistance of his own party in fulfilling his promises. He has drawn power to himself but not found the political courage to make that power effective."[49] Six years later, this remains an accurate description of his failures. With every concession, there has been a contradiction, like the black and white toilet facilities in the new "unsegregated" Carleton Hotel. While job reservation for whites was withdrawn by some companies, white trade unions will not tolerate a black supervisor of white workers. The pass laws were ended in 1986 but not the Group Areas Act. Winnie Mandela's banning order was lifted; but thousands of her followers were arrested.

## Right-Wing Reality

The unrepentant Afrikaner maintains that concessions are a sign of weakness and only strength is respected. Andries Treurnicht, a former leader of the right wing within the National party, and now the head of the Conservative party, opposes all change in apartheid. Concerning segregation in sports Treurnicht said: "If the white man shared the Rugby field, he would ultimately have to share the country."[50]

The Herstigte National Party (HNP), a right-wing racist group, made sensational gains in the April 1981 elections.[51] This *verkrampte* reaction was totally committed to fortress South Africa. Later, the Conservative party, created by Treurnicht and other right-wing M.P.s, won one seat in a series of by-elections in 1983 and in 1985 ousted a minister. Their power is largely rural, and the fear of guerrilla attacks and the liberation movements adds to their support. The right wing opposed the 1983 referendum on electoral changes; but the conservatives were decisively beaten by a ratio of three to two. However, the power of the right is a continuous drag and has prevented the extension of the franchise to urban Africans and other reforms.

A paramilitary force surfaced in 1985 in the Transvaal called the Afrikaner Resistance Movement led by Eugene Terre Blanche. Members trace their roots to the Boer commandos and have committed themselves to resist with force concessions to the black majority.[52] An emblem resembling the Nazi swastika is used, and they quote the Book of Revelation to support their violent claims. Yet, the major right-wing force remains the Conservative party, whose leadership opposes even the minor representation given to Coloureds and Indians. Dr. Treurnicht stands firmly in the path of negotiation.[53] And the intensification of the right-wing revolution in 1985 made him a realistic alternative to Botha, should the Boer *laager* ("ox wagons in a circle") mentality spread to a majority of whites.

The white electorate is badly divided. But mid–1985 polls showed a majority favored the gradual dismantling of apartheid. A substantial majority of whites believed the system would not survive ten years.[54] The attitude toward Mandela and the ANC remained negative; not a single white polled supported him for president. This may be because the government has portrayed him as a man of violence. Once a peace process has begun, this image could change rapidly as it did in the case of Ben Bella in Algeria and Robert Mugabe in Zimbabwe.

As a result of the African uprising and loss of business confidence abroad, a powerful corporate and financial group emerged in 1985. Led by both internal business leaders and external multinational spokesmen, this group sought to persuade the government to dismantle and "bury apartheid." Such figures as Anton Rupert of the Rembrandt Group and Roger B. Smith, chairman and chief executive officer of General Motors, as well as Henry Oppenheimer of DeBeers Consolidated, issued advertisements in newspapers and adopted resolutions requesting the "abolition of apartheid" and negotiations with "acknowledged black leaders."[55]

Representatives of this group met with the ANC in Lusaka, despite the charge by President Botha that this was disloyal. Several other groups also met with the ANC in Lusaka, including the opposition political party. Such actions showed that a powerful segment of the ruling class with important international connections had defected from the previous white consensus about excluding liberation movements from negotiations about the country's future. The majority of whites stood behind Botha, but for the first time a major crack appeared in the solid wall of apartheid.

President Botha was stunned, as this came at the same time that Western powers embraced limited sanctions, to be discussed in detail later. This meant that the external financial structure of support was crumbling. He was beginning to be perceived as no longer in command.[56] The question, then, arose in late 1985: Who would grasp the helm?

The direction the white electorate was willing to move had become a highly volatile variable. While it was changing rapidly, it became clear that a majority was ready to accept a significant dismantling of apartheid structures. The London *Sunday Times* poll showed only 5 percent supported the right-wing leader Treurnicht, who proposed a *laager* response. A majority were prepared to accept a change in the pass laws and even black representation in government.[57] However, the gulf was widening between the *verligtes*—who favored negotiation with the African nationalists led by Mandela—and those of the right wing who favored a military-led *swaardmag* against internal and external enemies of white rule. At the end of 1986, a bloodbath under a totalitarian state appeared more likely than a negotiated settlement.

## The Liberation Movement and the Progressives

There are numerous groups and movements that have emerged in South Africa in the contemporary period whom Cabral has called "the progressive petite bourgeoisie." Some have been repressed, like the United Democratic Front (UDF), while others have been tolerated for a time, like the Black People's Convention, and then banned. Trade unions have been important among them, such as the General and Allied Workers Union (GAWU), formed in 1980 and led by Samson Nku. The GAWU was nonracial and opposed to registration.[58] The most important democratic trade union federation is the Congress of South African Trade Unions (COSATU), formed in 1985 and the heir of South African Congress of Trade Unions (SACTU), which was banned and went into exile in the 1960s. Buthelezi and Inkatha have been encouraged by the government in the organization of the rival Federation of United Workers of South Africa (UWSA). These two movements have clashed over political issues as strikes and boycotts became important after 1985.

At a meeting in Cape Town in August 1983, the UDF, under the leadership of Allan Boesak, Albertina Sisulu, Oscar Mpetha, a veteran trade unionist, and Zac Yacoob of the Natal Indian Congress, was formed. The assimilationist groups of SABA and the National Forum Committee opposed the UDF at first, but it was soon evident that a movement which claimed two million followers and had the backing of the ANC was the wave of the future. However, the leadership was arrested and its followers brutally repressed by the thousands in 1985 and 1986. But the imprisonment and banning of the leaders could not abolish this major movement. The time had passed when such organizations could be eliminated by police action. Even total military repression in the emergency periods could not restrain the political consciousness of students, workers, and activists, which led to strikes, boycotts, and violent eruptions. Thousands of deaths have resulted from conflicts between blacks as well as with security forces.

The strength of the ANC in South Africa by 1985 could no longer be denied by the skeptics.[59] During the 1960s and 1970s, the exile organization had established a wide network of support, despite informers and repression. After 1974, its following mushroomed among workers, students, small shopkeepers, and the salariat. Its total strength is difficult to estimate accurately. Polls are notoriously unreliable, but a German survey found 27.1 percent willing to admit support for the ANC in 1980.[60] This was remarkable, since it was a crime punishable by immediate imprisonment without trial, and possible death through police torture. Professor Thomas Karis reported in 1984 that the ANC had become the most popular movement inside South Africa among the skilled and educated in urban areas.[61] His conclusions were later substantiated by polls such as the one conducted by Markinor, an affiliate of Gallup, for the London *Sunday Times* which reported a 49 percent black preference for Nelson Mandela as president.[62] The research of a South African sociologist, Mark Orkin, "found that 39 percent of 800 blacks looked to Nelson Mandela or the closely allied UDF for leadership" (*Manchester Guardian Weekly*, September 15, 1985). Buthelezi and his Inkatha ran far behind in these polls.[63]

The "Release Mandela" campaign received great impetus with the formation of the moderate UDF in 1983. Its support for Mandela received progressive white backing in South Africa.[64] This, in turn, sparked Western countries, such as France, to urge President Botha to release the ANC leader for negotiations and, in late 1985, the U.S. secretary of state publicly requested South Africa to negotiate with "representative black leaders."[65] However, the State Department maintained its ambivalent policy of nonrecognition while urging talks until late 1986, when it opened direct relations with Oliver Tambo of the ANC.

The history of the ANC goes back over seventy-three years. The ANC was one of the most well-developed nonviolent movements in the world until repression by Afrikaners in the 1960s convinced most of its leaders that passive resistance would not gain their objectives. It remained, however, a multiracial movement, representative of all major African ethnic groups, and in recent years it has received increased Coloured backing. The PAC was initially a militant group of younger leaders who, by the mid–1950s, had developed a black consciousness that rejected whites in the movement and turned increasingly to Pan-Africanist force. Paradoxically, it was at the same time strongly anti-Marxist and these differences have remained the dividing points between the two movements. Whites and Indians serve on the ANC executive committee. Three were elected at the Lusaka Conference of 1985.

Support for the PAC in exile and within the country has been small. For this reason, as well as the desire of the Organization of African Unity (OAU) to force a unification of the ANC and PAC, OAU backing for PAC has been limited. However, it has substantial support from several African states, notably Tanzania, where it is headquartered. Zimbabwe also recognizes the PAC. China has, in the past, given considerable backing to the PAC as a counter to Soviet support for the ANC.

While the Soviet Union is the principal international supporter of the ANC financially, and in terms of weapons supply, many other countries, including Sweden in the West, have backed it financially, and several Third World countries, especially Algeria, Nigeria, and India, have provided arms training and supplies. In an interview in 1985, Oliver Tambo stated bluntly: "The Soviet Union will give us what the West does not want to give us, namely weapons."[66] In the West, a strong antiapartheid movement has aided the ANC, providing financial and legal aid.[67] The internal politics of the ANC is a mixture of liberal, Marxist, and Christian ideas, with a liberation base. The claim that it is ideologically committed to the Soviet Union is a fabrication of the racial ruling class, and the counterrevolutionaries. Both Oliver Tambo and Nelson Mandela are moderate African nationalists with socialist convictions. They are lawyers who practiced together before the ANC was banned. Armed resistance has been forced upon them by the tactics of the Nationalist party. In 1961 Mandela became the leader of Umkonto we Sizwe, the military wing of the ANC responsible for sabotage and guerrilla warfare inside South Africa. In the 1963 Rivonia raid by the South African police, the top leadership was arrested and imprisoned, although Tambo and several others remained abroad to form the exiled movement. In time, they were supported by African states, the OAU, and many nongovernmental organizations, such as the World Council of Churches. The support of the Christian churches was highly controversial at the time and only later generally considered prophetic.

On the question of democracy and socialism, Nelson Mandela had stated at the Rivonia trial: "I have a great respect for British political institutions and for the country's system of justice. . . . The American congress, that country's doctrine of separation of powers, as well as the independent judiciary arouses in me similar sentiments."[68] According to a 1985 interview with him conducted by Lord Bethel of the Conservative party (U.K.), his views had not changed, despite twenty-three years in prison.[69]

Lacking the capacity to launch a major guerrilla war against South Africa, as SWAPO has done in Namibia, the ANC resorted increasingly to tactics of sabotage, strikes, and other disruptions of the economy. One of the leaders, Mr. Nzo, summarized its strategy as follows: "We know we cannot fight the same bush war the others have carried out; but we will use guerrilla tactics in the cities and towns. The people will be our bush!"[70]

Repression has held this resistance down because the police can be more effective in urban areas. The Portuguese territories, Rhodesia, and Namibia were not semiindustrialized countries. They have extensive rugged terrain in which guerrilla armies can operate. The Achilles heel of South Africa, as a semi-industrial country, is the African control over the production system, which can be exercised by withholding labor power and by general disruption. However, it is an economy built by the tribute system and dependent upon the continued flow of investment technology, weapons, and skilled manpower from the West. Disruption, if not severance, of this external support system, which would make the country ungovernable, Tambo has said, is one of the objectives of the ANC.[71] The economy provides the wealth on which the high living standards of the white population are based. The ANC has attacked police stations, banks, and vital sources of fuel.[72] These tactics are combined with further disruption through strikes, boycotts, and demonstrations. The effect of these actions is mainly to widen the base of support for the armed liberation struggle, through re-Africanizing the majority. It also weakens the position of those who want to compromise on both sides of "the two nations" of South Africa.

The strategy will succeed as the ANC gains the cooperation of the black population in South Africa. The battle for the political loyalty of the African has therefore become critical and has given rise to many splits and rivalries. There is little doubt that the Botha government, and even the white liberals, are attempting to hold their ground with the assimilationist leadership, particularly the homeland leaders, most important of whom is Chief Buthelezi. In the 1970s the Chief enjoyed ANC support, since he opposed the pass laws and independence for the homelands. However, since 1980, the two movements have become bitter rivals, with clashes between Inkatha and UDF followers spreading from the Natal province into a general conflict and even civil war in urban areas such as the squatter town of Cross Roads near Cape Town. The South African police have used the Inkatha and vigilantes to attack centers of African resistance.[73]

A large number of liberation groups have emerged. They are allies of the ANC, but maintain an independent status in order to prevent being banned. Like the Soweto Committee of Ten and some of the trade unions, such as COSATU, they seek a bargaining position for workers through which the big change can be brought about.

By late 1986, it seemed clear that the ANC and its allies were winning the struggle for the minds of urban Africans and, to a lesser extent, the rural Africans in the homelands. Building on ethnic loyalties and promises of wealth to the tribal elites, the homelands strategy has slowed down this advance. However, in the cities, the dramatic attacks on energy sources, police stations, military installations, and banks, as well as the strikes and demonstrations which have rallied millions of blacks, have presented a pattern of growing power, despite the national emergencies and fierce repression in the streets, arrests of thousands, silencing of the press, banning of trade union leaders, and the attacks on students in universities and schools. The over 2,300 deaths in 1985–1986, and the thousands of tortured in prison, have only increased support for the progressive position among all races.[74]

## Economic Dependence

The major source of pressure for reform on the Botha government has been the performance of the South African economy. Since the early 1980s, the balance of trade has declined because of the nonrecovery of the metals market. South Africa's industrial market, in the United States and Europe, has slowed. There is high unemployment and alternative supply sources have depressed prices. The reluctance of banks to make loans and the increasing withdrawal of overseas capital have further aggravated the decline. Unemployment has risen to 15 percent among whites and in 1986 was 50 percent among black workers, when the homelands are counted, according to a study by two Witwatersrand University researchers.[75] High inflation and interest rates precipitated the financial crisis of mid-1985. When the rand fell to one-third of its value the year before, the stock market was closed temporarily and a moratorium on debt repayments was declared. This, together with the State of Emergency Declaration, scared foreign banks and investors away.

This time, foreign governments and banks did not bail South Africa out, as they had in 1960 and 1976. In 1982, the United States, with a $1.1 billion International Monetary Fund (IMF) loan, delayed the day of reckoning. President Botha's failure to initiate major reform has alarmed the international financial and corporate community, and they have begun a campaign against the entire structure of apartheid, led by several of the major corporations.

Economists differ on how self-sufficient the South African economy is; but it is clear that when it has been disrupted, productivity falls off drastically, external capital drys up, and immigration of white skilled labor ceases. One prominent risk analysis firm, Frost and Sullivan, placed it in the "D" category in 1980. Many Western businesses have begun to see the writing on the wall and have sought to get out part of their investment or to end expansion. *The Economist* reported that some thirty major U.S. and U.K. corporations had either left or begun divesting their holdings in 1985.[76] By the end of 1986 more than sixty American corporations had left. Total U.S. investment was reduced from $2.6 billion in 1981 to $1.3 billion in 1986. Banks followed suit, reducing loans to private borrowers. In 1986 Barclays Bank withdrew from South Africa, following the decision by major banks such as Citibank and Chase Manhattan not to lend to private corporations.[77] This was reinforced by the U.S. government sanctions adopted in September 1985, which are discussed later.[78] The international campaign by the antiapartheid movement to persuade and force businesses to divest from South Africa began to take effect in the actual compliance by banks, businesses, and governments in 1985. Loss of revenue by municipal bonds sales and banks because of city and state divestment had a major impact. The South African government made vigorous attempts to counteract this loss of confidence. It has succeeded to some degree in creating an active pro-South African business and propaganda lobby in several Western countries, which has, nevertheless, completely failed to stem the tide due to political and economic conditions. The general trend to limit involvement has continued among U.S. banks and corporations.

The European and U.S. institution of sanctions in September 1985 launched a new phase in the struggle in which Western governments have been drawn into the antiapartheid movement. Maneuvering for position by disengagement from the inevitable collapse of apartheid, in order to preserve capitalism and Western security interests, has become their central external policy. This does not mean that the objectives of "constructive engagement" have been changed, as President Reagan has argued, or that the subimperial relationship has been abandoned. The strategy of the United States has shifted to use of its considerable international corporate and financial power to bring about a negotiated settlement with those Africans willing to accept the rules of the dominance relationship and with those whites prepared to maintain control under it.[79] These rules are that apartheid will be abandoned and Africans will participate in the system in the liberal Western sense of freedom, provided the fundamental economic and security relationships are maintained.

The nature of this compromise settlement was specified in the U.S. congressional joint resolution adopted in September 1986 and was contained in *Mission to South Africa: Commonwealth Report by a Group of Eminent Persons*. Both documents made it clear that the Western powers required an end to racial discrimination in living, voting, and working. Majority rule would be necessary, and minorities would be protected. African leaders should be released, and the emergency powers of the government must be relinquished prior to any negotiations. The final terms of the settlement were to be worked out between the parties, but according to the U.S. Congress sanctions would continue until a just settlement was reached. Thus began a sanctions program that had no early end in sight but would vastly change Western–South African relations. President Botha's mid-1986 rejection of a negotiated settlement along these lines indicated that South Africa's white rulers had decided, for the present, that the military and "siege economy" costs were acceptable to them.

## NAMIBIA: PLUNDER AND WAR

> Lord, remember what has been done to us.
> God, look how we are trampled down.
> Our inheritance has been turned over to strangers
> and our homes to aliens.
> Our heart of joy has disappeared.
> Our dance has changed into sorrow.
> Lord, you rule forever.
> From generation to generation.
> —"Namibian Lament"

Namibia is a prime example of the consequences of the subimperial system which subordinates the human rights of the vast majority of people to the security and economic interests of the dominant power in the region. While Western powers have supported Namibian independence, it has been conditional on the understanding that the dominance relationship not be disrupted.

The Reagan administration placed the issue squarely within the context of security matters when it insisted upon linking the withdrawal of Cuban troops from Angola with the end of South African occupation of Namibia. This implied a recognition of the right of South Africa to use force in the occupation of an internationally recognized independent country (Namibia) if Cuban or Soviet forces remained in Angola. The southern African Frontline States felt this doctrine threatened them, since several have been subject to South African intervention and have military ties with the U.S.S.R.

Thus, South-West Africa (Namibia), remains under the rule of South Africa because the dominant forces of the Western world basically have benefited from this relationship, though they seek some adjustment in equity and justice. The importance of South Africa to the West overrides the concerns about growing African hostility and the rising cost of the military occupation of Namibia. The clashes between the Angolan government and the South African forces, which have invaded Angola periodically since 1975, have risen along with the casualties in the fighting between SWAPO, supported by Angola, and the SADF. Through aggressive tactics, South Africa has widened the war by occupying southern Angola and supplying UNITA in an attempt to overthrow the Angolan government and drive the Cubans out of southern Africa. The MPLA government, formed in 1975, has been recognized by every major government in the world except the United States. By supporting UNITA, the Reagan administration in effect has endorsed the "total strategy" of South Africa.[80] In the eyes of the African Frontline States, the United States, even more than South Africa, bore the major responsibility for the failure of Namibian independence.[81]

The West, operating through the Contact Group of Five (United States, Great Britain, Germany, France, and Canada) since the mid–1970s, had sought to negotiate a settlement that would recognize the independence of Namibia. But since 1981 the United States increasingly supported South African military power against what it broadly defined as Soviet intrusion in the region. The effect was to create a deadly stalemate.

## The Plunder of the Economy and U.N. Decree No. 1

Mining and extraction have become the major industries and primary sources of wealth in Namibia, although the majority of whites, like the Africans, are engaged in agriculture. Lead, zinc, and coal are mined on the central plateau. Diamonds, copper, and uranium are the primary exports of companies like DeBeers, AMAX, Newmont, and Rio Tinto Zinc, and account for 90 percent of all mined wealth. These companies are owned primarily by North American and European multinational corporations, with South Africa a secondary partner.[82] However, most production transits South African ports and is subject to tax and export control by the South African government.

Thus, although the major Western powers own and control the most lucrative sections, South Africa benefits from taxes and currency control. The expatriation of profits from diamonds and copper has been, in recent years, over 35 percent, a very high proportion for a developing country. This needs to be seen in terms of redistribution through wages and reinvestment. In fact, the outflow of dividends in 1980–1983 exceeded the African workers' total wage cost by three times.[83]

The potential wealth of Namibian minerals is not fully realized. Namibia is the fourth largest copper producer in Africa, the largest refined lead producer, the second largest zinc source, and has the largest uranium mine in the world, with three more large mines available. This is downplayed by those who claim U.S. operations are minor in Namibia and therefore unimportant to control. The United Nations tried to retain these resources for Namibian development with Decree No. 1, passed by the Council for Namibia on September 27, 1974. This decree specifically forbade the continued development of these resources by South Africa or the granting of concessions without the authorization of the council.[84] Chester Crocker, assistant secretary of state for Africa, in testimony to the House Committee on Foreign Affairs Subcommittee on Africa in 1985, argued incorrectly that U.S. economic interests were secondary and that they were not subject to international law.[85] In point of fact, Namibia is potentially one of the richest countries in minerals in southern Africa, and American firms based in South Africa have recognized this. Moreover, the United States has adhered to a number of international treaties that U.S. courts have recognized as binding, not the least of which are treaties covering international air hijacking and international air traffic control. Torture and racial discrimination are generally recognized as international crimes today, and there is no constitutional reason Congress could not restrict firms or individual Americans who violate these generally accepted norms. Allan Cooper estimates that about 130 U.S. transnationals continued to operate in Namibia in 1982, although only about 35 have a direct presence in Namibia while others operate from South Africa. He notes that only 2 have ceased operation as a result of a U.S. government request.[86] Several oil companies have abandoned their quest without finding oil and one indicated protests at home was a reason, among others, for ending operations.

In a time of falling gold prices and drain on South Africa's balance of payments, the contribution of Namibia is more significant.[87] Thus, South African fears over the loss of Namibian profits and contribution are a factor in the strategic political calculations.

Farming is secondary to minir  for the white economy. Only 6,500 white farms occupy the central plateau.[88] Still, whites who are primarily of German and Afrikans origin exercise enormous political leverage.

The change in the world market for minerals and growing sanctions against South Africa have cut the profitability of the Namibian economy. Foreign companies have begun to withdraw, and South Africa is losing its market for steel and uranium. Therefore, the cost of keeping Namibia has risen beyond what rational economic argument alone could justify. Yet South African resolve to continue its control and occupation is stronger than ever.[89]

The Namibian economy is controlled by external interests, and the internal distribution favors the tributary class of whites and a few African local and central government personnel. While apartheid has declined in Namibia as an official policy, whites run the political economy, and a new tributary class of Africans who support the South African presence and multinational corporate development has emerged as a participant in privilege.

**Western Security**

The security dimension of the South African/Namibia tributary relationship is important to NATO powers who have made defense of the Cape Route a major priority.[90] Namibia is located on the western flank of the Cape with the only deepwater port, at Walvis Bay, and the strategic prospects of a long coastline. Great Britain had established the Walvis Bay enclave in 1878, and it was transferred to South Africa in 1922 under a League of Nations mandate.

Namibia has remained under the military occupation of South Africa, and the South African navy uses Walvis Bay, as occasionally do NATO task forces. A South African air force base at Rooikop was built as a support strike force and patrol area. The Second South African Infantry Battalion Group has been stationed at Walvis Bay.[91] Its importance is shown by South African refusal to even consider giving up the port city in the negotiations over Namibian independence. Some Western powers are sympathetic to this claim because of security considerations. But the U.N. passed a resolution, SC 432, requesting that Walvis Bay be reintegrated into Namibia; and this is the clear position of most Namibian nationalists.

The military occupation of Namibia by South Africa has revealed the scope of its strategic interest. The war with SWAPO's People's Liberation Army of Namibia (PLAN) has widened into Angola and occasionally Zambia. Southern portions of Angola are still occupied despite South Africa's pledge to withdraw. South African army and air force bases have been built along the border in Ovambuland and the Caprivi Strip.[92] The objective of defeating the internal SWAPO insurgency along with containing the Angolans, Cubans, and Soviets north of the border has been a central strategic aim of South Africa. The United States, while originally anxious to negotiate the conflict under the Carter administration, switched to support of South Africa under Reagan. The objective of preventing Cuban and Soviet influences from moving south into Namibia has become central. In 1985 South Africa maintained a standing force of 75,000 troops at a cost of nearly $2 billion a year.[93] (Costs have doubled since Botha claimed a billion dollars annual cost in April 1982.[94]) The price of this operation, plus the cost of administrating the territory, could not be sustained for long by

South Africa without international subsidy, which raises directly the question of the nature of U.S. interest.

For the Reagan administration, the major strategic issue was the linkage of Cuban troops in Angola to South Africa's occupation of Namibia. This issue was not originally raised by South Africa, but was introduced by Reagan's secretary of state, General Alexander Haig. Both Angola and SWAPO rejected the relationship and argued that Cuban assistance was important to the unity of Angola. South African support (and U.S. aid) for UNITA angered the Angolans and entrenched their opposition to any attempt to pressure Cuba out. The introduction of the issue did not lead to a "trade off," as Assistant Secretary of State Crocker maintained, but gave the South Africans an excuse to attack Angola at will in pursuit of PLAN and in support of Jonas Savimbi, the South African-backed leader of UNITA. Thus, the internal politics of Angola were injected by Crocker and Haig into the issue of Namibia. By the end of 1985, it had become a major controversy within the Reagan administration, as well as in the U.S. Congress and at the U.N. The American right wing, under leaders such as congressmen Claude Pepper of Florida and Jack Kemp of New York, succeeded in repealing the Clark amendments with the help of Reagan's endorsement and continuing CIA covert support for UNITA in Angola.[95] The State Department was said to be opposed, but the White House ideologues in the National Security Council had the bit in their teeth. By 1986, Savimbi was directly supplied by the CIA which, in the view of Angola and other African states, made America a direct ally of South Africa in the struggle.[96]

Not only would the Cubans not withdraw under these circumstances, but Angola was compelled to request more assistance from them and the Soviet Union. Given their long-term support of Luanda and the weakening trend of Botha in South Africa, the Soviets were not slow to take advantage of this opportunity to solidify their Angolan tributary relationship.

After the failure of the U.N. plan for a transnational authority and election, the Western Contact Group of Five presented various proposals for settlement of the Namibian problem.[97] Though they attempted to be impartial, as Elizabeth Landis has observed, they appeared to favor South Africa.[98] Based on a free and fair election which would be preceded by a cease-fire and withdrawal of military contingents, the election of a constituent assembly and the installation of an interim government would provide for the implementation of a new constitution under an independent Namibia. However, the key underlying issue has been which groups would win the election and control the new government. The Western proposals attempted to provide for minority protection within the framework of majority rule through a formula of a two-tier representative system, to give two votes to each citizen, one for the party and one for tribal candidates. Such a formula might, in fact, deprive SWAPO of majority control.[99] Because SWAPO rejected this, the proposal was later modified to count a single vote twice. This would enable small minority parties to gain representation and again prevent SWAPO rule, as no group would have a controlling two-thirds of the constituent assembly.[100] Moreover, the formula of tribal representation is regarded by SWAPO and the Frontline African States as a continuation of the earlier Bantustan policies of South Africa, which are rejected by Namibian nationalists as vehemently as they are in South Africa. In opposing the proposal of the Contact Group, Theo Ben-Gurian, SWAPO's permanent representative to the U.N., stated: "The Organization of African Unity . . . and SWAPO find this process fundamentally unacceptable since it is intended to keep Namibian people disunited and separate physically."[101] Thus, they have seen the Western proposals as connivance with South Africa to prevent the majority party, in this case SWAPO, from gaining power.

This attempt to impose a Western formula of "democratic" representation and protection of minority rights onto the conflict, in order to placate South Africa, is a continuation of Western colonial paternalism. It has been rejected because the formulas have added credence to the SWAPO and Frontline African States' belief that the West and South Africa have maneuvered to prevent a SWAPO victory. Thus, Western policy has failed, not because of Cubans in Angola but because it sought to preserve the tributary status of an "independent" Namibia, within the subimperial role of South Africa.

## South African Policy

South Africa is committed to a continuation of this dominance and control of Namibia under a settlement that will maintain an assimilated coalition in power. It has always suspected a U.N.-supervised cease-fire and election. The Botha government has created virtually its own version of independence which is illegal and unacceptable to the Contact Group and the U.N. Council for Namibia. Led by the white liberal Dirk Mudge, the Democratic Turnhalle Alliance (DTA) has established an "interim government." The DTA has only at best fluctuating African support but has incorporated Moses Katjinongua and Andreas Shipanga into it.[102]

The ruling coalition of DTA came unglued early in 1982, when Peter Kalungula, then president, withdrew his Democratic party, which is mainly based in Ovambuland. Kalungula attacked the DTA as promoting apartheid, and South Africa dissolved the interim government in 1983. But South Africa put them back together again in 1985 to form a puppet transitional government with limited powers. The smaller African-supported parties in the DTA, such as Shipanga's SWAPO-Democrats and SWANU, have only regional pockets of support. Mudge's DTA coalition has only a limited white base. It is generally conceded that the transitional government would be overwhelmed by SWAPO in a free election. White parties on the right are small and have been challenged by a Namibian branch of the Herstigte National Party (HNP) from the extreme right which accuses South Africa of selling them out. An alliance of right-wing groups in Namibia called AKTUR opposes the transitional government. AKTUR insists on an ethnic tier for homeland governments in the new constitution and absolutely opposes SWAPO participation in any form.

Prime Minister Botha considers SWAPO to be "Communist-dominated" and untrustworthy, in terms of South African interests. Moreover, the South African right wing of the Nationalist party and the new Conservative party are convinced that the Soviet Union controls SWAPO. These right-wing groups have threatened to resist with force any settlement that gives SWAPO an opportunity to form a government.[103] Liberal and progressive opinion in South Africa rejects this alleged direct link of SWAPO with Moscow, but their views have long been disregarded by the government. South African forces are locked in a deadly combat with SWAPO guerrillas, and it is clear that South Africa finds SWAPO unacceptable. It persists in seeking a formula that will at least give the appearance of democratic elections, thereby retaining U.S. support. The secret discussions in 1984 between Sam Nujoma and South Africa, as well as the All Parties Talks in Lusaka, ended in an impasse over the question of free elections.[104] From the beginning, SWAPO distrusted the Reagan initiatives, and it will be very difficult to regain the ground that has been lost.

## SWAPO

SWAPO, in the eyes of most informed observers, is the majority-backed party in Namibia. There is some opposition to it, but mostly among the smaller tribal groups such as the Herero. The largest African tribe, the Ovambo, has backed SWAPO since the early 1960s and South African occupation and repression has only intensified this attitude. Leaders like Chief Kalungula who originally supported the DTA broke with that party once it became clear that it was intent on maintaining a Bantustan system of tribalism. SWAPO has not been seriously weakened by fragmentation, as the SWAPO-Democrats who have joined the transitional government are a small group.

SWAPO began its armed struggle in 1965 and has continued it with the aid of Angola and other Frontline African States. Nonmilitary aid has been received from Sweden (in substantial quantity), the East European states, and Cuba. Castro has stated that Cuba will leave Angola once the South African threat to the MPLA government is withdrawn and the future of Namibia has been settled.[105] Cuban forces have not been involved in direct support of PLAN; but they have been the major protective force against South Africa's intrusive military actions into Angola. A SWAPO government would not be a Cuban or a Russian surrogate any more than Angola itself has proven to be. Marxist beliefs are heavily diluted with Western Christian values among the leadership.[106] The churches of Namibia, who have many martyrs who have died in support of SWAPO and independence, represent over 80 percent of the Namibian people. Over half of these are Lutheran with ties to the United States through the Lutheran World Federation. SWAPO is not illegal in Namibia and the churches have been able to back it openly as they have done on numerous occasions, though retaliation has often been fierce and deadly against Christian leaders who have supported liberation. These acts of heroism and repression have been recorded in numerous instances. One of the most notable was a statement read to the confidante of President Reagan, U.S. Secretary of State William Clark, during a visit to Windhoek in June 1981 by a SWAPO delegation. The authors included several clergymen and Mr. T. Hoebeb, vice-principal of the Martin Luther High School and president of the synod of the Evangelical Lutheran Church in Namibia. It stated, in part:

Your excellency, you have come here to Namibia in the hope that you would acquire credibility to take your so far unknown and amorphous proposals further afield. But your recent veto in the Security Council on mandatory sanctions against South Africa has already ruined your credibility, if ever you had any, with the Namibian people who see you collaborating with racist South Africa.[107]

One outspoken church leader, Dr. Zaphaniah Kameeta, who has been arrested in Namibia although he is vice-president of the Evangelical Lutheran Church in Namibia, stated in an interview in the United States that SWAPO turned to Eastern Europe because it had been turned down by the West. He urged the West to recognize that this was the Namibians' struggle against apartheid and that they should be assisted in opposing it in their own way.[108] SWAPO is committed to Namibia's control of its own resources and culture, and a SWAPO-formed government would clearly mean a retention of capital in Namibia for its own development.[109]

In Namibia, whites (12 percent) and Coloureds (11 percent) worry about their future. However, SWAPO does not want them to leave, as they contribute to the technical resources and growth of the economy. A SWAPO-formed government would, in all probability, continue the basic economic relationship, as in Zimbabwe, while initiating steps for a new international order through the Southern African Development Coordination Conference (SADCC), characterized by a more equitable system of exchange and a shift from South African strategic ties to nonaligned links with the OAU and Frontline States.

A settlement will be possible only when the rights of the majority are involved in the foundation of a new relationship with the West. This new relationship must create the prospect of the fulfillment of the aspirations of the majority while protecting the rights and interests of minorities and the external parties. The basic principles derived from a self-reliance strategy are (1) majority rule with constitutional protection for minorities, (2) social justice and redistribution of economic gains, and (3) strategic self-reliance.

## Toward a Settlement

As Congressman Wolpe has pointed out in U.S. congressional hearings, the issue of the Cuban presence in Angola is not a long-term concern, once the

Namibian conflict is settled and South Africa ends her incursions into Angola and support for UNITA.[110] The Cubans are anxious to terminate this costly responsibility and have made no commitment to provide logistic support for the ANC. The Namibians, while sympathetic to the ANC, are not likely to provide base facilities for an ANC guerrilla army. SWAPO has indicated that its intent is the liberation of its own country.

A very difficult issue is Walvis Bay, which South Africa has indicated it will retain. Under international law, the territory clearly belongs to Namibia.[111] As Elizabeth Landis has argued, this is true for several reasons, not the least of which is "since racial discrimination and apartheid are international crimes, a state which engages in these crimes is illegitimate and its claims to sovereignty over a non–self-governing territory cannot be recognized."[112] The U.N. Security Council should go beyond Resolution 432, which dealt ambiguously with the issue, to insist that Walvis Bay be a part of an independent Namibia. A self-reliant economy cannot be developed without this major hub of shipping and transportation inland. Namibia, under a SWAPO government, will opt to reject dominance and move toward self-reliance, which cannot tolerate a large foreign enclave for security purposes.

The Western (U.S.) dominance contains a contradiction of interests between the United States and Western powers and South Africa, which is far more than a difference over human rights and racial discrimination. South Africa is essentially a Western surrogate or subimperial state which is useful to the West as long as it can secure the continued stability of the region.

The South African government has been deeply divided over how to respond to this Western pressure. The rapid rise of the far right has forced the Botha government to respond more slowly to the external pressures than would otherwise have been the case. The dominant power can only manipulate the environment in such a way as to bring about a political change favorable to its policies. And in this case, the Reagan policy of "constructive engagement" has created an illusion of power and independence on the part of the South Africans, which has delayed the realization of the necessity for accepting the Western power solution. The argument that gentle persuasion would work better than coercion has not been borne out by the increase of militancy within South Africa and the pressure it has exerted on the government. As Senator Kennedy, Jesse Jackson, and the British Labour party have argued, isolation and restrictions on arms and economic investment might well be more effective. Congresswoman Patricia Schroeder of Colorado has submitted a bill that would enforce U.N. Council for Namibia Decree No. 1 by preventing the operation of U.S. businesses in Namibia, in mineral extraction and export, until independence is achieved.[113] The view of Chester Crocker and Jeffrey Gayner, counselor for International Affairs of the Heritage Foundation, that this action would violate U.S. law, has no standing in international legal circles, which over the past two decades have developed a very clear interpretation of the obligation of signatories, such as the United States, to resolutions and covenants of which it is a party.[114]

Western governments, now committed to a course of human rights action under the United Nations, will probably be forced to resort to means of economic coercion under Chapter 7, Article 41 of the United Nations Charter. U.S. and British vetoes have prevented such drastic action to date, but this is changing. The dominant powers will not permit South Africa to continue to prevent their access to the resources of Namibia and to jeopardize their general security positions through a policy that invites chaos.[115] Sanctions may well precipitate an even greater right-wing reaction and more intensive repression; but their long-term effect will be to weaken South Africa's position in southern Africa and Namibia.

A Namibian election under U.N. Resolution 435 is a desirable outcome, if it can be obtained under terms that will provide a fair atmosphere and not prejudice the results in advance. Such an outcome would be a great triumph for the principles of international order and human rights, as well as the liberation movement.

### Aggression

South African attacks on Frontline States have increased in severity and in the number of casualties. By repeated invasions into Lesotho, Botswana, Angola, and Zambia, South Africa has sought to intimidate them into cooperation.[116] And by backing mercenary forces such as the Mozambique National Resistance (MNR) in Mozambique, whose objective has been to destroy President Chissano's fragile economy, already devastated by drought, it hopes to force all southern African states into greater dependence on South Africa.[117] The effect of these operations on the ANC has been very limited. The Afrikaners have more effectively sealed the Swaziland border, but the infiltration of ANC military cadres continues, through migratory labor groups and other routes.

Several of these attacks have angered the United States, such as the Maseru killings of forty-two people in December 1982. Sabotage attempted against the Cabinda oil field refinery in northern Angola in 1985, and the political killings in a raid in Botswana in June 1985 brought denunciation after the fact. This has not removed criticism of U.S. policies by a number of African states and the U.N. for complicity with South Africa. The United States is accused of equipping and encouraging South Africa to engage in these activities, though publicly denouncing them at the U.N.[118]

The U.S. policy of "constructive engagement," which is a de facto alliance with the apartheid state, has become increasingly hypocritical and untenable. Exposure of South African association with the MNR in Mozambique and subversion of the Nkomati Accord—which was backed to the hilt by American diplomacy—as well as the decision officially to supply CIA aid to UNITA, and the third-party supply of the MNR have hopelessly entangled U.S. policy with South African subimperialism.[119] Knowing they have U.S. backing, the South

Africans have kept up their aggression to maintain economic penetration and military control of the region.

Despite the United Nations' bans of 1963 and 1977, a continuous flow of arms to South Africa has been well-documented by the Stockholm International Peace Research Institute (SIPRI). American complicity in this supplying of arms by private groups and government agencies has been documented in the United States by the American Committee on Africa and the Association of Concerned African Scholars.[120] Great Britain, France, and the United States have maintained an elaborate network to supply directly and indirectly sophisticated technology and advanced weapons systems, often deploying these transfers through third parties. The idea that South Africa is self-sufficient has been repudiated even by more conservative researchers such as Chester Crocker before he became assistant secretary of state.[121] While the Carter administration had reduced U.S. complicity, under Reagan, direct and, more importantly, secret indirect transfers of advanced antiaircraft surface-to-air missiles were made to the South African–backed insurgencies UNITA and MNR. Furthermore, the United States has helped to upgrade the military communications and intelligence gathering equipment of South Africa which was used against SWAPO-PLAN. When the administration could not secure congressional endorsement, they undertook illegally to supply these materials under the Reagan doctrine of so-called "support of liberation wars."[122] State Department denials of such activity frequently were passionate, but the devious channels of supply apparently were not even known to such officials as the secretary of state. The details of this "unholy alliance" began fully to emerge only after the 1986 exposure of the sale of weapons to Iran. This most recent action to equip South Africa was simply another chapter in a long history of deception and secret alliance.

The major U.S. aim in Namibia has been to keep Soviet influence out, and to date South Africa has been the primary force in achieving this objective. However, it is now in the U.S. government's interest to end the war in Namibia and compel South Africa to make peace with SWAPO and the ANC. Realization of this could bring an end to U.S. subimperial relations with apartheid.

The Frontline States are committed to a self-reliance policy and will continue to develop the Southern African Development Coordination Conference (SADCC) and strengthen their defenses against South Africa. They have detailed the cost of South African aggression to their economies, not only in destruction and disruption, but also in the increased expenditures needed for their own defenses. The SADCC group estimated that over five years South Africa had destabilized them to the extent of $10 billion.[123] This estimate did not include the Namibia war. The cost of sanctions by Frontline States against South Africa have risen rapidly, as South Africa has retaliated against bans in trade and has supported insurgencies to expand its hegemony.

The decisive element of change lies in South Africa itself where the ANC and its allies have captured African national consciousness. As noted, this power cannot be controlled in the long run by repression. The reforms have failed and not all the "total strategy" of the Afrikaners can prevent Africans, whose labor controls the economy, from creating a new revolutionary relationship. As this African power grows, and U.S.–core power subimperial support for South Africa weakens, the Frontline States will be able to accelerate the process of change.

In the long run, even the U.S.-run OECD will see the necessity for a shift to sanctions and recognition of the ANC and SWAPO because of the failure of white power to govern and control.

## SANCTIONS AGAINST SOUTH AFRICAN RACISM

The final collapse of white power racism in South Africa will be facilitated by the withdrawal of the support structure provided by U.S. and Western core dominance. Moral outrage may well supply the impetus, but the major dynamic will be the failure of the South African tributary leadership to maintain profitable and sure industrial supply and market for the goods and profits the Western industrial system has required of it. A related motive will be the inability of the Afrikaners to control the stability and security of the Cape Route in Western strategic planning. Whether African-led, multiracial governments can supply the needs of the Western dominance system is uncertain; but at least it has already become a desired alternative, even in some conservative minds. William Safire, a conservative columnist for the *New York Times*, expressed this view well when he wrote: "What's the best way for us to dissuade Prime Minister Botha from continuing to radicalize millions of Blacks?... We must disengage ourselves from Mr. Botha's crackdown to show that error has consequences."[124]

Support for disengagement and sanctions has grown in the United States. The Reagan administration was forced to act by the adoption of sanctions by Congress, which reflected the widespread divestment campaign.[125] The driving force is the deterioration of the South African economy and the related internal strife. Because its economy is semiindustrial, it depends upon cheap semiskilled black labor. But black trade unions and political organizations have disrupted the supply and reliability of this labor, and other sources in Africa or Asia cannot replace this need today. In the earlier part of this century, the Afrikaners would simply have imported tens of thousands of "coolies" from Asia. While labor from Mozambique and Malawi is available, it is unskilled and also politically dangerous, as it is infiltrated by political activists. South African authorities and some of the corporations have attempted to build a compliant labor force with the assimilationist leadership, but this has failed. They are therefore compelled to try to reach a compromise but are so divided among themselves that this has become impossible. The powerful reactionary groups of *verkramptes* in the rural areas, led by Treurnicht and E. T. Blanche, threaten civil war rather than yield to major concessions; but they cannot prevail any more than their Boer ancestors.

Another major characteristic of the economy is its dependence on foreign capital that has been content to invest and reinvest as long as prosperity was assured. High returns cannot be guaranteed and corporations and banks are eagerly seeking exit points, for "business reasons rather than morality," as they like to put it. The effect of this is to give impetus to political pressures for disengagement and sanctions in the United States.

Do sanctions mean the end of U.S. dominance in South Africa? Actually, it means a shift in strategy of the dominance system to one it hopes will bring to power a coalition of groups capable of governing and maintaining Western interests. The American far right opposes such a step, because it feels this will give the Marxists and the U.S.S.R. an opportunity to take over. At this point, most liberals in the West do not view that as a likely prospect and are therefore supporting increased pressures on the South African economy.

### Boers and Colons

Much has been made of the Afrikaner determination to resist to the bitter end; but most of these precedents stem from a different era. The Boer, at one time, could exist with his oxcart and rifle on a remote farm. Today, the economy is not only specialized but dependent upon black labor. Many will resist, though others will see the virtue of compromise as depression spreads and bread-and-butter concerns take over even Boer politics.

Because of the nature of the South African economy and its dependence on the outside world, a unique opportunity exists for liberal politicians, through the depression of the economy, to exert pressure on the Afrikaners for major concessions. This could have a startling effect. It would not be the first time. France went through a similar deprivation of her "Colons" in Algeria, who first revolted and then left. After initial instability, Algeria reasserted its close ties with France and the United States. The difference in South Africa is, of course, the more entrenched character of the Afrikaners, the advanced nature of the economy, and the high level of political consciousness among blacks.

Nevertheless, we should be prepared for a long, bitter struggle. An alternative relationship based on nonracialism, liberation, and self-reliance in the end may be possible for South Africa and Namibia. But reconciliation, after all these years, is not easy.

A new issue has arisen on the left, where sanctions are seen as an attempt to preserve capitalism through reform and thereby perpetuate new forms of racism. The argument is that Africans have to liberate themselves, and sanctions are only a new form of intervention. This view rejects a negotiated settlement and insists on continuation of the revolution until capitalism completely capitulates. There is some insight in this view; but it also has a very doctrinaire tendency that could block a settlement. The leadership of the ANC and SWAPO have repeatedly argued against the extreme forms of this position, as they believe in a gradual transition to socialism and are not convinced this is impossible through an accommodation of interests with whites and external capitalism.

Oliver Tambo and Sam Nujomo have characterized the international sanctions campaign as of great importance to their success:

We are far from suggesting that sanctions will bring the apartheid regime to its knees. We have to do that; we are doing that. All we are saying is that sanctions will weaken the apartheid regime and will make our struggle the lighter . . . sanctions against apartheid is a direct contribution to our struggle.[126]

They have no illusions about the difficulty in implementing such actions, but they have never varied in their advocacy of this approach. Bishop Tutu, as a middle-ground moderate, regards the international sanctions campaign as an important test of the support of the international community for the African position in negotiations and "the last nonviolent option left" for settlement.[127]

The issue is a complex one, but experience elsewhere in Africa has shown that the liberation leadership that has committed itself to a struggle for freedom is the best guide for those who seek to provide support from the outside. This is the meaning of solidarity that is truly universal in its faith in the ability of Africans of all races to determine their own destiny.

There is an absence of discussions on the nature of external support. Sanctions can take various forms—obviously, existing measures are almost meaningless. The walls of Jericho are not going to come tumbling down simply because of U.N. resolutions or the appeals of "enlightened capitalists." But the potential impact of U.N.-based and well-enforced financial, energy, and transportation embargoes should be given detailed consideration.

**Sanctions Strategy**

To date, the various government sanctions available have not been seriously implemented.[128] Major Western governments have not yet seen this step as an important weapon in their attempt to persuade the South African government to undertake changes. Moreover, the U.S. and British governments have considered such steps to be counterproductive and certainly counter to the Reagan objectives of "constructive engagement." These policies have failed as the South Africans have repeatedly marched up to the brink and marched down again. Public opinion in the Western democracies, therefore, has swung sharply against the South African attempt to maintain white control and dominance. Thus, there is a growing prospect that for the first time Western powers will undertake sanctions of a serious proportion with a major impact on the situation. These entail the prevention of military supply through third parties to South Africa; the institution of an energy embargo on oil; an end to all new investment in South Africa by nationals and corporations; the prevention of loans of all kinds, including refinancing; and, most important, a ban on the importation of South African minerals and agriculture products.[129]

Many other forms of sanctions have been proposed, such as the withdrawal by Western powers of tax-exemptions for corporations operating in South Africa.[130] But the major issue is the seriousness of the objective of these powers, which can only be assessed in terms of the creation of machinery to implement and monitor the functioning of these sanctions as well as legislation to penalize noncompliance.[131] Usually sanctions have been for internal political consumption rather than for the purpose of influencing the internal policies of another state. In addition, the United States has quite frequently undertaken sanctions policy unilaterally and with the minimal cooperation of other states. In this case, the support would be nearly universal. And for those noncomplying states, there could be penalties which would assure their cooperation, such as the loss of aid if they violate the ban on arms supply or loans. Since there has been a long history of failure of such sanctions at the United Nations, a considerable amount of cynicism will have to be overcome.[132]

One of the strongest objections is that the sanctions would not be effective and would damage primarily the Frontline States and those groups in South Africa we wish to assist. But such conclusions are usually refuted by the point that the states and groups concerned have requested sanctions and presumably best know their own interests.

The question of effectiveness has many related categories, such as the dependence of the economy and opportunities to break sanctions of the ruling class and the business and financial communities. The impact on these groups must be primary while the effect on nontarget groups needs to be secondary. The high dependence of the South African economy has already been demonstrated and the vulnerability of the business community and the white standard of living is also high. A cutoff of loans and oil would have an immediate impact because the costs of internal production would rise along with unemployment. Business would be forced to cut production, and more foreign companies would attempt to sell and leave the country. There would be increased unemployment among nonwhites, as suggested in the Porter study.[133] But the impact on whites would be much greater than he concludes, in terms of loss of income, employment, and standard of living. The already high level of unemployment among blacks, as well as their low standard of living, will enable them to absorb a cut far more easily than whites. Moreover, they are morally prepared for this, since they have generally agreed that sanctions will benefit them in the long run.

Many South African liberal whites have wondered if sanctions would have the desired effect of forcing the Nationalist Leadership to accept compromise and a settlement with representative Africans.[134] They fear the opposite effect through the ferocity of the right wing. Much would depend upon general public opinion and the reaction of the military members of government. The chances are that they would follow the direction of their own self-interest, which is to save as much of the system of production and wealth as they can, rather than see the whole economy destroyed. While their reaction against growing violence and bloodshed in the streets is to stiffen their repression, they cannot control sanctions except by coming to terms. The chances are, therefore, that their reaction to a determined and effective sanctions program would be at first considerable anger, followed by a sober realization of the way in which the system of dominance was now against them. They would then attempt to reach a settlement acceptable to internal and external opposition. It is similar to a negotiated settlement of a war in which the government is at first totally opposed to negotiation, but its power base, faced with losing all, insists on a settlement in order to preserve something. If the international sanctions are seriously implemented, the devastation could be quite similar to a conventional war that has often in the past persuaded ruling groups that coming to terms with more powerful world forces was in their best interest.

South African business and government have had a great deal of experience in defeating past sanctions such as the arms bans of 1963 and 1977 and the Rhodesian unilateral declaration of independence (UDI). They have skillfully continued to import oil despite the Arab ban by using multinational oil companies willing to ship oil under false papers substantially above the existing oil prices. Oil and shipping companies affiliated with Saudi Arabia, Israel, and Taiwan have facilitated the working of this black market. Furthermore, South Africa has responded to the U.S. and Commonwealth sanctions by establishing a program of shipping and importing numerous types of goods under false documents. South Africa would also like to extend its use of non–South African ports, especially Maputo, and airports like Gabaronne. Companies dependent upon spare parts and markets are quite prepared to engage in the "paper chase" operation that had been so successful between Rhodesia and South Africa during UDI.

It is clear that sanctions can be made to work only if there is general agreement among South Africa's major trading partners on compliance with major sanctions action. Token acceptance and subterfuge have often undercut sanctions in the past. And there can be no exceptions. Such action as an oil embargo, or a total loan and investment ban, if carried out according to international law, must be voted upon by the Security Council of the United Nations under Chapter 7. This would be one of the very few actions of that body in which support of the major powers could be expected. Implementation would have to be centralized and the U.N. Secretariat would be a logical place for it. Compensation funds would be needed for those countries whose economies were most directly affected. While costly, it would be considerably less so in the long run than the destruction of the South African and other southern African economies that is almost certain to be the case if this international intervention is not undertaken.

In addition, there would have to be agreement on the minimum objectives of the sanctions action, as was included in the U.S. congressional action in 1986. The objectives included the initiation of negotiations with representative African leaders and organizations in which the agenda included several of the basic requests of the African Freedom Charter, along with the latest reform proposals of the South African government. Whether sufficient movement toward a settlement was made would have to be decided by an international "good offices" committee established by the U.N.

One of the greatest problems for such international mediation and intervention proposals is, on the one hand, the right-wing's fear of the Soviet Union, and the attempt that South African and other Western conservatives would make to keep the Soviets out of any settlement process; and, on the other hand, the desire of the African leaders and liberation movements to have them a part of the discussions. There is little prospect for a reasonable and negotiated settlement in any major regional conflict of the Third World where this approach is not taken. This does not mean that the region will be handed over to Soviet intrusion as the radical right has so often warned. Rather, the conditions of self-determination are to include the recognition of the emergence of the self-governing rights of all these areas. They will then pursue their own policies of contact and trade. Evidence has shown that even in countries forcefully liberated by armed struggle, the shift from existing patterns of trade and linkages has been very gradual at most. The Marxist-led governments of Angola and Zimbabwe have not, in practice, cut their ties with the OECD trading system. They have, in fact, accepted the increased importance of these ties while diversifying their external linkages. The motive for South African aggression has been to destroy these Western links; for example, by attacking, under the cover of UNITA, the Gulf oil facilities in Cabinda, Angola, and maintaining a destabilizing pressure on the economies of Zimbabwe and Mozambique. The adoption of Savimbi, Botha, and the MNR by the American extreme right wing has clarified this "unholy alliance."[135] Those who want to keep the Soviets out of the settlement process ignore the fact that the East Europeans have been the primary source of arms for the Frontline States and the indigenous liberation movements and could be a disruptive force if their limited interests are excluded from the settlement.

This raises the final point about the realism of suggesting that the rival systems of dominance have reached today any grounds for adopting different policies that are not a continuation of their Cold War II rivalry and arms race or that tributaries and subimperial states are more than expendable pawns in "the great game." If the dominance arms race is sustained as basic policy, there is no prospect that outside forces can play anything other than a role of supporting one side against the other in a fight to the finish in South Africa.

As discussed earlier, the hope that some other prospect awaits Africa is based on the analysis that the two rival world systems have reached a stage in their own internal political/economic dynamics and their relationship with the Third World where they find nondominance in many respects a more viable policy than the continued indirect conflict through tributaries. The theoretical basis for this has been laid out in terms of the internal political pressures within each system. Both the U.S. and Soviet leadership are forced by these considerations to seek points of mutual interest and disengagement, to reduce the unacceptable costs as well as the fears of direct conflict. This argument leads to the conclusion that South Africa and southern Africa are Third World regions where the Soviets are most ready to reach agreement. And in the United States, as in Western Europe, the liberal side of the political spectrum has recognized the limited nature of any security interest because its economic stake cannot be preserved under an "unholy alliance" with apartheid policies.

Under these circumstances, the liberation movements and their supporters have a better chance of success in the long run. The liberation movements place much greater stock in private pressures and sanctions than in Western public policy change.[136] Their view is that the disinvestment of corporate operations in South Africa must take place in order to reduce the influence of international profit making on the support structure of apartheid. One wing of the liberation view has little confidence in the prospect of significant Western-led public sanctions. Their faith is in the growing strength of the indigenous African movement and its capacity to decide the outcome. In fact, they are inclined to suspect the compromises that might be exacted by the external liberal states if they are a major part of a settlement. Such views are held by some Africans in the liberation movement.

However, another wing is hopeful that the worldwide private and public pressures on South Africa can come together and create a combined force sufficient to make a significant difference in bringing about an early settlement. This view does not reject the help of any of the major groups pressing for the end of apartheid, whether they are conservative, liberal, or leftist, black or white. This is a new coalition made possible by the broadening base of the antiapartheid movement, which includes the church as well as Marxists, in this struggle. They have been able to bridge some of the ideological rigidities of the cold war and place their emphasis on the moral objective, rather than the purity of strategies. Solidarity with those ready to seriously combat the evil of racism and uphold justice is advocated—from civil disobedience, to the disinvestment of corporations, to the imposition of sanctions.[137]

The plight of South Africans has entered into the consciousness of the growing peace and justice movement in the Western world. The strongest parallel is with the nineteenth-century abolition of slavery movement. It is a faith issue that transcends class and status.[138] For this reason, it will grow as a political force until it is resolved. Leaders and politicians will not be able to ignore it as it has a growing constituency in all major organizations. Hopefully, it will be resolved before some great tragedy like the American Civil War ends this struggle for human rights. This movement is one of deeds more than words, as was stated by Dr. Martin Luther King in 1962: "We ask all men of good will to take action against apartheid in the following manner. . . . Don't buy South Africa's products; don't trade with or invest in South Africa."[139]

## NOTES

1. Edwin Munger, *Notes on the Formation of South African Foreign Policy* (Pasadena, Calif.: Castle Press, 1965).

2. Robert S. Jaster, "South Africa's Narrowing Security Options," Adelphi Papers, no. 159 (London: International Institute for Strategic Studies, 1980).

3. Ibid., p. 25. The importance of this development was noted by Michael MacGuire in his "Modes of Power Projection into the Indian Ocean" (Dalhousie University conference, "Indian Ocean Perspectives on a Strategic Arena," 1982).

4. Defense expenditures tripled in the 1970s, as reported in *World Military Expenditures and Arms Transfers, 1971–80* (Washington, D.C.: Arms Control and Disarmament Agency). Total military expenditures rose from $620 million to $2,043 billion. See p. 66 (Table 1).

5. W. Andrew Terrill, "South African Arms Sales and the Strengthening of Apartheid," *Africa Today* 31, no. 2 (1984).

6. Jaster, "South Africa's Narrowing Security Options":

South Africa is to all intents and purposes self-sufficient in the manufacture of small arms and small arms ammunition and produces a rather narrow range of military aircraft, rockets, artillery, armoured cars, small naval craft and communications equipment. But for a number of heavy and sophisticated weapons, including tanks, submarines, long-range maritime patrol aircraft, heavy artillery, radar and communications equipment and certain types of ammunition, South Africa remains dependent on imports (p. 40).

7. James Roherty, "Beyond Limpopo and Zambesi: South Africa's Strategic Horizons" (Paper presented at the Conference on the Indian Ocean, Perth, University of Western Australia, August 1979).

8. Patrick Wall, ed., *The Indian Ocean and the Threat to the West* (London: Stacey International, 1975).

9. Sean McBride refers to this meeting in the opening address to the Washington Conference on Namibia organized by the American Committee on Africa. Washington, D.C., no. 29, November 29–December 3, 1982.

10. Quoted by Patrick Wall in "Where NATO Must Not Drop Its Guard," *To The Point*, December 20, 1976.

11. Both Robert Price and Larry Bowman concur that the commitment to defend South Africa is limited and, moreover, the reality of the Soviet threat is much exaggerated by Reagan strategists. See Larry Bowman, "The Strategic Importance of South Africa to the United States: An Appraisal and Policy Analysis," *African Affairs* 81, no. 23 (1982).

12. Numerous studies have documented this transfer of weaponry, such as NARMIC, "Military Exports to South Africa: A Research Report on the Arms Embargo" (Philadelphia: American Friends Service Committee, January 1984).

13. Ron Walters, "Uranium Politics and U.S. Foreign Policy in Southern Africa," *Journal of Southern African Affairs* 4, no. 3 (July 1979).

14. The definitive research on unofficial arms transfers and the strengthening of SADF has been done by Richard Leonard, *South Africa at War* (Westport, Conn.: Lawrence Hill, 1983), pp. 131–166. Other reliable sources are numerous, but see especially U.S. Congress, House Subcommittee on Africa, *The Space Research Case and the Breakdown of the U.S. Arms Embargo Against South Africa,* Staff study, March 24, 1981.

15. U.S. Congress, House Committee on Foreign Affairs, Subcommittee on Africa, *Hearing on South Africa*, 96th Cong., 2nd Sess., October 19, 1980.

16. Bowman, "The Strategic Importance of South Africa to the United States."

17. Franklin Thomas, ed., *South Africa: Time Running Out,* Rockefeller Commission Report (Berkeley and Los Angeles: University of California Press, 1981), p. 135.

18. See Richard E. Bissel, "How Strategic is South Africa?" in *South Africa into the 1980s*, ed. Richard Bissel and Chester Crocker (Boulder, Colo.: Westview, 1980), pp. 214–16.

19. Michael Samuels, Chester Crocker, Roger Fontaine, Dimitri Simes, and Robert Henderson, *Implications of Soviet and Cuban Activities in Africa for U.S. Policy*, Center for Strategic and International Studies, Significant Issues Series I, no. 5 (1977).

20. U.S. Congress, House Committee on Foreign Affairs, Subcommittee on Africa, *Hearing on South Africa*, p. 87.

21. Gerald J. Bender, "Angola, Left, Right, and Wrong," *Foreign Policy*, no. 43 (Summer 1981).

22. Larry Bowman outlines this Soviet support in "African Conflict and Super Power Involvement in the Western Indian Ocean," in *The Indian Ocean in Global Politics*, ed. Larry Bowman and Ian Clark (Boulder, Colo.: Westview, 1980), pp. 92–93.

23. Kevin Danahar, *In Whose Interest? A Guide to U.S.–South African Relations* (Washington, D.C.: Institute for Policy Studies, 1984), pp. 49–50.

24. M. C. O'Dowd, "The Stages of Economic Growth and the Future of South Africa," in *Change, Reform, Economic Growth in South Africa,* ed. Lawrence Schlemmer and Eddie Webster (Johannesburg: Raven Press, 1978), p. 45.

25. *Minerals Yearbook* 1980, vol. III (Washington, D.C.: U. S. Government Printing Office, 1982), p. 871.

26. U.S. Congress, Senate Committee on Foreign Relations, Subcommittee on African Affairs, *Imports of Minerals from South Africa by the United States and the OECD Countries*, 96th Cong., 2nd Session, 1980, pp. 9–10.

27. The policy outlined in the 1977 Defense White Paper and its implications are discussed by Richard Leonard in *South Africa at War*, pp. 198–222.

28. Kenneth Grundy observes that General Malan and others, like Harry Schwartz, favor a ratio of 80 percent politics to 20 percent force. The question of force as the decisive variable in the total strategy, however, remains. Kenneth W. Grundy, "The Rise of the South African Security Establishment," The South African Institute of International Affairs, Bradlow Series, no. 1 (August 1983), p. 35.

29. "Destabilisation in Southern Africa," *The Economist*, July 16, 1983.

30. See Chester Crocker's statement in U.S. Congress, House Committee on Foreign Affairs, Subcommittee on Africa, *Hearing on Namibia*, 99th Cong., 2nd Sess., October 29, 1985.

31. O'Dowd, "The Stages of Economic Growth," p. 45.

32. Heribert Adam, *Modernizing Racial Domination* (Berkeley and Los Angeles: University of California Press, 1971).

33. "The Sullivan Principles, No Cure for Apartheid," American Committee on Africa, Public Statement, 1980. The statement was signed by fifty specialists and activists in African affairs.

34. Gail M. Gerhart, *Black Power in South Africa* (Berkeley: University of California Press, 1978), pp. 21–34.

35. Ben Magubane, *The Political Economy of Race and Class in South Africa* (New York: Monthly Review Press, 1979), p. 15.

36. Amilcar Cabral, *Return to the Source: Selected Speeches*, edited by Africa Information Service (New York: Monthly Review Press, 1973), pp. 54–55.

37. Ibid., p. 45.

38. Magubane, "Political Economy."

39. Buthelezi has attacked those who will not negotiate with the whites, as he feels even the smallest concession should be exploited. "We as blacks dare not prejudice any white initiatives which even remotely promise to move the country in the right direction." *Sunday Times* (Johannesburg), October 28, 1979.

40. Roger Southall, "The Beneficiaries of the Transkeian Independence," *The Journal of Modern African Studies* 15, no. 1 (1977): "These groups do not actively support

apartheid in its narrowly racial discriminative sense; but they are prepared to accept the marginal gains offered as an alternative to the costs of struggle for a meaningful liberation" (p. 21).

41. Joseph Lelyveld, *New York Times,* March 6, 1981.
42. John F. Burns, *New York Times,* September 21, 1980.
43. Barry Streak, "Organizing the Struggle: Cyril Ramaphosa, General Secretary of the National Union of Mineworkers," *Africa Report* 31, no. 2 (March–April 1986).
44. Elizabeth Schmidt, "The Sullivan Principles: Decoding Corporate Camouflage," New York: United Nations Center Against Apartheid, March 1980, p. 53.
45. John Kelly and Murray Waas, "Behind Reagan's Embrace of South Africa" (cited in a U.S. Consulate General report and substantiated by a confidential International Monetary Fund report which documented the gap), in *Africa Asia,* no. 1 (January 1984), pp. 12–13.
46. This was documented by a two-year study financed by the Carnegie Corporation, headed by Professor Francis Wilson of Capetown University, and reported in the *New York Times,* April 22, 1984.
47. "Human Rights in South Africa" (an interview with Patricia Derian, *Current Policy,* no. 181) details the actions taken in support of the international campaign against the violation of human rights.
48. John Dugard, "Commentary," *Race Relations News* no. 1, (Johannesburg: South African Institute of Race Relations), 1977.
49. *The Economist,* June 21, 1980.
50. John Burns, *New York Times,* April 13, 1980.
51. Joseph Lelyveld, *New York Times,* May 1, 1981. Also, *X-Ray* (London) reported that Botha was mainly preoccupied with the fight against the *verkrampte* elements in his own party: "The army leadership is strongly identified with the Verlichte elements in the Afrikaner political establishments." September/October 1980.
52. Alan Cowell, *New York Times,* August 25, 1985.
53. Robert Davies, Don O'Meara, Sipho Dlamini, *The Struggle for South Africa,* vol. 1, (London: Zed Press, 1984), pp. 155–56.
54. Seventy-two percent of English and even a majority of Afrikaner speakers thought apartheid would not survive ten years. *The Sunday Times* (London), September 1, 1985.
55. *New York Times,* September 30, 1985.
56. View expressed by a South African editorial writer to the author in October 1985.
57. *The Sunday Times* (London), September 1, 1985.
58. Davies, *Struggle for South Africa* 2, p. 344.
59. Joseph Lelyveld commented in 1983: "From a military point of view, the African National Congress has been one of the world's least successful 'liberation movements.' " *New York Times,* October 12, 1983. By 1985, the military role could not be separated from the political.
60. Professor Theodore Hauf, "Report on Urban Blacks and Whites" (Berlin: Arnold Bergstraesser Institute for Socio-Political Research, 1980).
61. Thomas G. Karis, "Revolution in the Making: Black Politics in South Africa," *Foreign Affairs,* Winter 1983/84.
62. *Update* (New York), September 1985.
63. The Institute for Black Research's Special Report, *Unrest in Natal* (Durban: August

1985), reported that Buthelezi had 4.8 percent support among Africans, down from 45 percent (p. 84).

64. Even retired General Handrick van den Bergh, formerly head of the Security Police, said: "Mandela has served his debt to society." *New York Times,* May 21, 1980.

65. Secretary of State George P. Schultz said: "Therefore, the centerpiece of our policy is a call for political dialogue and negotiation between the Government and representative Black leaders. Such an effort requires that we keep in touch with all parties, Black and White." *New York Times,* October 10, 1985.

66. Blaine Hardin, *The Manchester Guardian Weekly,* September 1, 1985.

67. For details, see the author's *Anti-Apartheid: Transnational Conflict and Western Policy in the Liberation of South Africa* (Westport, Conn.: Greenwood Press, 1977), pp. 117–34.

68. Nelson Mandela, *No Easy Walk to Freedom: Articles, Speeches and Trial Addresses,* ed. Ruth First (New York: Basic Books, 1965), p. 183.

69. Jack Simons, "Our Freedom Charter," *Sechaba* [London], June 1985, p. 10.

70. *New York Times,* January 27, 1980.

71. Oliver Tambo, "Making the Country Ungovernable," *Sechaba* [London], March 1985.

72. The attack on the SASOL (oil) plant was the most sensational. *Africa News,* April 27, 1980.

73. Alan Cowell, *New York Times,* July 8, 1986.

74. Extensive documentation has been made of these human rights violations by several reputable sources, such as the "African Rights Monitor" in *Africa Today* 32 and 33, nos. 1, 2, and 4 (1985/86), *Africa News* 17 (1986), and the reports of the Lawyers Committee on Civil Rights in South Africa (Washington, D.C.: 1985–86).

75. Jeremy Keenand and Michael Sarakinsky, quoted in *Lincoln Letter* [London], October 1986.

76. *The Economist,* September 21, 1985.

77. *New York Times,* August 30, 1985.

78. Ibid.

79. Kenneth S. Zinn stated: "The sooner the West withdraws its economic and political support for apartheid, the sooner the White military government will be forced to the conference table with the legitimate leaders of the Black community." "Economic Pressure and the Ending of Apartheid," *Manchester Guardian Weekly,* September 8, 1985.

80. Douglas G. Anglin, "The Nkomati Accord in Retrospect" (Paper delivered at the African Studies Association Conference in New Orleans, Carleton University, Ottawa, Canada, 1985).

81. Julius Nyerere represents this view. See Margaret Novicki, "Interview with Julius Nyerere," *Africa Report,* November-December 1985, pp. 7–8.

82. In mining, South Africa owns 40 percent, while U.S. and European interests control the rest. If all production, including farming and fishing, is considered, then South Africa owns 75 percent of production. SWAPO, *To Be Born a Nation: The Liberation Struggle for Namibia* (London: SWAPO and Zed Press, 1982), pp. 46–48.

83. Allan D. Cooper, "An Overview of American Corporate Investments in Namibia" (Paper delivered to the American Committee on Africa, Washington, D.C., November 29, 1982).

84. Based on U.N. General Assembly Resolutions 1514 and 1603 (December 14, 1960, and December 14, 1962).

85. Chester Crocker, statement on legislation concerning the U.N. Council for Namibia, U.S. Congress, House Committee on Foreign Affairs, Subcommittee on Africa, October 29, 1985.

86. Cooper, "An Overview," p. 2.

87. Richard V. Green, "From Sudwestafrika to Namibia: The Political Economy of Transition," Scandinavian Institute of African Studies (Uppsala), Research Report no. 58, (1981), p. 8. South Africa has a large favorable balance in foreign currency from Namibia and South African companies like DeBeers pay only one-half the taxes in Namibia that they pay in Botswana (p. 55).

88. People are still forceably removed from areas to provide for white interests and protection. International Defense and Aid Fund, *Namibia: The Facts* (London: IDAF, 1982), p. 22.

89. Green, "From Sudwestafrika to Namibia."

90. A confidential document of the U.S. National Security Council proposed a South Atlantic alliance, including South American countries like Argentina, in order to defend the Cape Route. "Reagan Alliance Woos South Africa," *South* (London), October 1981, p. 24.

91. International Defense and Aid Fund, *Apartheid's Army in Namibia: South Africa's Illegal Military Occupation* (London: IDAF, 1982), p. 7. Also, United Nations Council for Namibia, *The Military Situation in and Relating to Namibia* (New York: United Nations, 1983).

92. The extensive deployment of SADF is outlined in *Apartheid's Army in Namibia*, pp. 4–5.

93. Ibid., p. 15.

94. *New York Times,* March 24, 1982.

95. Ibid., October 29, 1985.

96. "A Letter From Luanda," *Africa News* 26, no. 6 (March 24, 1986); and "Savimbi Visit Spotlights Gulf Again," *Africa News* 26, no. 5 (February 10, 1986).

97. "Proposal for a Settlement of the Namibian Situation," *Objective Justice* 10, no. 2 (Summer 1978). Security Council Resolution 431 (July 27, 1978) established the U.N. Temporary Assistance Group (UNTAG).

98. Elizabeth Landis, *Namibian Liberation: Self-Determination, Law and Politics* (New York: Episcopal Churchmen for South Africa, 1982), pp. 8–9.

99. The original idea was that half the members of the constituent assembly would be elected on a national basis by proportional representation and half on the basis of single member constituencies. Each voter was to have two votes, and this would enable tribally-based candidates as well as national party candidates to win seats. See "Revised Contact Group Proposal," in "Issue Brief," *Transafrica Forum* (February 1982) *Africa News,* May 24, 1982, carries the full statement of SWAPO views.

100. *Africa News,* February 22, 1982.

101. *Update* (African American Institute), February 10, 1982.

102. Allan J. Cooper, "Political Developments in Namibia," Association of Concerned African Scholars (ACAS) Newsletter, no. 16 (Fall 1985), p. 35.

103. *Africa News,* May 24, 1982, carries a full statement.

104. *Namibia: The Facts,* pp. 48–50.

105. Randall Robinson, *New York Times,* April 22, 1982.

106. Interview with Sam Nujoma, *Africa News,* July 16, 1984. Also see "Namibia, A Nation Wronged," a report of the British Council of Churches, Division of International

Affairs, London, 1982. "They found a belief that SWAPO was the 'amiti' (friend) of the people" and "many SWAPO leaders are Christians."

107. *Newsletter,* Episcopal Churchmen for South Africa, New York, (July 1981), p. 2.

108. Ibid.

109. *Dateline, Namibia* (New York), no. 1 (1984), pp. 4–5. These proposed changes have been published in the research reports of the United Nations Institute for Namibia, Lusaka, headed by Hage G. Geingob. See *UNIN News,* quarterly and other reports, such as R. H. Green, *Manpower Estimates and Development Implications for Namibia* (Lusaka: UNIN, 1978).

110. U.S. Congress, House Committee on Foreign Affairs, Subcommittee on Africa, *Hearings on Namibia,* 98th Cong., 1st sess., February 21, 1983, p. 32. This point has been affirmed by Congressman Solarz who believes the Angolans will remove the Cubans as soon as aid to UNITA from the outside is ended. President Dos Santos reiterated this on October 24, 1985, and said that the attacks had deepened their reliance on Cuban troops. Gretchen Eick, *UCC Peace Priority* 4, no. 8 (December 1985), p. 4.

111. Richard Moorsom, *Walvis Bay, Namibia's Port* (London: International Defense and Aid Fund, January 1984), p. 15.

112. Landis, *Namibian Liberation,* p. 15.

113. Patricia Schroeder, statement before the Subcommittee on Africa, U.S. Congress, House Committee on Foreign Affairs, 99th Cong., 1st sess., October 29, 1985.

114. Jeffrey B. Gayner, testimony before the Subcommittee on Africa, U.S. Congress, House Committee on Foreign Affairs, 99th Cong., 1st sess., October 29, 1985.

115. See David J. Stephenson et al., "Enforcing Decree No. 1 in the Domestic Courts of the United States," *Africa Today* 30, nos. 1 and 2 (1982), pp. 69–82.

116. Richard Leonard, *South Africa at War,* pp. 86–96.

117. South African denial of its support for the MNR has been exploded by the capture of an MNR officer's diary that specifically implicated the South African military, notably General Constand Viljoen, Chief of Staff in Supply Operations. Michael Bole-Richard, *Manchester Guardian,* October 27, 1985. Also, see extracts from the diaries published in *Africa News,* Nov. 4, 1985, by William Minter.

118. The United States has supported U.N. Security Council denunciations of these killings. But criticism of U.S. complicity has grown. U.N. Council for Namibia, *The Military Situation in and Relating to Namibia,* pp. 12–13.

119. *Africa News* (November 4, 1985) reported that anti-Communist groups were increasingly influential in Angolan policy-making in Washington, D.C. Details of the U.S. right-wing support is reported in *Africa News* 27, no. 10–11 (December 8, 1986). Also see *The Independent* (London), December 9, 1986, on secret arms transfers from the U.S. to South Africa.

120. Kevin Danahar utilizes their work in his *In Whose Interest?*

121. Chester Crocker, *South Africa's Defense Posture: Coping with Vulnerability,* Washington Papers, no. 84 (Beverly Hills: Sage Publications, 1981), p. 46. The self-sufficiency interpretation has been given by Christopher Coker, *The United States and South Africa 1968–1985:* (Durham, N.C.: Duke University Press, 1986).

122. "News in Review," *New York Times,* December 14, 1986.

123. *Africa Report* (November-December 1985), p. 49.

124. William Safire, "Disengagement Time," *New York Times,* August 8, 1985.

125. These five initial sanctions were specified in the *New York Times,* September 10,

1985. Divestment is the withdrawal of funds from corporations doing business with South Africa in order to force them to disinvest from South Africa. The scope of the campaign is detailed in Jennifer Davis et al., "Economic Disengagement and South Africa: The Effectiveness and Feasibility of Implementing Sanctions and Divestment," *Law and Policy in International Business* 15, no. 12 (1983).

126. *Sechaba*, Editorial, December 1985.

127. Desmond M. Tutu, "Sanctions vs. Apartheid," *New York Times*, June 16, 1986.

128. In discussing sanctions undertaken by the Reagan administration, Professor Wright argues they are negligible but represent a victory for the antiapartheid movement. Sanford Wright, "Constructive Disengagement: U.S. Sanctions against South Africa," *The Black Scholar*, November-December 1985, pp. 2–10.

129. A review of these sanctions proposals was made by Clyde Ferguson and William Cotter in *Foreign Affairs*, October 1978. More recently, see Elizabeth Schmidt, "Impose Tough Sanctions on South Africa," *New York Times*, January 17, 1986.

130. Jennifer Davis, James Cason, and Gail Hovey, "Economic Disengagement and South Africa: The Effectiveness and Feasibility of Implementing Sanctions and Divestment," *Toward Policy in International Business* 15, no. 2 (1983), p. 556.

131. Ibid., pp. 559–63.

132. D. C. Clarke, "Policy Issues and Economic Sanction on South Africa," no. 1 (Geneva: International University Exchange Fund, 1980).

133. Richard C. Porter, "The Potential Impact of International Sanctions on the South African Economy," *Journal of Conflict Resolution*, December 23, 1979.

134. Martin Bailey and Bernard Rivers carried out a study for the U.N. which answered many questions about implementation. See "Oil Sanctions Against South Africa," *Notes and Documents* 12, U.N. Center Against Apartheid, June 1978.

135. John B. Judis, "Savimbi: New Darling of the New Right," *In These Times*, February 12–18, 1986.

136. From the Carter to the Reagan administration, there has been consistent government support for American businesses in South Africa, and opposition to pressures on U.S. firms to disinvest and withdraw. Kevin Danaher has an excellent discussion of this proinvestment policy. See especially chapters 5 and 6 in *The Political Economy of U.S. Policy Toward South Africa* (Boulder, Colo.: Westview, 1985), pp. 137–219.

137. The chairman of the Washington, D.C. Retirement Board wrote to the *New York Times*, October 31, 1985, after it had divested $45 million from its $470 million portfolio: "In the three quarters since September 30, 1984, the performance of the two South Africa Free Index Funds has been 19.3%. The performance of the stock market, as measured by Standard and Poors 500, has, over the same period, been virtually identical." Others such as Michigan State University, working through South Africa Free (SAF) investment funds, have experienced an increase in their revenue. Such SAF "risks" are slightly higher than traditional portfolios, according to a study by Daniels and Bell, though returns are greater and well within prudent guidelines.

138. See resolutions passed at the National Conference of the South African Council of Churches, Johannesburg, June 28, 1985.

139. Statement issued on Human Rights Day, December 10, 1962, quoted in *Southern African Perspectives*, no. 2 (New York: ACOA, 1985).

# 3

# War on the Horn among Tributary States: Intervention from Above and Revolution from Below

> Behold how the Infidel lays traps for you [Somalis] as you become less wary. The coins he dispenses so freely now will prove your undoing.
>
> —Last words of Sayid Mohammed Abdille Hassan, the turn-of-the-century leader of the Somalis against the British, French, and Italians, as quoted by Abdi Sheikh Abdi.

Recent failures in African state policies have led to war and famine and many other tragedies for the peoples of the Horn of Africa. But can the inept, aggressive, and foolish decisions of indigenous leaders be regarded as only the actions of pawns in "the great game"? There is a very important interrelationship between the tributary governments of the region and the dominant powers. Responsibility for the famine in Ethiopia and civil war in the Sudan cannot, however, be simply explained as a continuation of "neocolonialism." The superpowers who dismiss their own responsibility for the wars and the Africans who blame their own rulers for the millions who have perished are both wrong. There are several lessons to be learned here about tributary states and the use of regional rivalries by the superpowers for their own interests on the giant chessboard.

The Horn of Africa should be seen as an extension of the major security and economic interests of the United States and the Soviet Union into the Persian Gulf and the northwestern Indian Ocean. This region became a new security zone for both powers in the mid–1970s, but the roots of this policy go back earlier, to the postwar settlement that brought both superpowers fully into the region.

The chief conditioning factor has been the creation by the superpowers of new security zones, for political strategic reasons. Since 1945, northeast Africa has seen the extension of the superpowers' rivalry over the Middle East. Since the mid–1960s, the Persian Gulf region and the countries along the Red Sea have been caught up in the growing arms race and increasing warfare.

The wars between Ethiopia and Somalia have been in part a product of this extended rivalry. And the revolutions in Ethiopia, Somalia, and the Sudan have been enormously influenced by it. Secessionist movements have found militant fuel and subsidy for their internal wars in the arms that have spilled over from the major conflicts between states. Conflicts between the regional states of Libya, Sudan, Chad, Uganda, and Tanzania have added to the turmoil. The usual explanations of tribal and elite rivalry are only a small part of an adequate analysis. External intervention and the dependency of these states are not the sole explanations, but these have had enormous influence.

## U.S.-SOVIET RIVALRY AND THE ETHIOPIAN REVOLUTION

Superpower rivalry in the Middle East has been indirectly caught up in the ancient conflicts of the Horn of Africa through their tributaries. The Arab and Islamic politics of the Middle East, as well as the Arab-Israeli conflict, have spread to the new states of northeastern Africa. From Egypt to the Sudan and Somalia, majority Arab and Islamic populations are supercharged with the issues of Iran, Iraq, and the politics of oil prices. Saudi Arabia and Libya have emerged as two major regional contenders for leadership. Qaddafi has sought to establish a radical tripartite among Libya, Ethiopia, and South Yemen, while the Saudis have coordinated their politics with the Sudan, Somalia, and Kenya.[1] Only Tanzania has disengaged herself from this network of rivalry.

Behind these maneuvers, the dominant powers have supplied arms, money, and moral support in pursuit of their major strategic and economic objectives. No other region of the world presents a greater confusion and conflict of regional and global interests. Thus, a pattern of tributary development has clearly emerged in this new phase of imperialist rivalry.

Geopolitically, the countries of Ethiopia, Somalia, Djibouti, Sudan, and the two Yemens guard the southern access to the Suez Canal through the Red Sea. Their resources are considerable, but very underdeveloped. They have virtually no oil (except the Sudan), and they number among the poorest countries in the world, yet their seaports have provided bases and communications facilities of major importance to the two superpowers. While the full strategic significance of the region was not apparent until the 1970s, the United States had established, in 1953, a communication base at Kagnew in the Eritrean highlands and the U.S.S.R. began aiding Somalia's armed forces in the mid–1960s. Anglo-Egyptian withdrawal from the Sudan took place in 1956, and Chad became independent in 1960. Superpower rivalry penetrated into the Sudan and Chad in the 1970s, when they became part of a total struggle for control of the trade routes, the strategic position, and the resources of northeastern Africa. Underlying rivalries between the Eritreans and the Amharas and between the Africans and the Arabs have flared periodically into civil wars and have involved the superpowers indirectly in dangerous, unsettling conflicts. To the south, Kenya and Tanzania have strategic facilities and provide different types of leadership. Kenya has become a center for multinational corporate development, and Tanzania is the titular leader of the self-reliance movement against the dominant powers.

The U.S.S.R. has had tributary relations with Somalia, the U.A.R., the Sudan, Libya, and Ethiopia through whom it has intruded into the regional conflicts of Eritrea, the Ogaden, southern Sudan, and Chad, as well as gained important surveillance posts over U.S. naval operations in the Arabian Sea. In competition, the United States has set close tributary links with the Ethiopian monarchy, Kenya, Somalia, the Sudan and Egypt. From bases in these countries, it has tried to project its power into the Indian Ocean, to offset Libyan and Ethiopian influence on the African-Arab conflicts and prevent Soviet predominance on the Horn, which is close to the Arabian Peninsula. Through the wealth of Saudi Arabia, the population of Egypt, and the strategic positions of Somalia and Kenya, the United States has attempted to contain both radical Arab influences and Soviet penetration into the Nile Valley basin as well as Soviet influence in black Africa to the south. The vital oil route partially flows through the Suez, but the primary U.S. preoccupation is with the strategic bases needed to protect its tributaries in the Middle East, especially Saudi Arabia and Israel.

U.S. dominance designs in the region were predicated upon the security links and limited economic interests established as a result of the British and Italian withdrawal from the Horn following World War II. After the defeat of Italy on the Horn, Great Britain and France collaborated with the United States in the creation of Somalia, Libya, and Djibouti, and in returning Eritrea to Ethiopia. The Sudan gained independence in 1956, with southern Sudan as a reluctant inclusion.

Unification of British and Italian Somaliland formed the Republic of Somalia in 1960. Ethiopia protested against an independent Somalia, but the British government, which favored a unified Somalia, rejected Ethiopia's claims of prior control.[2] The British thereby opened the door to further Somali demands on the Ethiopian territory of the Ogaden, Kenya's Northern Frontier District, and the territory known as French Somaliland until 1977 when as Djibouti it finally gained independence in an agreement which left France with an important military base and naval facilities.[3] Eritrean aspirations for nationhood following the defeat of Italian colonialism in the war were bargained away by the U.S. and Great Britain in return for strategic positions on the Red Sea in Ethiopia.

Initially, the U.S. interest in Ethiopia as a client and tributary state was as a buffer against radical Arab nationalism, which had begun in the Middle East wars over Israel and culminated in Nasser's revolution in Egypt and the struggle over the Suez Canal. Sudanese nationalism established a republic in 1956, which became increasingly pro-Egyptian, particularly after the military coup in 1958 led by General Abboud. The British position in Aden and Yemen, across the Strait of Bab 'el Mandeb, was under attack by pro-Nasser insurgents, assisted by the Soviet Union. Therefore, the United States saw the Ethiopian highlands as a strategic center, as well as an important communications base for its nascent nuclear submarine activity in the Indian Ocean. As Tom Farer concluded, concerning this U.S.-Ethiopian alliance, "The Ethiopian armed forces fly U.S. planes, fire U.S. rifles loaded with U.S. ammunition, and roll on U.S. tanks and trucks. Most of the officer corps has gone through U.S. training programs. Dependence on the United States for spare parts is virtually total."[4]

Ethiopia was recognized as a tributary state, not only because of its strategic location on the Red Sea, but also because its Coptic ruling class was both anti-Muslim and non-Arab. The emperor was pro-Western and the Amharic aristocracy trained in English and European values. The regime appeared stable and willing to provide the facilities the United States needed to deploy its forces and counter the growing influence of Abdel Nasser south of Suez. The colonial areas of Africa were not available to U.S. intrusion at the time. But the reinstated government of Emperor Haile Selassie was an obvious target for U.S. military links. Naval and air bases were established under agreements that gave the United States naval facilities at Assab and an air force communication base at Kagnew near Massawa. At their peak, these facilities had between three and four thousand American personnel.[5] Thus, the United States had direct land-based air facilities for twenty-five years under the agreement, as well as another stage in the global network of communication facilities for the strategic submarines it had begun to deploy in the Arabian Sea by late 1950s. The Indian Ocean served as another launching area for strategic missiles against the U.S.S.R. and the Kagnew base participated in the sophisticated (LV3) sonar system, established on the northwest cape of Australia in the 1950s for guiding submarine-launched ballistic missiles (SLBMs) against U.S.S.R. targets.[6]

The prominent position of the United States in the disposition of Eritrea gave it the needed opportunity to begin discussions with the emperor regarding base facilities.[7] The close coordination of these policies with Israel, the principal subimperial state for U.S. policies in the Middle East at that time, led to the establishment of diplomatic ties and an Israeli military training unit for counterinsurgency in Eritrea.[8] American training of Ethiopians through the Military Assistance Advisory Group (MAAG) was the largest in Africa, covering a 40,000-man army. The air force was a priority, and the United States helped establish, through Trans World Airlines, the new Ethiopian airlines.

By the early 1960s, the United States had established a tributary relationship with the emperor's government. His Majesty could be counted upon by the United States to take the moderate line in African and Arab circles. He even retained diplomatic ties with Israel until the Arab-Israel October War of 1973.

American economic interest in Ethiopia was marginal, and the bulk of Ethiopian trade in this period was with the U.K. and the European Economic Community (EEC). At most, one hundred American corporations operated in Ethiopia. A large U.S. AID mission, especially concerned with agriculture, was established and thousands of Ethiopian students studied in the United States. The majority of Ethiopia's principal crop—coffee—was exported to the United States. However, the real economic interest was the protection of the oil route from the Middle East. The Horn of Africa became a geopolitical strategic center for this reason. In addition, the support of nuclear SLBMs made the region into a security zone to contain the U.S.S.R. within its borders.

The lack of a significant economic base and the Ethiopian revolution in 1974, plus the change in U.S. strategic policies in the mid-1970s after the Vietnam War debacle, meant that Ethiopia was not raised to subimperial status in the tributary system. It is doubtful that the revolution alone led to this decision, since the United States was not opposed initially to the take-over by military officers in 1974, most of whom had been trained in the United States. Military aid and training on a reduced scale continued until the new government requested the withdrawal of MAAG in 1977. This disengagement policy of the United States was a significant example of how a shift in superpower strategic policy resulted in the hastened demise of the feudal comprador class and aided the take-over by anti-Western revolutionaries. The interpretation of the step as an example of small power autonomy is quite erroneous, since the U.S. decision to shift its interests facilitated the revolution. The United States could have intervened in the civil war against the Derg through arms supplies to Somalia and support for a Sudanese-backed invasion of the north, but it did not.

However, before the Ethiopian revolution in 1974, U.S. policy began to change toward Ethiopia, as its center of security for the northern Indian Ocean shifted to the new pro-American governments in Egypt under Sadat and in the Sudan under Nimeiri. The Shah of Iran was viewed as a more reliable anchor to the new security system. Moreover, the decision was made to build Diego Garcia in the Indian Ocean as a major communication point, and to phase out the Kagnew base. Soviet influence in Somalia was a worry from a strategic standpoint; but detente with the Soviets was believed to restrain them. In addition, Ethiopia was caught between the Arab states and Israel. The former were backing the growing Eritrean secession, and the latter trained the emperor's counterinsurgency forces until 1973.

Unable to obtain from the United States all the aircraft, M-60 tanks, and air-to-ground missiles he sought for his army, the aging emperor was surrounded by his enemies and losing to the Eritrean insurrection at home.[9] Thus, the Amharic aristocracy, which had become dependent upon U.S. and Western protection, was unable to hold back any longer the tides of revolution that broke over Ethiopia in 1974. The United States did not intervene to save the Lion of Judah, who had been such a close ally, because he was expendable. More defendable tributary relations had been worked out with Nimeiri to the west and Sadat to the north. While the initial phase of "the officers' revolt" was not seen as anti-Western or a threat to the feudal system, this changed as the old empire began to fall apart under the attack of external enemies and the rebellion of long-oppressed minorities.[10]

## Soviet Policy

Somalia's invasion of the Ogaden region of Ethiopia in 1977, while not planned by the U.S.S.R., was made possible by Soviet aid. By 1974, the Soviets had transformed Somalia's armed forces into the best-equipped force on the Horn and had made Somalia essentially their tributary in an attempt to counter U.S. influence in the Indian Ocean.[11]

The Soviets began in the mid-1960s to build surrogate links with the Somalis, and when General Barre came to power in 1969, proclaiming his particular brand of "Islamic scientific socialism," the Soviets seized the initiative. Their own trading interests through the Red Sea and the Suez Canal-Indian Ocean connection had matured. With the help of Nasser, they had gained direct access to the Indian Ocean, and they were looking for ways to strengthen their defenses against U.S. SLBM deployment in the Arabian Sea. Somalia's banana exports and nomadic tribes held little economic prospect for them; but the position of the port of Berbera, and Somali antagonism with U.S.-dominated Ethiopia, fitted their new strategic interests to protect their shipping and promote revolution in the northwestern region of the Indian Ocean.[12] The Soviets had increased the number of shipping supply lines to North Vietnam, which were through the Suez Canal, and they wanted to protect them against U.S. hostility with antisubmarine warfare naval surveillance.

A new factor was the growing military capability of the U.S.S.R., which by the 1970s had begun to match that of the United States in the Indian Ocean. The Soviet navy was a rapidly expanding force, with long-range submarines and small attack carriers. Thus, both the United States and the Soviet Union entered the region simultaneously with new military technology. The northwestern zone of the Indian Ocean became a major security objective for both.

The political changes in Egypt following the October War convinced the Soviets to consolidate their position at the southern entrance to the Red Sea and the Suez Canal, which was their major link between their Mediterranean and Pacific fleets. The new relationship between the Soviet Union and Somalia became a full tributary one in the early 1970s, after the U.S.S.R. was ousted from Egypt by Sadat, and the Sudan by Nimeiri. The Berbera base gave them virtual control over the access to the Red Sea and direct surveillance over U.S. operations in the Arabian Sea and into the Gulf of Persia.

In return, the Soviets provided Barre with heavy armored cars and tanks, as well as MIG fighters, which more than matched the Ethiopian forces. Economic aid and training ties with Moscow began to transform this small Islamic republic into a center of radical influence in northeastern Africa. Indirectly, this sparked the growth of the leftist Eritrean People's Liberation Front (EPLF) in the Eritrean secessionist province of Ethiopia. Also, the Western Somalia Liberation Front (WSLF) in the Ethiopian Ogaden was even more directly aided by the Soviet presence and arms supply.

When the Somalis attempted to use this Soviet support in 1976 for their own pan-Somali ambitions in the Ogaden against Ethiopia, Brezhnev sought to restrain them and to arbitrate with the help of the Cubans. Fidel Castro made a final effort to find a compromise by a flying visit in 1977 to the Horn of Africa, in which he visited both Ethiopia and Somalia and suggested that a socialist federation be formed of the three "socialist republics"—Ethiopia, Somalia, and the Peoples Republic of Yemen—which would be backed by the Soviet Union.[13] This idea caused alarm in Saudi Arabia and the Sudan. However, Castro had underestimated the force of Somali irredentism and Ethiopian imperialism. General Barre agreed to the federation, provided the Ogaden was returned to Somalia and Eritrea was allowed to enter as a separate state. This was immediately rejected by Mengistu and the Somali forces pressed ahead.[14] With their modern weapons, they soon routed the Ethiopian army.

The Soviets were therefore faced with the choice of continuing to back Somalia or disengage. By this time, the Ethiopian revolution had declared itself "scientific socialist," had defeated pro-Western socialist insurgents of the All-Ethiopian Socialist Movement (MEISON), and had requested Soviet assistance.[15] The United States had already disengaged and was at this stage not backing either Ethiopia or Somalia in the spreading war. Thus, the Soviet decision not to resupply Somalia and to throw its support to Ethiopia was a classic in tributary politics. Despite their treaties with Barre and many professions of solidarity, the Soviets suddenly switched sides in late 1977. In less than a year, Soviet commanders with Cuban troops were assisting the Ethiopians before the gates of Harar and reversed the tide of war that was almost certain to have defeated and divided Ethiopia into several parts. The Derg had been besieged on three sides, by a Sudanese army in the northwest, by the Eritreans and Tigrans in the northeast, and by the Somalis and Oromos attacking in the south.

The importance often cited of the Somali ouster of the Soviet Mission in 1977 had little to do with the reasons why the Soviets chose the Ethiopians against Somalia. Soviet strategy had been shifting for some time. The rise to power of Mengistu gave them the tributary leader they wanted to defeat the counter-revolution and obtain a strong base. They were worried over the success of conservative Arab backing of Eritrea, and the defeat of the Derg might well have returned pro-Western feudal groups to power in Ethiopia. Ethiopia's manpower, combined with its strategic position, could make it a major force in the region in time. The naval and air facilities on the Dahlak islands off Massawa and the Aden base gave the Soviets control over the entry to the Red Sea.[16] Their air surveillance and anti-submarine sonar equipment operated more effectively from communications stations in the Ethiopian highlands. In the late 1970s, the U.S.S.R was worried about war with China, and the Red Sea link was important to them in the event of the severance of rail connections to Vladivostok. They saw China's submarine capability in the Gulf of Aden as a threat to their shipping. It was a difficult choice for which Brezhnev's doctrine of defending "socialist revolution" gave them an excellent rationale.

The lesson that this "great game" holds for world politics is not the triumph of ethnic irredentism over superpower policy, but precisely the reverse. Traditional ethnic animosity was used, directed, and abandoned by this dominant power, whose short-term interests were served by the intervention that preserved the Derg's revolution.

## The Ethiopian Revolution and the Soviet Tributary State

On September 15, 1974, the Provisional Military Central Administration took over Ethiopia, with General Aman Michael Andom as chairman, and the country was officially declared a republic. The emperor was deposed and taken off to prison, where he died, supposedly of natural causes. However, the revolution was far from over and the groups who had instigated it began to fight among themselves for power.

There were five major fronts on which the Derg fought. The first was among themselves, junior officers and southerners versus the senior Amharic group. The second was against various counterrevolutionary factions in the countryside such as monarchists and ethnic groupings. Many of these had external backing. The third was against the comprador bourgeoisie who wanted a republic but not a socialist state. The fourth was against radical students and socialists who distrusted the military and wanted to institute their own brand of socialism. And the fifth was against national secessionist groups especially in Eritrea and the Ogaden, backed by foreign intervention.

### Conflicts within the Derg

Unlike many military coups in Africa and the Third World, the Derg instituted a revolution in a class and ethnic sense, expropriating land and property. However, they soon fell out among themselves and destroyed other groups who sought to participate in the new order, rather than share power with them in a new representative system.

Because the rebellion was led by noncommissioned and younger officers, most of whom came from the southern tribes and were non-Amharic, the same division continued into the revolutionary regime. While the lower-class non-Amharic initiated the revolution, eliminating all senior officers who did not pledge their loyalty, in later stages the Amharic dominance was reestablished. Much of the resistance to the Derg was led by provincial lords who sought to rally the peasantry by appeals to feudal and ethnic sentiments. They failed because the serfs could clearly see they benefited from the changeover. Widespread conflict arose with secessionist movements in the north, south, and western provinces. The Eritrean conflict was not resolved but intensified, despite the initial policy of reconciliation after the elimination of the old regime. Eritrea was a turning point in the conflict. Despite sympathy for the older Eritrean Liberation Front (ELF) position on the part of a few northern officers, particularly General Aman, who was himself Eritrean, the imperial policy was reasserted. General Aman wanted to grant the rebel province regional home rule and compromise the "national issue." But Lieutenant Colonel Mengistu, the vice-chairman of the Derg and a young rising star, insisted on integration and no compromise. General Aman was eliminated when he resisted arrest.

Pressure was also exerted in the south against the Ogaden tribes who rose against their feudal lords and joined the WSLF. In the west, a coalition of moderates, who wanted to restore the monarchy but not the power of the emperor, received the backing of the Sudan. Ras Mangesha and General Nega marched to within a few hundred miles of Addis Ababa before being turned back.

The internal conflicts of the Derg, with civilian factions, helped lay the ground for the turn to the Soviets. Mengistu had little or no contact with socialism, as was the case with most of the Derg, until he took power. The Derg attempted to form an alliance with the radicals and socialists but were rebuffed by them, especially the MEISON and the Ethiopian People's Revolutionary Party (EPRP) who were the leading socialist factions. These groups wanted the Derg to give up power and turn the government over to civilian rule on the grounds that they did not know how to govern and were unable to lead the country on a path of "scientific socialism."

Unwilling to relinquish power, the Derg sought to utilize the radical socialist groups in the achievement of a new society through the Political Bureau. For a brief time, many students and intellectuals worked closely with the land reform and socialist programs. However, intense rivalries broke out between the two groups that had ethnic, ideological, and personality aspects. These differences became caught in the struggle for power, and for a time a virtual civil war and reign of terror existed in a three-cornered fight between the MEISON, EPRP, and the Derg. The latter armed assassination squads to route out the socialist opposition in what Mengistu himself described as a "Red Terror" to counter the "White Terror." Thousands were killed. This reached its height in November 1977, with sharp disagreements among the Derg and a shoot-out in the grand palace in which Mengistu's bodyguards eliminated the moderate Chairman Tefri Bante. His "Red Terror" in the streets also outgunned the socialist underground, in what amounted to a counterrevolution against the democratic ideals of the original revolutionaries, leaving Ethiopia in the hands of a military dictatorship unwilling to share power.

In 1984, the Derg finally established a "vanguard party," after much prodding from the Russians and the Cubans. However, the military officers retained control over the civilian workers and peasant councils convened to inaugurate the Workers' party of Ethiopia.[17] Many observers believe the failure to end Amharic imperialism while attempting social reform was the fatal flaw of the regime. The Derg came to be dominated by an ethnic military group and failed to bring other nationalities and civilians with popular interests into the center of government. As Addis Hiwet put it: "In the final analysis, the Ethiopian experience demonstrated that no progressive social reform can be sustained internally, while an imperial war is being pursued abroad."[18]

### Brezhnev's Intervention

The Soviet airlift of some ten to eleven thousand combat-ready Cuban forces, plus equipment, including four hundred tanks and fifty MIG fighters took place in February 1978.[19] These forces turned the tides of battle first in the Ogaden and later in Eritrea. Extensive Soviet technical assistance as well as financial aid had been provided for the state-run farms and production plants. Within a year, the Soviets and the East Europeans had provided over $2 billion in military and economic aid. From 1978 on, Ethiopia was a Soviet tributary state. The 1978 airlift was the second major example of the Brezhnev Doctrine in action in Africa, which committed the U.S.S.R. to preserving socialism when it deemed a friendly state was threatened by counterrevolution.

The intervention was used essentially to turn the revolution in the direction of Moscow's own blueprint of socialism and effectively to wipe out indigenous socialist groups like MIESON that opposed the Derg's subservience.[20] While the unity of Ethiopia was preserved, the repression of autonomous groups in Eritrea, Tigre, and the Ogaden only aggravated the revolutionary national question and further mortgaged the Ethiopian economy to the purchase of billions of dollars of Soviet arms. In addition, the effect of land reform on agriculture production was negligible, and later production dropped drastically due to national disputes, peasant rebellions, and internal strife. In the 1980s, millions of Ethiopians again faced starvation because the drought multiplied the impact of failed policies.[21]

The outcome of intervention has been the frustration of most of the revolution's democratic and socialist aspirations. Such a result can only be termed counterrevolutionary, subordinating the prospect of a better life for most Ethiopians and bringing fierce repression to ethnic and political minorities. Unlike the Communist revolutions in Russia, China, and Cuba, the "workers' state" of Ethiopia under Colonel Mengistu is not likely to survive. The army sergeant's son occupies the Menelik Palace and has created a new ruling elite who are dependent on the U.S.S.R. to survive. The economy has been devastated and the starvation of millions, especially in the Tigre and Eritrean provinces, has created an atmosphere of fierce repression. Millions have been "resettled" from Eritrea to the western provinces of Ethiopia for political reasons as much as because of food shortages. The upheaval of a million and a half people and forced marches have taken the lives of tens of thousands.[22] The famine of 1984–1985 was not entirely the result of government policy, as the drought was the worst in nearly a century. However, the failure to settle the Eritrean and other minority claims, and the heavy investment in war and arms, have militarized the society. The amount spent on arms imports in 1983, principally from the Soviet Union, was five times that of Somalia's and four times that of the Sudan.[23] Their ratio of three to one of arms versus social expenditures was the highest in Africa.[24] Kenya, for example, had almost the reverse amounts in favor of social services.

Since the Derg took over the revolution, the country has become a militarized and aggressive tributary that has lowered the quality of life for the majority of its peasants and workers. Repression by the Mengistu regime can only contain the resistance for a time, and once the U.S.S.R. can no longer afford the billions annually—that the Ethiopians can never repay—the next revolution may return them to a more self-reliant and representative path.

## THE SOMALI AND ERITREAN PAWNS IN THE GREAT GAME

In 1960, after the establishment of the Republic of Somalia, the United States supplied primarily economic assistance to this country of nomadic, predominantly Muslim people and sought to restrain their pan-Somali ambitions of acquiring the lost provinces of the Ogaden, the northern frontier district of Kenya, and to the north the lands of the Afars and Issas, including Djibouti, then still under French administration. At this time, the United States was looking for Islamic states to check Nasser's ambitions. East Africa was just becoming independent; and the Polaris SLBM had been deployed in the Arabian Sea. Revolutionaries in Oman, South Yemen, and Eritrea were providing an opening for Soviet influence. Thus, Somalia, with its pro-Western British tradition, presented a stable balance against a Mau Mau upsurge in Kenya and a Nasserite regime in Southern Yemen.

Little attention was paid to the fact that the Somalis claim that one-third of their population still lives outside of their boundaries and fervently wish to be reunited into greater Somalia. They have an unusual determination to bring about unity, as symbolized in their five-pointed star of Somalis. There is an Arab quality to the Somalis who take their nationalism very seriously, and it is undoubtedly true that if a plebiscite could be organized to assess the wishes of the poetic desert dwellers—who without noticing cross boundaries looking for pastures—they would opt for Somalia. However, neither Ethiopia nor Kenya has ever entertained notions of agreeing to such a plebiscite. Periodic clashes have given way to wars such as the Ogaden War in 1964 and again in 1975–1978. Fighting in Kenya's Northern Frontier District occasionally has led to serious clashes between the Kenya forces and what they refer to as *shifta* (bandits). After the 1964 attack on the Ogaden, the United States suspended military aid and refused to renew it until the Somali forces were routed by Ethiopia with Soviet and Cuban assistance in 1978.

### The 1969 Coup

Irredentist frustrations led to increasing instability and on October 15, 1969, the president of Somalia, Dr. Abdar-Rashid Ali Shermarke, was assassinated during a visit to a remote desert area. In the scramble for power that followed in Mogadishu, the army seized power under Major General Mohammed Said Barre. Barre was a political unknown, who unexpectedly launched his country in the direction of an "Islamic socialism." Barre's brand of socialist development was similar to that of Nasser's and Qaddafi's—more nationalist rhetoric than substantive change. In search of arms to reunify Somalia, Barre soon established close ties with the U.S.S.R. after the United States turned him down. The Soviets, at this stage (the early 1970s), had just begun to enter the Indian Ocean. The U.A.R. was lost to them and they needed bases for their navy squadron and land-based aircraft to counter the U.S. SLBM system, and their fear of Chinese intrusion.[25]

The Soviets were not misled by Barre's overnight conversion of his country of nomads to "scientific socialism," but took advantage of the new opportunity and later signed a friendship and cooperation pact to establish the Berbera naval base.[26]

In a few short years, with the help of the Soviets, Somalia acquired the most powerful mechanized land force in Africa, equipped for desert warfare with T-34 and T-105 tanks, fitted with 103mm guns. Their air force was also updated with MIG fighters and IL-28 bombers, as well as surface-to-air missiles. This put them in a position to challenge the larger but less well-equipped Ethiopian forces. After the signing of the 1974 Friendship and Cooperation Treaty with the Soviets, which provided bases at Berbera and the port of Kismayo in return for Soviet planes, ships, and guided missiles, the Somalis had what they needed to renew the war for the Ogaden.

The Somalis, however, did not have access to the Soviet facilities at Berbera, which were run in the old colonial style. The agreement was of interest to the Somalis because of their plans to recapture lost lands, and the Soviets gained a major strategic position on the Arabian Sea and a choke point on the access to the Red Sea through the Strait of Bab 'el Mandeb. The Soviets had no love for Haile Selassie and were aiding the EPLF at the time in order to disrupt the U.S. position in Eritrea at Kagawa and Massawa.

General Barre was willing to play this game because he believed he could manipulate the protector to help him fulfill the "Greater Somalia" dream. What the general never learned is that tributary states are pawns in the interests of the patron power and do not fulfill their dreams, unless these complement the short-term interests of the superpower. Barre believed that Soviet anti-Americanism could be counted upon to provide him with continued backing in a war against Ethiopia. While there were some grounds for this, the Barre policy failed to take into account the growing U.S. disengagement from Ethiopia, which had begun with the 1974 revolution but was also motivated by technological and strategic shifts to the Diego Garcia base in the Indian Ocean. The Somali rejection of the Cuban offer to mediate was perhaps inevitable but a major error in their calculations.[27]

Thus, when the Somalis began to move in mid–1975 into the Ogaden in support of the WSLF and against the weakened and disunited Ethiopian Derg, the Soviets warned them they would not support such adventures. Using the cover of the WSLF, Somalia militarily backed an uprising in the Ogaden which derived in part from anti-Amhara interests in the region.[28]

Finally, in late 1977, with the help of Cuban forces using modern Soviet arms, the Derg was able to rally its forces in defense of Harar, deep in its own territory. The Ethiopians once again repelled the invasion of their highlands as they have done for centuries. The Somali defeat turned into a rout, as the Soviets refused to resupply them. The United States also failed to deliver on earlier supportive signals the Carter administration had given to Barre in return for his promise to break diplomatic relations with the Soviet Union, which the Somalis did with great flourish in 1977.

Somalia's defeat was complete. The Ethiopians would have taken Mogadishu but for the intervention of the outside world. Islamic Somalia was saved by the insistence of Iran that the Ethiopian forces stop at the existing boundaries. The Shah threatened to intervene, and Saudi Arabia sent money and arms to Barre, who had by this time joined the Arab League. The United States and the Soviet Union exerted their influence on Ethiopia and other states for a settlement over existing boundaries. Fortunately, the Derg did not insist upon its condition that Somalia renounce forever its claims on the Ogaden, and the war was settled before it could go further.

No one appears to have learned any lessons from this humiliating and tragic defeat. General Barre soon entered the great game again as a pawn, this time of the Americans. No one in Somalia believed that the Americans made better friends than the Soviets, but the Somali government agreed to make available to them the Soviet-constructed base at Berbera in return for military and economic aid. Barre has consistently ignored the advice of Sayid Mohammed Abdille Hassan, who fought the British intrusions in the nineteenth century.

This small state has become one of the key tributaries in the U.S. counterforce doctrine of response to the "Soviet threat" following the invasion of Afghanistan. In return for the base or "facilities," as they are termed, the United States rearmed Somalia's forces and assisted with the refugee problem.[29]

## The Refugee State

There were one and a half to two million refugees in camps in Somalia in mid–1986, a decade after the war. One out of three of the total population is a refugee. Many are from the Ogaden that Somalia sought to liberate. Some have fled their drought-stricken lands, others refuse to return home as long as hostilities continue.[30] The United States and other countries have tried to help them reconstruct their shattered lives, but famine and war have made Somalia into a huge refugee camp. The simple people, the villagers and the nomads, suffered the major casualties in this war. Far fewer soldiers died and the generals continue preparing for the next one. The regime has damaged the economy and created "dejection, despair, and distrust."³¹ General Barre had some opposition for a time and once fled into hiding, but his American aid has restored his power. Many Somali revolutionaries are unhappy over the U.S. deal. Abdullahi Yusuf Ahmed heads the opposition Somali Salvation Front, with headquarters in Ethiopia, which has opened a periodic campaign in the Ogaden. But Barre continues to eliminate his enemies and to regroup, with the help of U.S. money, Chinese-built fighters (M-16s, M-21s), and Egyptian-supplied spare parts for the previously supplied Soviet weapons.

Though the exile groups have the backing of Ethiopia, they are not strong enough to overthrow Barre as long as he has U.S. and conservative Arab backing. But the oil glut, with its depression of Arab economies, weakens one of these supports. The United States may well discontinue its costly presence in the Arabian Sea, with its tributary requirements. At that time, Somalia will find itself once again abandoned. Barre's regime could not survive and a new move towards independence under a united front of opposition groups would have a chance. New civilian governments in Addis Ababa and Mogadishu are indispensable if the peoples of the Horn of Africa are to have freedom from dominance and a better life.

### The Eritrean Question

Many liberation and nationalist movements have failed because of the superpower rivalry, while others have flourished as a result of the aid provided by the competitive cold war environment. Tributaries often have used the military assistance provided them for external defense on their own rebels. The cases of SWAPO and the ANC in South Africa and the Polisario in Western Sahara are better known than the Eritrean struggle. The Eritreans, who have had as good a case for independence as most African states, have been bound to Ethiopia by postwar superpower rivalry and the arms provided Ethiopia first by the Americans and then later by the Soviets.

*Intervention.* The Soviet and Cuban intervention in Ethiopia in late 1977 at the request of the Derg has, among other things, prolonged the war over Eritrea that appeared to be nearly won by the rebels. "Eritrea affects everything," said a one-time resident foreign economist.³² The Eritreans have carried on a direct military rebellion for over twenty years, with fortunes that have ebbed and flowed. As a former colony of the defeated Italians, Eritrea qualified under U.N. criteria for independence following World War II, just as Libya had earlier. However, international superpower politics persuaded the U.N. to accept Ethiopian claims to incorporate the former colony into a federation. The decisive factor was U.S. backing for Haile Selassie, who provided strategic requirements in Eritrea.

The initial plan for Eritrean independence was laid aside in favor of a federation plan presented by Ethiopia. Contrary to the usual U.N. procedure, the proposal was not put to a referendum before the U.N. vote in 1950 approving the scheme. U.S. policy had begun to search for a tributary relationship with Ethiopia. And in 1953 the initial Eritrean base concessions to the United States were made by Ethiopia.[33] While there is no direct evidence of a deal, the fact that these bases at Kagnew and Assab were in Eritrea and were granted only three years after the U.N. settlement, points to a remarkable coincidence of interests.[34]

*Repression.* The repression of the Eritrean independence movement that followed constituted human rights violations that grew in massive proportion in later years. U.N. provisions for Eritrean self-rule under a federation were abandoned by Ethiopia, and after the armed struggle began in 1962 the repression became extremely severe with the massacre of pro-ELF members in villages.[35] These violations, along with the colonial period of Italian rule, provided the case for independence. However, this case was rejected not only by the U.N., but also by the majority of African states who have refused to consider these claims. This reflects the status-quo orientation of governments who fear the spread of secession demands at home, as well as the long-term preeminence of Haile Selassie at the OAU meetings. Nevertheless, the rebellion grew, because of its legitimate claims.[36]

The Eritrean secessionist movement from Ethiopia is a combination of ethnic religious differences and a comprador bourgeoisie class that emerged more rapidly in Eritrea under Italian occupation than in the rest of Ethiopia. Islam is dominant in Eritrean culture, although Muslims were discriminated against in terms of political privileges and representation under Ethiopian rule during the federation. After the 1974 revolution, the Islamic population marched in the streets for the first time. For 50 years the Italians had cultivated different elites opposed to the return of the Amharas. Initially, Coptic Eritreans played a prominent role in the opposition to Ethiopia. The ELF, founded in 1961, was at first primarily a middle-class nationalistic movement whose members were better educated and more Westernized than the Ethiopians. Later, the resistance grew, with the younger and more radical EPLF, formed in 1970. In 1981, these groups split again and the ELF became little more than an exile group.[37] The EPLF has waged the war and supported a program of extensive self-reliant development within Eritrea where it has administrative control. They have initiated land reform, cooperative production, health, and education programs. Militarily, they control the countryside, while Ethiopia occupies urban areas.

Under the Haile Selassie regime, these liberation movements made their major gains. They deliberately avoided attacking the U.S. bases, although much of their assistance came from the U.A.R. and radical Arabs and the U.S.S.R. and Eastern Europe. Their failure to achieve independence at this stage was as much a result of the opposition of African states in the OAU as of U.S. backing for the emperor. Unlike the liberation movements in southern Africa, the Eritreans were opposed by a combination of Westernized and conservative African interests that viewed secession on the African continent as subversive of all newly established authority. In addition, Soviet aid for the Eritreans was covert and indirect, channeled through radical Arab states, as the U.S.S.R. had outwardly good relations with Haile Selassie, who also received Soviet military aid.

The revolution brought a brief respite between Ethiopia and the Eritreans, as General Aman, an Eritrean, was chairman of the Derg. But after Aman was killed, the repression returned and fighting spread. This time, Cuban forces and Soviet planes were a part of the central government's attempt to reimpose its rule.

*The Eritrean De Facto Independence.* In 1978, the Eritreans fought a pitched battle for the occupation of the Eritrean capital of Asmara, and were finally driven out as a result of intervention by Cuban forces equipped with Soviet weapons. After fierce hand-to-hand combat and many casualties, the fronts retreated back into the mountainous terrain bordering the Sudan in the west. As masters of guerrilla warfare from long years of experience, they have proved impossible to dislodge, even with the aid of Soviet helicopters and skillful antiinsurgency training. Today assistance comes from the conservative Arab world, particularly the Sudan and Saudi Arabia. Sudan's sanctuary is important, as are its routes of supply, and the Saudis provide the money and weapons. The guns are Western-made, mainly American, and there is some East European captured equipment. Supplies are sometimes run across the Red Sea in Arab sailing dhows from North Yemen; but the Sudan is their primary source of supply. This has greatly strained Ethiopian-Sudanese relations, though there have been periodic detentes. Hostilities emerged more directly after 1982 when Ethiopia used the continuance of internal warfare in the Sudan to provide a base for the forces of Colonel Garang in the south fighting the Sudanese government. A long-standing feud with Libya added to the instability of Sudan and its suspicion that Ethiopia and Libya were fueling the rebellion (as will be discussed in the next section).

While the United States is anti-Derg and would like to prevent the Soviets from using the Eritrean bases, especially the port of Assab, it has never cut off all assistance to Ethiopia, especially food. Despite its differences with the Ethiopian government, the United States has been the primary supplier of food during the 1984–1985 famine. And the U.S. AID has been very careful not to openly support the Eritreans, despite the appeals of Eritrean relief groups, based in the Sudan, who charge Ethiopia with a deliberate policy of starvation and population removal in the insurgent regions.[38] Paradoxically, much of the equipment of the Ethiopian forces is still American, so that the Eritreans are bombed and strafed with both American and Soviet weapons.

The ELF has begun negotiations with the Derg and may well accept a settlement, but the EPLF is unlikely to agree to a cease-fire, though many more will starve to death. If the Derg falls apart, the disunity would give the Eritreans another chance. Their strongest opponent is the U.S.S.R., which argues that the EPLF is counterrevolutionary. The Cuban troops have generally refused to engage in repression of the EPLF, and have a different interpretation, urging settlement of "the national question" on both parties.

The Cuban view is that ethnic differences can be reconciled within a socialist state. Eritreans and Tigreans respond that the opportunity for this existed shortly after the revolution but was rejected by Mengistu, who will not compromise even though it will cost millions of lives, and they, too, will pay the price needed for freedom.

Eventually, the scene of U.S.-Soviet rivalry will shift to other areas of the Indian Ocean and the Third World. A superpower arms agreement could bring this about, or a crisis in Central America or Europe. At that point, Arab support for the Eritreans may well finally provide the margin that enables them to occupy the urban areas. Freedom has been subordinated to dominance, and the Eritreans have a right to self-determination. The Eritrean claim will one day prevail, first as a de facto military achievement and later as a state recognized by the OAU. There has emerged a bitter but durable spirit against the superpowers which a young Eritrean rebel expressed to the author in Khartoum: "You Americans bombed us and now the Russians are bombing us and eventually we will survive both of you." Their sufferings are trials by fire and their self-reliant response shows the growth of a group consciousness that has historically molded nations. That process of nationalism, under the new class consciousness, has not ended in Africa.

## THE SECOND SCRAMBLE FOR THE NILE: THE AFRO-ARAB SUDAN

The Sudan is the largest state in Africa, yet among the poorest. The discovery of oil in the western province of Darfur by Chevron adds to its importance, as a great deal more oil wealth may be found. But the major role of the Sudanese government has become, in the eyes of the United States, to contain Soviet expansion from Qaddafi's Libya to the north and Mengistu's Ethiopia to the east. Chad is less strategically important, though it has valuable minerals in the north and may have substantial oil.

The Sudanese are masters at milking the superpowers in the cold war. Until 1972, the U.S.S.R. had a close working relationship with Nimeiri. And the United States was then well entrenched in Ethiopia. But the politics of the Horn of Africa are fickle and suddenly explosive. This was well demonstrated when the Soviet-backed coup in 1971 against Nimeiri, led by the Sudan Communist Party, was turned back by Colonel Nimeiri, who survived several rebellions. His overthrow in April 1985 came as no surprise but shifted only slightly the tributary balance of power in the region.

Neighboring Chad had been stable and united only by virtue of French intervention. When the French withdrew in 1979, civil war again broke out. External pressures can have highly destabilizing consequences for the delicately balanced internal politics of the Sudan and Chad, as Libya and Egypt have demonstrated, acting as surrogates for superpower interests. The Soviets have an interest in Qaddafi, primarily because he is one of their best arms customers, and also because he provides radical leverage within the Arab and African worlds.

The Sudan therefore has become a keypoint of struggle between the two superpowers, not because it is wealthy or has oil potential, but because of its strategic location and manpower for tributary armies to fight in either northeast Africa or the Persian Gulf. Once again, as when Lord Kitchener marched down the Nile from Egypt to defeat the Mahdiya at Khartoum, the peoples of the Nile are caught up in the rivalry of world dominant powers who view them as important pawns in the power game.

## The Divided People of the Sudan

The first impression of the Sudan is its immensity. One can see that it is not desert but semiarid, on which dryland farming is carried out by people in the western and eastern regions. In the south, there are great mountain ranges, swamps, and much higher rainfall. The desert lies to the northwest, where the great Sahara begins, the land of the nomads who still travel by camel caravan.

The people are as diverse as the land. In the northern regions, nine million swarthy Arab-speaking peoples dominate. They control the urban areas and the politics. (Though less than half the population of the Sudan is Arab, most speak some Arabic.) The eastern Sudan is inhabited by the Beja, whose antiquity predates that of the Arabs. The Nubians in the western and northern Sudan are the last black vestige of the Nubian era, ended by the Arab invasion in the 7th century. And in the south are several Bantu and Nilotic tribes, including the Shilluk and the Dinka—black Africans who have been only partially arabized. The close affinity of the northern Arabs with Egypt is one of the major cultural characteristics of the country.[39]

## The North-South Split

The major political division is the north-south racial and cultural division. Since the Turko-Egyptian period, the southerners have attempted to resist the arabization of the country. After independence, attempts by the north to assimilate the southern tribes have led to repeated rebellions and secessionist movements. The latest is the Sudanese People's Liberation Movement (SPLM), headed by Colonel John Garang.

The south has remained animist and Christian, with economic links to Uganda and East Africa. British colonial power protected the southerners against northern Arab intrusion, while at the same time insisting on their inclusion in a united Sudan, oriented toward the north. This north-south split has been the basis of immense instability in the modern Sudan. The first major secessionist movement—the Anya Nya guerrilla campaign in the equatorial forests of the southern region—ended in 1972 with the Addis Ababa agreement.

Thus, a major compromise was struck, giving the southerners hope that they would receive large new benefits from the north. However, Dunstan Wai, a southerner educated in England and the United States, in summarizing the failures of the Nimeiri government, has said, ''To eradicate the memories of the past, the Arab Sudanese must still learn to share political power and the highest political positions in the Government." He saw very little progress in terms of actual allocation of development funds and social change since the 1972 accords. "So far, the South remains at the periphery of central decision-making and has been allocated not more than one-tenth of the planned development projects in the next decade."[40]

A new guerrilla movement of the SPLM calling itself the Sudanese People's Liberation Army (SPLA) has been formed, with its base in Ethiopia and major recruits from the Dinka and Shilluk.[41] There was reputed to have been some Libyan support for this southern rebellion, though after Nimeiri's overthrow this ended. What is distinctive about this latest rebellion is Garang's claim to lead a revolution of the whole Sudan, rather than only a southern movement. His forces are better organized and equipped than previous rebellious forces, and they have a well-established sanctuary in Ethiopia. Few Arabs have joined them, and with the overthrow of Nimeiri in 1985 the northern parties remained loyal to the reforms of the new Dahab and Sadiq al Mahdi governments. The transitional cabinet made new concessions to the south, such as ending offensive Islamic laws and restoring development. However, Garang refused to accept these as adequate and insisted the SPLA must fight until they win. Garang accused the junta of "snatching victory from the people" and continuing the unpopular rule of the military and its subordination to the United States. Although the caretaker government ended the 1983 legal decree of unification that had been "a primary source of grievance," General Siwar el Dahab's attempts to achieve a cease-fire were rebuffed by Garang.

Libya's support for the rebels ended with a new understanding with the Sudan in mid–1985, but the refugee exodus from Eritrea strained relations with the Ethiopian Derg. The long border provided ideal support for a guerrilla insurgency and the struggle appeared to be long-term.

Southerners, as usual, are divided. The former leader of the Anya Nya, General Joseph Lagu, has supported the new regime. Leaders of the SPLM are drawn from the southern front.

Economic failures have contributed to this renewed rebellion; but the main issue is southern suspicion that political repression is a revival of Islamic conservatism. To many southern political leaders, the prospects for an integrated nation are directly related to the ability of the northern moderates to build a central coalition. In the early days of Nimeiri's Sudan Socialist Union, they had hopes, but as the messianic Muslims have grown in power, that hope has waned.

## The Status of the Sudan as a U.S. Tributary

The basic economic problem of the Sudan has not been resolved by Western economic investment and aid. Development is for the benefit of a small privileged class, notwithstanding all the slogans of equal rights of Islamic Africa and scientific socialism, or the well-laid plans of the World Bank and the U.S. AID missions. The comprador class and Western technicians enjoy a quality of life that is a hundred to a thousand times better than that of the peasants who never see a doctor or a trained teacher, and whose children die in their arms, rather than a hospital bed.

The economy is oriented to the desires of the Westernized elite. This is reflected in the export cash crop economy, which does not produce enough food for its own population. Exports are a few raw materials—cotton, gum, durra, and hides with minimal processing—while imports are machinery, flour, petroleum, cars, TV sets, and numerous luxury items, producing a deteriorating balance of trade. The Sudan had a $9 billion foreign debt in 1982. Repeated devaluation has not solved this problem which is a fundamental one for all African economies tied to Western markets and capital.[42]

Between 1971 and 1985, Sudan slowly swung toward a full tributary relationship with the United States. Sudanese leaders repeatedly profess a desire to remain nonaligned, but they are worried about the Soviet Union's intentions in Chad, Ethiopia, and the Red Sea regions. They view the United States as the only power able to prevent the intrusion of the Soviets into the region and a new Ottoman empire under the Ethiopian Coptics. This represents a remarkable turnaround in their attitude toward the United States, which the author experienced in the Sudan in the mid–1960s, while a visiting professor at the University of Khartoum. The elite has gone from one extreme to the other, while the masses of peasants remain solidly in the middle, worried more about the price of flour than whether Sudan has MIG-21s or F-15s in its air force.

Over the 1973–1977 period, the largest supplier of weapons was the Soviet Union ($20 million), apparently based on pre–1971 agreements, and the United States is recorded as supplying no weapons during that period. U.S. aid has dramatically increased since 1979 with U.S. realization of the key strategic role of the Sudan. The Carter administration approved a $140 million aid program, mostly for military purchases.[43] The Reagan administration has agreed to supply sophisticated aircraft and desert warfare tanks, as well as F-6s. In 1983, the U.S. Air Force, based in Egypt, deployed AWAC air surveillance against Libya on behalf of the Sudan. General Nimeiri invited the United States to establish several military airfields, similar to those in Egypt, and with these the United States set up a chain of supply for CENTCOM from the Red Sea into the Persian Gulf and Pakistan.

## CIVILIAN RULE AND RECONCILIATION

People danced in the streets when General Abboud was overthrown in 1964 and demanded a return to civilian rule. They danced again when General Nimeiri was ousted by a popular military coup in April 1985. "Al Bahlawan," the tightrope artist, was gone. He had survived so many previous attempts to remove him from office by the military and civilian groups. A University of Khartoum professor, Mohammed O. Beshir, recalled the similarity between the two periods and circumstances when civilian rule ended in the return of the military, but stated hopefully that "perhaps history does not always repeat itself." The new leader, General Abdel Rhaman Siwar el Dahab, had promised that after one year of interim government there would be elections and the political party system would be restored. In the meantime, the government would attempt to reestablish peaceful relations with the south and work on resolving the country's economic problems.[44]

The overthrow of Nimeiri was a result of the growing austerity he had imposed on the urban classes in an attempt to meet the stringent requirements of the World Bank and the IMF for the extension of further loans. Restrictions on imports increased the price of bread overnight by more than 30 percent and gasoline was rationed to less than a gallon a week, if it could be obtained. Intensification of the fighting in the south resulted from an attempt to extend Islamic law into the region, including the punishment under the Sharia law of cutting off the hands of thieves. Inclusion of Moslem Brothers in his cabinet had further alienated southern leaders. On another note, the generosity of the Sudan in opening up its borders to the huge influx of refugees from Ethiopia (and previously Chad) had worsened the food shortage caused by the drought. At the root of the government's difficulty was the fact a country that once exported food and was regarded as the prospective breadbasket of the Middle East could no longer feed its own population. And in 1985, Sudan was placed on the list of the twelve most endangered countries by the United Nations Emergency Relief Program.

It is to the credit of the Sudanese that they have managed fairly bloodless change and that the military stepped in from popular demand, as demonstrated by the huge crowds that filled the streets for weeks before the overthrow. Fortunately for Nimeiri, he was out of the country at the time and went into exile in Cairo. His own defense minister had taken over. General Abboud himself, after his eclipse, walked the streets of Khartoum untouched, and quite probably Nimeiri will be allowed to return from Egypt after memories have mellowed, in particular over such cases as that of the elderly reformer Mohamed Taha, hung by Nimeiri for opposition to his religious views.

The role of the protector is of some significance when such a change occurs. There was no evidence of direct U.S. involvement, but the choice of a successor such as General Abdel Rahman Siwar el Dahab was not objectionable to Americans who had made it clear something had to be done about the deteriorating state of affairs if the $180 million worth of new credit was to be extended. A petition had been presented to Vice-President Bush by a group of intellectuals during his visit to the Sudan earlier in the year. Nimeiri was on his way back from Washington, D.C., presumably with President Reagan's promises in his pocket, when the coup took place. It had all the characteristics of a staged turnover. Loans and military agreements were to be honored on all sides. And Egypt, the closest ally of the United States in the region, was amenable. However, the first government to recognize the new leader was Libya and hostilities ended between these two states. The left put forward a demand for the removal of foreign bases and in 1986 the newly elected government under Sadiq al Mahdi of the Umma party announced a nonaligned foreign policy, and relations with the U.S.S.R. were resumed. Ties with Iran, for economic as well as religious purposes, were established. The U.S. tributary relationship with the Sudan has basically not been altered. Nevertheless, under the new Sadiq civilian government, there are certain demilitarization and self-reliance tendencies that could now become predominant. Especially if the Sudanese have learned from past failures and genuinely seek reunification of the country through a settlement between Arabs and southerners, they can make a new start.

Clearly, the militarization of these countries' economies leaves them without the foreign exchange, petroleum, and other resources so desperately needed for economic development. The arms race with Ethiopia is not in the interests of either country and agreements should be reached to limit number and types of weapons imported. Sudan, as well as Egypt and Somalia, might well become parties to a regional disarmament agreement covering arms transfers, bases, and nuclear weapons. If both superpowers lessen their rivalry, Sudan will have the resources for development in the south. A political settlement under a new federal constitution, giving real autonomy to the south, is one prospect now being considered.

Agreements with internal rebel groups are a necessary part of such a demilitarization process. In the Sudan, this would appear to be much easier than in Ethiopia, though major concessions by both governments will be needed. Southern Sudanese clearly resent the attempt to impose Sharia law and other forms of arabization on them. Moderate and secular Arabs in the north understand and respect these differences, and a civilian government is more likely to represent these secular trends than the military. If the militant Islamic groups such as the Moslem Brothers can be kept out of the government, grounds for peace may be found. Under the leadership of Sadiq al-Mahdi the Ansar and Umma are apt to be more reasonable. Of course, economic development has to move forward equitably as well. This is possible, even in divided African societies, provided the greed of the comprador class is controlled. Colonel John Garang's SPLM seeks social justice rather than secession at this point. (The EPLF in Ethiopia has passed beyond that stage of reintegration.)

Reconciliation is more easily talked about than accomplished because the rebels have become very powerful internally and have the support of external powers, whose interests they serve. But if African governments can reach agreements about arms transfers and refugee flows, these can be used to deflect the demands of the superpowers, rather than play into their hands. And there are grounds for the case that the real interests of the superpowers in the military buildup on the Horn are beginning to fade. The Persian Gulf is far less crucial than it had been in the late 1970s. China is not a threat to the U.S.S.R. in the Gulf of Aden, and the Iranian revolution seems contained, at least for the present, in terms of U.S. and conservative Arab state concerns. Libya is outspoken and anti-American, but the issues are much less military and far more diplomatic than generally accepted. The new Soviet leadership under Gorbachev appears ready to discuss differences in all parts of the world as well as in the Middle East. And the Reagan administration is beset with the financial problems of a huge deficit at home which expanded military operations like CENTCOM only aggravate. Thus, the underlying interventionary forces are shifting to new grounds of rivalry and may well leave the tributaries of the Horn and northeastern Africa the opportunity to work out their differences in greater freedom than they have had since the time of independence.

This should not be interpreted to mean that the economic causes of tributary status have also became favorable. They are still and will be, for many decades, endemic to the comparative disadvantage of tributary states; but they are not crucial deterrents in northeastern African countries, where resources such as oil are minimal. Distribution is much the greatest problem, such as in the southern Sudan. But if the economies can be demilitarized, and redistribution seriously undertaken even before development, chances are good that reconciliation can take place.

## CONCLUSION

Superpower rivalry has given new significance to the security origins of imperialism and the role of a comprador class. Because global powers are able to establish new fronts from which to threaten each other, their traditional theaters of the European and Asian pacts have been extended to the Persian Gulf and the Horn of Africa. Within this new theater, each has assembled a group of tributaries by using its military and economic aid systems. They have, therefore, been able to achieve their objectives indirectly through the elites, military coups, and ruling classes.

The ruling comprador class of the new states of the Horn have accepted this new dependence because they have been convinced they could carry out their particular version of the revolution with the help of a superpower. They entered into pacts, and accepted military aid and training and economic assistance in the pretense that it was for development. Their enemies, they believed (with some justification), were deterred by the presence of the superpower's arms and protection system. However, they thought that they would be able to use the superpowers for their own ends and, by playing them off against each other, advance their own interests of class and ethnicity, rather than serve the ends of their protectors.

The results have shown this to be illusion. Their revolutions have been coopted by foreign interests. Advanced technology and expensive arms transfers have distracted them from sound economic policy into shows of military power and often fatal aggression. Their economies have produced what they did not consume and failed with the heavy debt and waste they have acquired.

The disaster from famine has been as much the result of policy failures as of drought and technology. The incapacity of these governments to deal with the postdrought problems, such as refugees, is a further indication of their lack of perception and concern for lives.[45]

And instead of coming to terms with internal opponents and honestly resolving the national and class issues, they have engaged in civil war. Increased militarization has intensified the repressiveness of these regimes. Attempts to give them the cloak of "scientific socialism," "self-reliance," or "Islamic brotherhood" have been fraudulent and have led to the intensification of insurrection against them.

To assume the democratic revolution has been spent in Africa is the illusion of ruling classes. The leaders of the liberation movements know that a dominance system of five hundred years is not quickly ended, especially when its origins in the centers of power are changing very slowly. Counterrevolution has been repeatedly fueled by the superpower rivalry. The ensuing conflicts have had horrendous effects—wiping out tribes, intellectual groups, causing racial and genocidal strife. But the resilience of people despite their suffering, in southern Sudan, Eritrea, and Somalia, is beyond comprehension in its courage and belief.

Western dominance has begun to recede. The rivalry is less intense over the Arabian Sea and the Gulf. The Red Sea has become again an open waterway. And the cost of maintaining tributary regimes in Somalia, Sudan, and Ethiopia is increasingly questioned. Once this becomes recognized, new political possibilities appear. As dominance withdraws its grip, it intensifies the paranoia of the repressors while it weakens their capacity to control. Therefore, new opportunities for revolution, negotiation, and settlement have begun to appear. Ethiopia and Somalia have begun negotiations. Chad and the Sudan have settled their differences. Federation in the Sudan is again under consideration.

When revolutionary regimes emerge, they will be more self-reliant, less militaristic, and more ready to undertake regional forms of collective action. As will be discussed in the next chapter, one of the most difficult steps for tributaries is to break with dependency. But some of the ways to accomplish this have been charted, and many of the pitfalls are known. Hopefully, these experiences will help the long-suffering peoples of the Horn to find their way to a better way of government and a more humane existence.

## NOTES

1. Colin Legum, ed., *Africa Contemporary Record: Survey and Documents 1981–82* (New York: Africana Publishing Co., 1982), p. B150.

2. Margery Perham, *The Government of Ethiopia* (Evanston, Ill.: Northwestern University Press, 1979), pp. xxv–vii.

3. Fantu Aganafar, "The Independence of Djibouti" (Ph.D. diss., University of Denver, 1980), p. 10.

4. The United States supplied Ethiopia from 1953 to mid–1975 with virtually half of all military aid to sub-Saharan Africa. Tom S. Farer, *War Clouds on the Horn of Africa: A Crisis for Detente* (New York: Carnegie Endowment for International Peace, 1976).

5. Based on interviews with diplomatic personnel in Addis Ababa. Such figures are disputed by U.S. official sources. Marina Ottaway uses the figure of 3,200 in her *Soviet and American Influence in the Horn of Africa* (New York: Praeger, 1982), p. 51.

6. John Markakis and Nega Ayele, *Class and Revolution in Ethiopia* (London: Spokesman, 1978), pp. 40–42. T. B. Millar, writing in 1969, saw this development:

> Yet as the Polaris and Poseiden submarine systems developed, it became obvious that the Arabian Sea and Bay of Bengal would provide a most valuable area for missile operations if necessary against Southern and Central Russia and Western China. The VLF (very low frequency) communications station was accordingly built at NW Cape in Western Australia.

"The Indian and Pacific Oceans: Some Strategic Considerations," Adelphi Papers, (London: International Institute for Strategic Studies, May 1969), p. 6

7. John H. Spencer, *Ethiopia, The Horn of Africa and U.S. Policy* (Cambridge, Mass.: Institute for Foreign Policy Analysis, 1977), p. 150.

8. Ottaway, *Soviet and American Influence*, p. 29.

9. Colin Legum, *Ethiopia, the Fall of Haile Selassie's Empire* (New York: Africana Publishing Co., 1975), p. 21.

10. Farer, *War Clouds*, p. 98.

11. Admiral Elmo Zumwalt, Jr., testimony before the Subcommittee on Near East and South Asia, U.S. Congress, House Committee on Foreign Affairs, *Hearings*, 93rd Cong., 2nd sess., March 21, 1974, p. 132.

12. Some controversy exists over whether the Soviets were ousted from Somalia in 1977 or made their own decision to leave. The best assessment of this is found in Michael A. Samuels, "White Paper on the Horn of Africa," *Washington Review of Strategic and International Studies*, (1978).

13. Marina and David Ottaway, *Ethiopia: Empire in Revolution* (New York: Africana Publishing Co., 1978), pp. 27–28.

14. Bereket Habte Selassie, *Conflict and Intervention on the Horn of Africa* (New York: Monthly Review Press, 1980), p. 11.

15. Michael Chege has a comprehensive account of this in-fighting, in "Revolution Betrayed, Ethiopia 1974–79," *Journal of Modern African Studies* 17, no. 3 (1979), pp. 359–81.

16. *Newsweek*, July 6, 1981.

17. *New York Times*, September 9, 1984. Seven of the eleven members of the Politbureau are from the Derg.

18. Addis Hiwet, "Analysing the Ethiopian Revolution," *Review of African Political Economy*, November 30, 1984, p. 30.

19. *New York Times*, February 25, 1978.

20. Markakis and Ayele, *Class and Revolution in Ethiopia*, p. 190.

21. James Kanu, "Holding Back the Facts of Famine," *South*, December 1984.

22. *The Denver Post*, February 19, 1985.

23. "The Africa Rights Monitor," *Africa Today*, 32, no. 3, March 31, 1986, pp. 78–79.

24. Soviet concern in early 1970 to protect the supply route of arms from Eastern Europe to North Vietnam was also a consideration. Not only was Soviet access to the Suez Canal at stake, but the United States had also cut off all aid to Somalia after it was

discovered that ships flying her "flag of convenience" were being used to supply North Vietnam. See Gary D. Payton, in *Africa Contemporary Record*, pp. 106–107.

25. Selassie, *Conflict and Intervention in the Horn of Africa*, p. 111.

26. Bereket Habte Selassie, "The Dergue's Dilemma: The Legacies of a Feudal Empire," *Monthly Review*, July-August 1980, p. 27.

27. Anthony Hughes, "Reagan and Africa: Policy Options in the Horn," *African Affairs* 26, no. 3 (May-June 1981).

28. David D. Calten, "War in the Ogaden," *Journal of Modern African Studies* 17, no. 1 (1979).

29. *Africa Confidential* 22, no. 6 (March 11, 1981). Also *Africa Today* 32, no. 3 (1985).

30. The Africa Rights Monitor in *Africa Today* 32, no. 4 (1985).

31. Ahmed I. Samatar, "Underdevelopment in Somalia: Dictatorship Without Hegemony," *Africa Today* 32, no. 3 (1985), p. 39.

32. *New York Times*, April 6, 1980.

33. "Upheaval on the Horn," *MERIP Reports* 7, no. 9, (November 1977), pp. 19–23.

34. Spencer, *Ethiopia, The Horn of Africa and United States Policy*, p. 150.

35. James Firebrace and Stuart Holland, *Never Kneel Down: Drought, Development, and Liberation in Eritrea* (Trenton, N.J.: The Red Sea Press, 1985), pp. 29–45.

36. Randolph Harrison, "Eritrea's Double Curse: Famine, 23 Years of War," *Orlando Sentinel*, February 10, 1985.

37. Firebrace and Holland, *Never Kneel Down*.

38. U.S. AID has condemned the mass removals which threaten hundreds of thousands of lives. "Relief Under Fire," *Africa News*, July 21, 1986, p. 6.

39. P. M. Holt, *A Modern History of the Sudan* (London: Weidenfield and Nicolson, 1961), and K. Henderson, *Sudan Republic* (New York: Praeger, 1965), provide excellent background studies of the land and its history.

40. Dunstan Wai, "Revolution, Rhetoric, and Reality in the Sudan," *Journal of Modern African Studies* 17, no. 1 (1979), pp. 88–89.

41. *Africa News*, May 7, 1983.

42. Ali Ahmed Suliman concluded in 1975: "Therefore, if we take per capita income as an indicator of economic development for the Sudan, no economic development seems to have taken place over these years between 1962 and 1970/71. On the contrary, some economic decline has taken place." *Issues in the Economic Development of the Sudan* (Khartoum: Khartoum University Press, 1975), p. 135.

43. *New York Times*, March 12, 1980.

44. "What Next for Troubled Sudan," *Africa News*, April 22, 1985.

45. "Recipe for a Second Famine," *South*, no. 68 (June 1986).

# 4

# The Struggle for Self-reliant Development against Dominance: The Kenya Comprador Class Rule and Tanzania's Self-reliant Transition

The critical link is between the dominant power system and the tributary class, that is, the small segment of the population that emerged from the colonial system as prosperous, educated, and technologically sophisticated, and which respected and reflected Western values (Marxist as well as Christian). Members of this class used their new power to dominate and exploit their own people in the name of modernization. Their actual role has not been that of independent entrepreneurs, although they are frequently found on the boards of local companies and in the economic agencies of government. While appearing to exercise independent and even representative judgment, their decisions are indirectly influenced and controlled by the centers of world dominance. They govern in their own interest, while mouthing the slogans of populism.

Whether this group can be properly termed a class is a matter of much debate. There is a strong tendency for them to be reflective of the interests of a dominant tribal or religious sect and in some cases racial differences are important. But these characteristics are secondary to their political-economic role of comprador leaders on behalf of the dominant power interests of the global system. This role is hidden in the nationalistic and ideological mirages of the indirect imperialism of tributary states and must be carefully analyzed.

The tributary state is not simply on the periphery of the international capitalist system; it is an integral part of the international security system of the hegemonic superpowers who have replaced the colonial powers with their indirect linkages of power. A tributary class that emerges out of the new production and security relations provides the essential link of control for the dominant power.

This is not to argue that the tributary states do not have some autonomy or indeed that there is not considerable interdependence between them and the hegemonic powers. There is substantial mutual interest and exchange; but the essence of the relationship is unequal because the subordinate states operate within narrow limits of choice laid out by the interests of the hegemonic powers.[1] As noted, regional, cultural, and economic conditions have a great bearing on their decisions, but the major direction is charted by the intrusive powers who stand outside the region and control the decisive factors such as military supply, bank loans, and technology transfers. The transnational tributary class serves the intrusive powers in a comprador relationship. In some cases, it is well developed as a ruling class. In others, it is a bureaucratic-military elite, able to cling to power, after a coup, for example, only with the support of one of the superpowers and its allies. The role of this class in its external relationship is our chief focus in this chapter.

East Africa has emerged since the 1960s as a highly important strategic area within the Indian Ocean system, developing important connections with the Middle East, the Gulf, and southern Africa and intensifying the conflicts of ethnicity and race in the politics of Kenya, Tanzania, and Uganda. The struggle between South Africa and the Frontline States has involved Tanzania directly in a number of the major issues and new relationships of southern Africa. The collapse of the East African Community left the separate states of East Africa to drift apart in increased and often intense rivalry and conflict. These crises have been intensified especially by the arms race in the Indian Ocean between the superpowers, who are prone to exploit differences when it benefits their own interests within the wider arena of conflict. Thus, global and regional issues are constantly interacting and complicating the problems of individual East African states.

The East African states are at various stages of this tributary relationship, as demonstrated by the role of the governing class in Uganda. At the height of the Idi Amin regime, Uganda had become a Soviet tributary, with a ruling officer elite who controlled a divided comprador class. This professional and commercial petite bourgeoisie was divided tribally and religiously, with Amin favoring the northern tribes and Muslims against the previously dominant southern tribes and Christians. The economy remained primarily Western-oriented, though it was badly crippled after the expulsion of the Indians. The British-trained army came increasingly under the influence of the U.S.S.R.

A considerable degree of military dependence on Soviet supplies developed, primarily for the air force, with training and support coming from radical Arab states. After the 1979 defeat of Amin by Tanzania and the restoration of Milton Obote as president of Uganda, the Ugandans extricated themselves from this Soviet network, but they have fallen out among themselves. Baganda landowners have repeatedly resisted northern Moslem military rule. Their support made it possible for the army to overthrow Obote first in 1971 and again in 1985. In 1986 Yoweri Museveni, leader of the National Resistance Movement (NRM), came to power after a people's armed struggle that was aided by the southern landowning comprador interests. But the NRM is also popular and opposed to military rule. In the past the political parties could not agree among themselves and the military stepped into the breach. Museveni has created resistance councils based on the liberation movement and has banished the former Caesers along with Obote's Uganda People's Congress. There has been a start toward demilitarization, which could lead to a break with the tributary system.

Kenya has been a well developed Western tributary state with a ruling ethnoclass that has, from the days of Kenyatta on, accepted close economic and military links with the Anglo-American powers. Tanzania, in contrast, has been an Anglo-American tributary that has struggled to extricate itself from dependence on the West through a program aimed at building self-reliant socialism. Global and regional rivalries, as well as her own internal conflicts, have made this transition more bureaucratic and a much longer road than President Nyerere intended.

For a tributary state to become self-reliant, a class change is necessary.[2] The comprador class must be replaced by an industrious and democratic petit bourgeoisie. As Cabral has described this class, it is culturally indigenous and dedicated to the rediscovery of its own past, the rejection of Western dependence, and the establishment of an egalitarian society at home and a socialist state to rule it. Aware of the dangers of militarism and dependence upon a foreign power for protection or development, a self-reliant state is one in which military and economic links with the dominant powers have been greatly reduced. Internally, the redistribution of wealth and opportunity has moved the country toward greater equality; and some representation of workers in the production process has replaced foreign control. Legal protection of the people's rights as citizens has been proclaimed but seldom honored. Self-reliant societies in Africa, which contrast most directly with tributary states in their economic relations, distribution patterns, and security ties, can be numbered on the fingers of one hand.

But a few have begun the serious steps toward delinkage and the development of alternative economic plans and security management. The critics are legion and ridicule the possibility of shifting to new production systems or ending dependence on centers of power. Others view the problem as one of internal revolution and a shift to new modes of production. They view the nature of the state as an instrument of the production system. More conservative critics believe self-reliance will only compound the problem of bureaucracy and mass poverty.

This chapter focuses primarily on the comparison of Tanzania and Kenya as they have faced the problems of development, regional conflict, and superpower rivalry.

## KENYA AND THE *MATAJIRI* COMPRADORS

Kenya is the most important country in East Africa from a Western viewpoint. There are, however, several important questions to be answered about her role and her future. What some observers saw as rapid development has given way to a series of military insurrections, tribal conflicts, comprador rivalry, and growing repression of students and opposition leaders. Kenya's relations with South Africa and her ambivalence toward neighboring African states, as well as her growing association with U.S. Indian Ocean security policy, show that the former white-settler state is today controlled by a new tributary class which defines its own interests in close association with the U.S.-OECD-CENTCOM axis.

## New Tributary Class

A small group of teachers, lawyers, trade-union leaders, and tradesmen were responsible for the transfer of power in Kenya, rather than the peasant rebellion of the Mau Mau. This group gradually transferred power from the white settlers who at one time had attempted a unilateral declaration of independence (UDI), similar to the coup of the white settlers in Rhodesia in 1965. The settlers' fear of the growing power of Kenyatta and his friends made the Mau Mau rebellion much more significant than it would otherwise have been. The British Labour government had enough presence of mind to negotiate with Kenyatta in prison and other Kenya African Union (KAU) leaders on the outside such as Tom Mboya, a trade-union leader, recognizing that these men were not revolutionaries but potential comprador, middle-class African nationalists. Kenyatta, a graduate of the London School of Economics, was a Fabian socialist and pan-Africanist, who wanted for his own people freehold land and a share in the potentially wealthy, agrarian-based, Western-oriented economy of Kenya.[3] The Africans were not racist like most of the settlers, and were quite willing to allow Westerners and Asians who would help the new country with capital and technical aid to remain.

Thus, the KAU leadership, which came to power with Jomo Kenyatta as president in 1963, used a peasant rebellion to ease the settlers out of power, replacing a white tributary class with an African one. The new leaders very quickly used their control of the state to Africanize the sources of wealth and created a new bureaucracy serving their own tribal class interests.

Within a decade, a comprador bourgeoisie had emerged in Kenya, which controlled political power and shared economic power with those expatriates, mostly English, who controlled the major companies and financial enterprises.[4] Many African cabinet ministers bought large estates in the former White Highlands, where they became, for the most part, absentee landlords who commuted on weekends from Nairobi. Some of these coffee and wheat farms were very profitable enterprises, employing cheap migratory labor, very much as the previous white owners had done. The combination of incomes from various enterprises in farming, exporting, and even political payoffs has produced a small but very wealthy group, primarily Kikuyu, many of whom are closely related to Kiambu, the home district of Kenyatta, Mbiyu Koinange, Charles Njonjo, and Dr. Njoroge Mungai. A Swahili term has been applied to this new class: *matajiri*, meaning literally "the rich." Alan Amey and David Leonard have concluded they are a separate class and function differently from the European bourgeoisie in Marxian terminology in that they have a tribal base and use their control of the state to repress rival groups and advance their own wealth. The English-speaking members of the upper levels of the bureaucracy have joined this class, as they are free to take part in politics and business. Like Peter Kenyatta, the son of Jomo Kenyatta who became very wealthy, they thrive on their contacts and close tribal or family ties with the sources of contracts and patronage. They are, in short, a tributary class, with overseas links through business and cultural ties to Western countries, especially the United States and Great Britain. From their domestic power base in the bureaucracy, the business world, and tribal politics, they control all of Kenya using the power of the state.[5]

## *Matajiri* Politics

A struggle for power goes on within the *matajiri* and against rival groups who have been kept out of the center of power and wealth. This is the key to the nature of the Kenya political process—which to the outside observer is a vociferous display of competition for positions on the executive committee of the only political party, the Kenya African National Union (KANU), and for seats in the National Assembly.

Several Luo have become compradors and cooperate with the government. President Moi appointed three Luo to his 1980 cabinet.[6] Violations of the political rights of the opposition by the state have ranged from press repression to detention and assassination.[7]

In the late 1970s, a major struggle for power took place within the *matajiri* over the succession to President Kenyatta. The *mzee* was elusive about who should succeed him, but Vice-President Moi, as one of the very few non-Kikuyu leaders, was seen as a compromise. Intimidation and repression resulted in the death of J. M. Kariuki, an M.P. and critic of the government, and an alleged assassination plot against Moi and Njonjo was uncovered, in which local police in the Kikuyu district were involved.

Kenya has effectively had a one-party system of government since 1969, as all the candidates have to be first nominated by KANU; yet the scramble for seats is like that for bleachers in the World Series play-offs. This has been used to give an image of democracy. In many cases, several candidates for a single seat have been approved by the party. The press and observers have pointed out that there has been well over a 50 percent turnover in Kenyan parliamentary representation. However, the preselection of the candidates by the *matajiri* has assured that their interests would not be diluted through the populist spectacle of elections. Moreover, the continuation of Kikuyu control of the expanded ministries of the cabinet further enables this tribal class to rule.

Few states in Africa have avoided the pitfalls of a coup during such a period, and the contrast with Uganda is often made, where Obote, the nationalist hero, was overthrown twice, with disastrous results. The basis of Moi's success has been the basic cohesion of the *matajiri* and their ability to project a popular image despite increasing failures. Inflation and unemployment have caused unrest among the trade unions, who are under the control of a non-Kikuyu leadership. And the intellectuals associated with the universities and press have been major critics of the growing gap between rich and poor.

Several attempts to overthrow Moi have failed; but each has left a wider crack in the comprador front. The abortive August 1982 coup by junior air force personnel stemmed from a broad-based dissatisfaction and reflected the attempt of a rival faction who feared the growing instability and sought to take over to guarantee their position of privilege more securely.[8]

The *matajiri* are firmly entrenched in power; but indications are (from the Njonjo affair) that they have begun to fall out among themselves. Moi's control of the economy has continued to deteriorate, as the 1986 failure of *matajiri*-controlled banks revealed. And there is a growing scramble among the rich. The armed forces may well emerge as the final benefactor. Military coups in Africa are usually not revolutionary but preserve the stability of the ruling class. As long as the *matajiri* can rule the state, the military will stay out. And behind the *matajiri* stands the power of the Anglo-African corporate and Indian Ocean security interests.

### Anglo-American Dominance

English-speaking expatriates have very skillfully cultivated the emerging African ruling class, which reflects so closely their own values, tastes, and economic interests. Most of the white settlers in the former White Highlands have gone. Their huge estates have been broken up into smaller holdings, which have been purchased with government help by African growers or by wealthy African government ministers.

The extremes of poverty and wealth remain, while the settlers have taken their capital and invested it in new industries or returned to England.[9] Thus, the predominant expatriate interest has shifted to the processing and manufacturing sector of the economy. There are two major interest groups: those who own the large firms, such as Imperial Chemical Industries and Brooke Bond, and reside in the United States and Europe, and their agents and managers who live in Kenya as residents. Many of these possess dual citizenship under British law. They are supported by a well-paid cadre of professionals—lawyers, accountants and technicians—who though possessing foreign passports pay Kenya taxes and form the comprador bourgeoisie. They are predominantly British, but they have been joined by the nouveau riche Africans.[10]

Related to this group are the Asians, mostly Indians, who run family-owned enterprises from shops to large industries. Socially discriminated against by both Europeans and Africans, Asians have been especially restricted by the *matajiri* through regulation and nationalization. Nevertheless, they maintain their precarious prosperity by supporting the comprador Africans and government officials with favors, contracts, and bribes. No longer British subjects, they are more vulnerable than their white counterparts, as few elect to return to India.

In the late 1970s, Kenya appeared to be a model of African capitalism and prosperity which was not only profitable to multinational corporations but also provided access to the wider markets of East Africa, the Horn, and, to some extent, Central Africa. Moreover, Kenya had great prestige among other African states because of the pan-African role of Jomo Kenyatta. Even more significant, it was anti-Communist and willing to supply the United States with bases for the air and naval operations of the new American Indian Ocean forces. With Ethiopia under the Russians to the north, Uganda struggling back from the chaos of Idi Amin to the west, and Tanzania to the south leading the Frontline attack on western interests in southern Africa, Kenya became the center of hegemonic Western interest in East Africa.

The foreign-owned, multinational corporate economy was well established by the mid-1970s. A survey in 1972-1973 showed that twenty multinational corporations dominated 69 percent of the employment, 84 percent of the turnover, and 86 percent of the capital employed in the fields of cigarette manufacturing, soft drinks, footwear, leather, synthetic textiles, rubber, petroleum refining, industrial chemicals, paint, soap, cement, metal products, cotton textiles, and wood products industries.[11] Banking was British-dominated, while the U.S. companies entered the manufacturing sector.

The *matajiri* embraced this foreign control because Africanization meant not only managerial jobs but also positions on the boards of the multinational subsidiaries. (These were payments for favors in contracts and protection.) Though a small capital-owning class emerged among those Africans who controlled political power (at most they owned a few manufacturing subsidiaries[12]) the foreign-owned corporations, such as Lonhroes, East African Industries, J. Warren (Africa), and General Motors remained the decisive decision makers on investment, technology, and pricing. African socialism in Kenya meant the partnership of the state with foreign and domestic enterprise. Thus, national production-control boards and state finance were employed to serve the objective President Kenyatta had stated shortly after he was released from prison: "We will encourage the investors to carry on their business here and bring prosperity to Kenya. We want to run our country in the most peaceful and friendly way."[13]

Toward this objective, the nationalization of industry was rejected, and government-run boards, such as the Agriculture Finance Corporation, were established to aid farming and the Industrial and Commercial Development Corporation for industry.[14] African participation was, of course, encouraged, and in practice the *matajiri* received the opportunities and formed the core of the comprador bourgeoisie. Initially, this resulted in rapid expansion, and dependent development appeared to be providing even general prosperity, as Kenyatta had envisioned. However, inherent problems existed.

## Tributary Economy

Tourism in Kenya is a prime example of the exploitation of resources and export of value of the tributary economy. The Kenyan tourist industry is largely in private hands, and its contribution to development is minimal. It has created very few jobs, and most of the income is siphoned abroad through foreign-owned tour agencies, airlines, and hotels. It provides luxury goods and five-star hotels that add to the atmosphere of inequity. While providing recreation for Europeans, its effect has been to direct resources and attention away from the major production problems of agriculture, food supply, and employment. The revenue and foreign exchange from tourism is recycled to import the luxury goods and build the amenities of life that only the rich can enjoy. The *matajiri* enjoy the five-star hotels, but the man in the street looks on enviously.

The major contribution tourism has made is the preservation of wildlife—because of the interest in game parks among visitors. But the *matajiri* have plundered the animals in these parks for their ivory and skins. Under President Moi controls were finally imposed, but probably too late to save the black rhino. This precious heritage has been sold by the wealthy tributary class, while the poachers, when caught, have received the blame and prison sentences.[15]

## Inequities

In the 1960s and early 1970s, the economy appeared to be working, as Kenya's economic growth rate was high and prosperity came at least to the upper levels. However, a decline had set in by the end of the 1970s, associated with high fuel costs, falling export prices, inflation, and the high luxury living of the ethno-ruling class. The distribution pattern has been one of the most inequitable in Africa, showing a growing gap between rural and urban income. This has been accompanied by growing levels of unemployment, as school graduates continue to flock into the urban centers at the rate of 150,000 a year.

An International Labor Organization report in 1972 first pointed out the inequitable trends and suggested that redistribution take place in favor of the middle-income African, who could provide a more stable dynamic than the *matajiri*.[16] These inequities were also noted in a comparison study done by Amey and Leonard in which they concluded that in employment and education Kenya was falling behind Tanzania. In income terms of trade, the World Bank has shown that Kenya did better than Tanzania between 1970 and 1979, because of her diversified exports, but in net barter terms of trade Kenya has slipped more than Tanzania between 1970 and 1979.[17] With one of the highest population growth rates in the world, per capita economic gains are negative for the average Kenyan. One of the most familiar sights in Nairobi has been streets full of poorly dressed Africans walking ("tarmacking") by the shop windows, gaping at tape recorders, expensive clothing, and other gadgetry they cannot buy. Nairobi also has beggars who sit beside the curio shops and remind the tourists of the other side of Kenya.

A major slump in the balance of payments began in 1979, as a result of the high cost of oil and the world price decline for coffee. This, together with the necessity for food imports and the continued demand for luxury goods for the tourist economy, has forced Kenya to borrow heavily. Kenya's agricultural productivity has fallen off, due to disease and the poor management of the large farms by absentee African owners. The decline in production of the wheat crop is particularly worrisome to foreign aid officials, as it means more importation of food. The high costs of luxury goods, together with industrial needs, has made it very difficult to introduce the kind of austerity and exchange control necessary for improving the terms of trade.

Major income and opportunity gaps between rich and poor have widened rapidly since the mid–1970s, and the world recession and depression of export prices has aggravated the inequalities. With population growth unrestricted and the *matajiri* preserving their privileged position by the increased repression of the petite bourgeoisie, working-class, and peasant tribal protest, the pressures for explosive rebellion are enormous. While the military may well replace the civilian government, this is unlikely to resolve any of these problems. The usual role of the military in Africa has been to constrain rebellion and maintain the position of the tributary class. Attempts to establish an opposition socialist party have been dispersed by Moi's repression.

## Militarization Trend

The increasing militarization of Kenya is primarily a result of the extension of the strategic zones of superpower rivalry from the Persian Gulf and the northeast quadrant of the Indian Ocean to the northwest. Soviet bases in Eritrea and Aden have been countered by U.S. facilities in Berbera and Mombasa. Extensive naval and air activity has grown steadily during the 1970s. The Arabian Sea on Kenya's coast has been a key area for SLBM and antisubmarine warfare deployment by the United States. As noted earlier, the Soviets have intensified their shipping through the Suez Canal and the Red Sea. The U.S. search for bases for the rapid deployment force of CENTCOM has led it to identify Mombasa as critical, because of its facilities for carriers and inland airbase backup.

Soviet influence in this region has grown rapidly since 1969 when Said Barre seized power in Somalia and invited Soviet aid. Kenya has constantly opposed Soviet intrusion from the time Jomo Kenyatta became angered by the Soviet role in the 1964 Congo crisis, which he had attempted to mediate. Later, he believed the Soviets were involved in plots against him. One such plot involving the then Vice-President Oginga Odinga was discovered in 1965, in which a shipload of arms was uncovered in the basement of the vice-president's office.

The presence of the Soviet fleet in Indian Ocean waters has disturbed Kenya, and it has joined in the resolutions of the U.N. Ad Hoc Committee on the Indian Ocean seeking superpower withdrawal. The Kenyans' fear that the U.S.S.R. might use neighboring states against them in support of internal opposition was aroused when Idi Amin in Uganda sought to import Soviet arms, and Obote's new government later became suspect, especially after it invited the North Koreans to help train the Ugandan army. The curious role of Kenya in a series of coup attempts in the Seychelles against President Albert René is perhaps related to high Kenyan officials' fear of communism. René has accused Kenya of giving support to the two 1981 coup attempts and of directly working with South Africa to overthrow him.[18] The left-oriented politics of the Seychelles are disliked in Nairobi, and rumors that a Russian base, comparable to Diego Garcia, might be established in one of the Seychelles islands have unsettled Kenya as much as its patron powers, the United States and Great Britain.

Middle Eastern Arab politics have been mixed with the politics of the arms race in Kenyan Indian Ocean policy. Saudi Arabia has sought to build a conservative bloc against the radicalism of Libya, Ethiopia, and South Yemen and the backwash of the Iranian revolution. The Saudis have therefore generously aided those Indian Ocean countries, such as Kenya, who have taken a strong stand against the spread of Soviet influence. This has taken the form of both money and arms. A road between Somalia and Kenya was built with a Saudi loan of $23.5 million.[19] Since trade has always been minor between these two East African states, the military value of opening a supply line from the south to Mogadishu to support the Somalis against a feared Ethiopian-Soviet expansion is a possible major motive. The Saudi billionaire arms merchant Adnan M. Khashoggi is alleged to have been involved with Charles Njonjo in the attempted coup against René.

## U.S. Tribute

The United States, concerned with its rivalry with the Soviet Union in the Gulf and Indian Ocean and interested in the expansion of trade and investment in Africa, has found Kenya to be an important and receptive tributary.

The tributary relationship is more clearly seen in this case than with most other states in this region, including the oil-producing states. The combination of economic expansion with U.S. military intrusion, encouraged by the *matajiri* ruling class, has been well documented. It is tributary not only in the sense of neocolonial dependence, but in its obvious and growing strategic role for U.S. force projection and military deployment in the Indian Ocean. Kenya's government has willingly entered into this new relationship while maintaining all the nominal trappings of independence. The United States protects it against the perceived threat from the Soviet Union.

As for the traditional protection of East Africa, the British have long since abandoned the arms race with the U.S.S.R., though they and the French provide supply support for the American operation.

Early in 1980, the United States obtained a preliminary agreement with Kenya for the upgrading of the naval facilities at Kalindini Harbor in Mombasa by dredging, at an expense to the United States of $50 million.[20] These facilities are to be made adequate to service the largest U.S. carriers and battleships. The scope of the agreement is classified. However, suspicions have been aroused that Kenya has become a central base in plans for the rapid deployment force. This is corroborated by the fact that the United States has leased territory thirty miles inland at Mariakoni, where large underground shelters are being built. The United States is also building two new airfields, making Kenya the largest recipient of military aid in non-Arab Africa. Kenya has pressed for more sophisticated jet aircraft than the ten F-5 Tigers supplied in 1976 and the agreement upgrades them to sophisticated weapons status with F-11s and F-14s.[21] U.S. close ties with the development of the air force, in training as well as supply, came under a cloud following the implication of the air force in the abortive August 1982 coup. Between 1975 and 1979, the United States was the largest supplier of the Kenyan air force, with a total $90,173,000. Canada was second with $30,000,000, and Great Britain third with only $10,000,000. The United States has supplied sophisticated weapons and training to the air force, while the British and Canadians have been the major training source and supplier of weapons, tanks, and armoured cars.[22] Many Kenyan officers have Sandhurst and Mons cadet training backgrounds. Few foreign forces remain in Kenya, but the British retain basing privileges and the United States and Israel have training units there. The Israeli training units are reported to have provided President Moi with some protection during the August 1982 coup attempt.[23]

The American ambassador to Kenya, who had been engaged in some of these arms negotiations in 1979, stated that Kenya primarily feared Somalia rearmament, which was going forward with French and Saudi assistance at the time. In addition, he believed they saw the Russians as a threat, and that the American presence was felt to be an assurance against an inside coup with Russian backing.

These matters are not debated in the Kenya National Assembly, nor is the press allowed to comment on them in any detail, as President Moi has used his power to curb expressions of opposition. However, there is considerable dissatisfaction and fear that Kenya may be caught in a war between the superpowers, or that she might become a target for Soviet intrigue to offset U.S. influence.

There is no concrete evidence that the Soviet Union or indigenous Communists were behind the coup attempt of August 1, 1982, nor was it apparently anti-American in character or origins. However, as the fighting progressed, it took on an anti-American tone as the university students and working classes joined in. Uncertain as to who was responsible, Moi imprisoned virtually all his left-wing opponents at the universities and in the party and press.[24] Later, he directed his criticism against the right wing of the Kiambu faction which was led by Charles Njonjo, who had ambitions of replacing him.[25] Numerous accusations were made in the National Assembly and the press that Njonjo was involved with foreign corporations, including businesses in South Africa. He was clearly a wealthy Anglophile who had many business interests and had used transfer pricing of corporations he controlled to sequester millions of Kenyan shillings abroad. Moi's followers, including Vice-President Kibaki, were convinced he had plotted against the president. His close connections with individuals involved in the two major coups looked suspicious. Never convicted, he was forced to resign from office and stripped of his seat. Several of his followers went with him into the wilderness. The lesson for ambitious *matajiri* was clear—that "if you strike at a king, you had better kill him." More important, unless Moi can succeed in rallying the indigenous *matajiri* against the compradors who serve foreign interests, one day they will seize the state, probably with the help of the Kenya military and its foreign advisers.

Writers like Ngugi Wa Thiongo believe that, in time, a liberation movement may provide an alternative. But any signs of it in the universities, churches, and political party have been vigorously repressed; in mid-1986, twenty-eight people were jailed for membership in the Mwakenya organization of "Kenya freedom fighters." This reveals the internal weakness of the tributary state. Hatred for the repression and failures of the ruling class is directed against its internal leaders and external supporters. In Kenya, the intellectuals have turned left and become more anti-American because U.S. power is blamed for the continuing failures of Moi and the *matajiri*. While it is not the full story, it is the same tale that was told in the bazaars and coffee shops of Iran. Just as colonialism bred nationalism, the new tributary system breeds revolution.

## TANZANIA'S TRANSITION TO SELF-RELIANCE

In assessing self-reliance as an alternative to the tributary system, it is important to view this system as a method or strategy for accomplishing political and economic development goals. Self-reliance is one widely advocated way to freedom from dominance in Africa through the establishment of democratic control over the economic and political institutions that determine the level of human rights. Its proponents are not utopian or necessarily advocates of a classless society. They propose a method of democratic political control over the major financial, trade, and labor supply factors in the production system and the equitable redistribution of economic benefits to all classes and groups.[26] There are many forms that democratic political control can take—multiparty or single-party—and there are several ways in which the "heights of production" can be controlled, especially in former colonial countries. These methods are determined by the historical conditions of culture; the class system of production, which is in turn influenced by the level of technology; the patterns of trade; and the security framework. Human rights are more than nineteenth-century liberal objectives. They can be defined as the basic human needs of peace, security, shelter, food, and health, as well as legal and political freedoms.[27] These rights were given recognition in the *African Charter on Human and Peoples' Rights*, drafted at Banjul in 1982 and finally ratified by a majority of the OAU in 1986.

Tanzania has become a major experiment in the application of these principles to Third World and African conditions. It is also the most important example of the attempt to break out of the tributary relationship with the great powers of the world which characterizes so many of the new states of the Indian Ocean region. The idea of independent development through self-reliance, expounded by former president Julius Nyerere, is more than ideology; it has become a strategy of economic and political activity calculated to build up the internal resources and self-confidence of the people of Tanzania so that they can set their own African political pattern of life.[28] No man or nation is an island that is independent of what happens elsewhere in the world. Former President Nyerere and his successors, who have continued the Mwalimu's policies, are not seeking autarky or martyrdom. They believe it is possible to establish sufficient internal strength, in cooperation with other self-reliant states, to free themselves from external control and exploitation and develop greater internal equity and freedom. They are quite unaware of the difficulties, and considerable differences exist over the appropriate policies.

## Critics and Skeptics

There is a great deal of skepticism about the prospect of self-reliance, both inside and outside of Tanzania. Criticism has arisen on both the right and left, in the West and the East, as well as in Africa.

Nyerere's most scornful African critics were Kenya's *matajiri*, who opposed his state-directed economic system and ties with the Peoples Republic of China. Nyerere's strongest critics at home have been among the "scientific socialists," especially at the university, and to a lesser extent within the Chama Cha Mapinduzi (CCM) party. Since he is a non-Marxist and has taken some pains to differentiate *ujamaa* from scientific socialism, the more ideological critics, such as Issa Shivji and A. M. Babu, have attacked the Arusha Declaration and the failures of reformist African socialism.[29] The argument has many points, but basically it is that the state has been seized by a comprador class similar to Kenya's. Others maintain that the bourgeoisie have stalemated the achievement of a socialist state.[30] Critics on the right believe the bureaucracy has stifled the growth of the economy. These critiques cannot be simply dismissed, as the tributary analysis has shown. Yet they can be answered. The basic question to raise is not, "Has self-reliance succeeded?"—because it obviously has not—but "Has self-reliance provided a start in the direction that ends the deterioration of basic human needs and provides a hope for real independence from dominance and greater freedom?"

## Self-reliance

The concept of self-reliance as a strategy for the optimum development of Tanzania's resources began with the Arusha Declaration (1967) which was the product of the frustration and failures of the first few years of independence. This was a period of growing conflict with Western powers, highlighted by the controversies with the British over UDI in Rhodesia in 1965 and the American Embassy spy charges.

The idea of self-reliance is not autarky or even self-sufficiency, but utilization of one's own resources. The Tanzanians intend to build their own resources and strength to the point where they are not dependent upon the goodwill, financial, or technical ability of foreign powers. During the first years of independence, Tanzania's leaders came to realize that a policy of nonalignment and working with the various great powers did not free them from dependence. A Nigerian professor, formerly at the University of Dar es Salaam, Okwudiba Nnoli, pointed out eight major areas of dependence on foreign powers:

a) The dominance in the national economy of foreign ownership of the means of production, distribution, and exchange.
b) The consequent foreign exploitation of indigenous resources.
c) Various forms of socio-cultural and political dependence which sustained these ownership and exploitative relations.
d) The external orientation of the national economy.
e) The confinement of national participation in the international division of labor to primary production for export and the importation of manufactured goods.
f) Confidence in the salutary nature of external conditions.
g) High hopes of benefits from foreign relations.
h) Appeals to the humanitarian sentiments of the advanced countries, as the major means of international influence.[31]

Nnoli argued that the way to deal with these detriments to development was first and primarily to be prepared to reject links with foreign assistance that unnecessarily reinforced this dependence.[32] He maintained that it was possible to replace these old links with new ones, making new transactions possible and leading to a decline in dependence on foreign power.

According to Nyerere, building self-reliance meant an end to the colonial mentality of waiting for others to "do it for you." As he said:

Self-reliance is a positive affirmation that we shall depend upon ourselves for the development of Tanzania, and that we shall use the resources we have for that purpose.... We are not saying to other people: Please come and develop our country for us, and if you insist, we will stop being socialist or believing in equality.[33]

In a later address, as the recipient of the Third World Prize, he stressed the idea of South-South cooperation as an alternative based upon not catching up with the North but building with all Third World nations ready for self-reliance in a collective effort.[34]

Nyerere maintained that *ujamaa* is a cooperative socialist way of life, derived from the traditional African cultural values of the extended family in which production is for the use and benefit of all, rather than for profit. Individualism is a Western value, while communalism is African.

Thus, self-reliant socialism, according to Nyerere, is based upon the following principles:

1. Traditional African ethics, which provide for the basic needs of all members of the "family." "From each according to ability and to each according to need."
2. Self-control and development of one's own national resources with carefully limited external assistance.
3. Establishment of external trade and aid linkages with foreign powers prepared to accept Tanzanian self-reliance.
4. The struggle for self-reliant development for all of Africa, particularly with those who oppose neocolonial and racial rule.

However, Nyerere has conceded that these goals have not been achieved in Tanzania.

Self-reliance in one country is an impossibility. Without collective self-reliance among African and other Third World countries, the attempt will fail. Nyerere has been one of the primary advocates of South-South cooperation in the Indian Ocean region as one of the founders of modern pan-Africanism in the OAU. He has also become the recognized leader of the Frontline States in their diplomatic interventions in the conflicts of southern Africa, and Tanzania has formed a mutual defense alliance with Mauritius, Mozambique, and the Seychelles.

Tanzania has recognized the importance of attempting to control and limit superpower activity in the Indian Ocean, as well as within its own boundaries. It has backed the Indian Ocean Zone of Peace and the Ad Hoc Committee of the U.N. in the hope that it could dampen the arms race and lessen superpower presence. The American buildup in Kenya and Somalia worries the Tanzanians a great deal, as does the increasing Soviet presence in Mozambique, especially the use of port facilities by the Soviet navy. Nyerere has long maintained that direct use of Soviet aid in the liberation struggle was counterproductive as it gave the Western powers a stronger incentive to interfere through South Africa on the side of colonialism and racism.[35]

Tanzania, like Kenya, is a part of the northwest quadrant security zone of superpower rivalry. She has excellent ports and from the island of Zanzibar a big power could control the Mozambique Channel, strategically important to shipping around the Cape from the Gulf. Because of her close connections with southern African states as a political leader, this East African state is also very important within the southwest quadrant. Thus, the rival powers take Nyerere's policies very seriously, despite Tanzania's poverty and lack of military strength. But there has been considerable indirect rivalry to influence Tanzanian policy through third parties, such as Machel of Mozambique and Kaunda of Zambia.

Tanzania, despite her self-reliance policy, is still in transition from a tributary status. It has not been easy to cut military and economic ties that have bound it to the West. Arms are needed as is financial and technical aid. The process is a long-term one, fraught with controversy and opposed by the two major powers and some internal groups. If it succeeds, then a Third World alternative to tributary subservience will exist.

Relations with the two superpowers have as a consequence been cool, and they entered a new low with the United States after the American veto of Ambassador Salim Ahmed Salim as president of the U.N. General Assembly in 1982. He became prime minister in 1984, but stepped down when Ali Hassan Mwinyi became president in 1985. The U.S.S.R. has, however, made little headway even after the withdrawal of major Chinese aid. A delegation of the Supreme Soviet, led by I. P. Kalin, visited Tanzania in March 1982 and a joint communiqué reiterated support for liberation in Namibia and South Africa and criticism was made of the international economic system.[36]

Cuba has signed cultural agreements; and following the depletion of arms used in the Uganda war, the Soviet Union and Eastern Europe (1975–1979) became the major arms sources.[37] The pattern of diversified arms supply of self-reliance was only partially reestablished in the 1980s.[38] The Tanzanian army was developed and trained with Chinese aid that used old Soviet supplies and it is still dependent on the Soviet arms standardization.

The Chinese connection is a firm one that continues to bloc Soviet inroads. Nyerere, after Mao's death, repeatedly visited Beijing. China made a new loan for the repair and modernization of the TAZARA railway line in 1980 and a new textile mill was completed for childrens' clothing, together with cigarette and sugar manufacturing works.[39] China remains the largest customer after Europe for exports and the most important model for Tanzanians. Insofar as China has become an Indian Ocean power, Tanzania and Mozambique have been her two chief points of interest for trade, arms supply, and diplomatic support.

**U.S. Influence**

U.S. leverage on Tanzania is primarily financial, since there are few U.S.-based multinational corporations that have entered the economy. (Tanzania has no oil and few minerals.) Technical and economic aid has declined, especially under the Reagan administration which resented Nyerere's opposition through the Frontline States to its policies in southern Africa. Food assistance has been provided during the two emergencies by the United States and other Western states, though not in large quantities.[40] Other AID programs exist, primarily ultural, but Tanzania has increasingly relied upon European and U.N. sources for technical assistance. Difficulties with the World Bank and the IMF over the terms of loans have arisen from what the Tanzanians believe to be unjustified U.S. attempts to interfere with their self-reliance and socialist policies. Pressures from the World Bank to introduce greater reliance on "the individual entrepreneur," as suggested by the American World Bank President Alden Clausen during a visit to Dar es Salaam in 1981, were especially resisted.[41] Tanzania has refused loans from sources that attempted to pry it away from government-led industry toward a free market system, and has continuously resisted IMF pressures for devaluation and the limitation of social expenditures.[42] In the light of this resistance to U.S. economic and military intrusion, it is difficult to accept the argument of critics like Issa Shivji that Tanzania has capitulated in its struggle against dependency to the U.S.-OECD capitalist system. Even Nyerere's successors under Ali Hassan appear committed to continue this struggle to find a basis for self-reliant development, despite their continued dependence on external capital.

Economic and military aid from Canada, Great Britain, West Germany, and the Scandinavian countries clearly has sustained the Tanzanian economy over difficult years in the 1970s.[43] When one adds to this the EEC's trade and investment in Tanzania, the reality of a continuing tributary dependence in transition is seen. This has changed little despite the policy of diversification for self-reliance that Thomas Bierstaker found.[44] European aid indicates an interest on the part of democratic socialist states within OECD in assisting Tanzania to make a transition to self-reliance. By changing the terms of trade, Sweden in particular has provided assistance for equalizing exchange and technical aid. Diversification of sources of assistance rather than less dependence has been Nyerere's achievement in moving self-reliant development forward.[45]

## Tanzanian Collective Self-reliance

Tanzanian attempts to build security and economic ties with neighbors to the south have met with considerable success and some failure. The alliance with the Seychelles has benefited President René, as noted earlier, and the active intervention of the Frontline States, headed by Nyerere, has had several major achievements, not the least of which was the independence of Zimbabwe. Nyerere's vigorous leadership has won him the respect of the nine states that make up the new Southern African Development Coordination Conference (SADCC), and, in turn, the enmity of South Africa and those in the West, like the Reagan administration, who protect South Africa from censure and boycott.

Tanzania, in helping to found SADCC at Arusha in 1979 and in leading this group of nine states in a program of economic and security independence from South Africa, made a long-term commitment. Success is slow and difficult. Tanzania's adherence to the Preferential Trading Agreement of East and Central Africa in 1986 was an indication that it can be, one day, the basis of an East and Central African self-reliance alternative.

Leadership of the Frontline States gave Nyerere a major role in the negotiations over the Zimbabwe settlement and the continuing Namibia crisis. Robert Jaster traces perceptively the diplomatic influence of Nyerere in facilitating an agreement that at one point prevented Cuban and Soviet intrusion into the fighting, and at another stage vetoed the acceptance of a deal between Smith and Nkomo that would have prolonged the war.[46] And finally Nyerere and Kaunda, together, succeeded in turning Mrs. Thatcher around on the internal settlement with Bishop Muzorewa, and in turn, persuaded the Patriotic Front to accept an all-parties conference. "Nyerere was seen as more or less neutral as well as being a strong supporter of the Patriotic Front."[47] He was therefore able to work on both sides toward a final settlement that virtually all sides agreed was a remarkable outcome.

### Frontline States

Tanzania also has played an important leadership and mediating role over Namibia. The Frontline States have backed SWAPO and Angola from the start. They pushed SWAPO to accept an electoral settlement under U.N. auspices in 1978. And they have kept up the pressure on the Contact Five states, who have sought a settlement through negotiation with South Africa. Nyerere has backed Angola and SWAPO in their opposition to the U.S. proposal of a Cuban linkage to the agreement. Kaunda has been a channel of contact with Prime Minister Botha. He supported a negotiated outcome, while others, such as Nyerere and the Frontline leaders, have gone back to the U.N. for a full-scale economic boycott. Economic effects would be drastic on other SADCC countries like Zimbabwe; but they have not opposed measures by the U.N. which they could not entirely embrace themselves, given their trade dependence on South Africa.[48] If the Frontline States have their way and the U.N. adopts comprehensive economic sanctions, enforcement will become an issue, involving the superpowers and the small states in the Indian Ocean region.

### Step by Step

The criticism, from the right as well as the left, that Tanzania has failed as an African socialist and self-reliant system is widely spread, but it is based more on ideological preference than careful examination of the empirical basis for change that has been introduced.[49]

The question of the ethical or scientific basis of socialism is best answered in terms of the class character and redistribution accomplishments since independence. Nyerere and his party have maintained that the class struggle was not essential because African society was inherently communal and nonclass. The question of whether African society was class-based prior to and during the colonial period is highly contested.[50] However, Nyerere and TANU set out to prevent the emergence of a privileged class and with the Arusha Declaration initiated a program of deliberate redistribution to prevent inequities from becoming too great. This policy has been criticized for preventing growth by destroying incentives to produce. While there is some evidence that this has happened, especially in the agricultural sector, the Tanzanians have succeeded in preventing the emergence of an African comprador bourgeoisie. Many inequities exist; but even Nyerere's critics agree he has succeeded in redistribution far beyond most other African leaders.

These redistribution measures have greatly reduced sharp class differences.[51]

As Nyerere and others foresaw, the materialistic environment of postcolonial Tanzania produced a wealthy village elite whose children received the best education and entered the government bureaucracy and growing numbers of foreign firms. Restraints, however, were placed on their consumption through leadership codes. Roger Yeaker commented: "Inequality has also been lessened under the second Plan . . . by 1976 the ratio of the top government salary to the minimum wage was reduced to about fifteen to one, far below the seventy to one ratio that Tanganyika had inherited with independence."[52]

The cooperatives that favored the rich peasants were dismissed in 1976, and the *ujamaa* program in the villages reduced the tendency toward a "kulak" class. In addition, participation in the multinational subsidiaries was brought under government supervision. As a consequence, the comprador bourgeoisie did not gain control, as Amey and Leonard have demonstrated.[53] Instead, the major struggle has been between the privileged bureaucracy and party leaders, who have tributary tendencies, and a petite bourgeoisie based on the progressive peasants, workers, and unassimilated intellectuals whose commitment is to self-reliant development.

Tanzania's rulers are a self-reliant, progressive group, which has limited corruption and dealt severely with the comprador black market. The government has been very harsh with those who try to siphon off the foreign reserves. This is not to say that the black market does not drain the economy.[54] But no one tribal group has been permitted to emerge as the predominant beneficiary of the system, though again, differences resulting from historical location and cultural habits (such as with the nomadic Masai) obviously make for inequities in adaptation to modern life.

## *Ujamaa* Villages

The attempt to achieve development through the *ujamaa* campaign (cooperative villages) was the most controversial and most analyzed agricultural program in Africa. Critics and even officials agree the campaign failed to achieve its main objective—self-sufficient food production—and a serious cash-crop production problem exists. But it did accomplish several secondary goals toward the building of a new way of life that could turn out, in the long run, to be as important for self-reliant development as increased agricultural production.

During the decade 1970–1980, over 90 percent of the rural population were transferred from individual huts and plots to the *ujamaa* villages. The idea of village life changed the basis of agricultural production from isolated plots to communal agriculture and related cottage industries. It was also argued by government planners that the long-standing isolation of the rural peasant from education and technology could best be changed through village communities, and that the worst effects of rapid migration to the urban areas could be avoided by the decentralized growth of small units. These villages were to create a network of links between themselves and reduce the exodus to the coastal cities that so frequently has been the pattern of the export-oriented dependent Third World economies.

Farmers and tribesmen left their isolated plots very reluctantly. The main resistance came from the larger landholders and well-to-do shopkeepers who lost considerable property and, more importantly, political authority. This class resistance was not broken entirely peacefully. They were eventually forced to comply by the army who burnt huts and packed off the resisters in trucks to their new homes. Much attention was given to this resistance by the Western press, while the voluntary cooperation of 2 million was hardly mentioned. Unlike the communalization in China and the Soviet Union, where millions died, the change was comparatively humane.

The new system is not that of state farms. Families are encouraged to have their own private plots as well as work on the communal land. The major mistake was in assuming the peasants would work industriously on the communal project although the benefits received were indirect. Most of the communal profit was turned back into the payment for buildings or machinery, and the villagers received very little additional cash in labor compensation. Therefore, the tendency grew to spend time on private crops and subsistance as in the past. Such behavior, combined with the effects of the 1974–1975 drought, resulted in extensive food shortages. In 1976, the government policy changed and encouraged private food production. There was a recovery in 1976–1980, but again drought in 1980–1981 caused severe shortages.[55] In order to meet consumer needs, Tanzania was forced to import grain, and again the chief critics proclaimed the failure of *ujamaa*.[56]

However, the success of *ujamaa* as a means toward greater equity as well as production has been suggested by several observers. Hybrid seeds and mechanized production as part of a green revolution for Tanzania has begun under the auspices of the World Bank and the Food and Agriculture Organization (FAO). This new form of agriculture requires a type of knowledge and cooperation greatly facilitated by village life. Cooperative marketing and production has been taken out of the hands of government agencies and placed under the control of the villages themselves. Pragmatic adaptation to these methods of agricultural production has been made by Tanzanian officials.[57] Critics who claim this is a retreat from socialism have little evidence that greater success has been registered with state farms. State farms in Mozambique have been mainly adapted from previous Portuguese estates, and have encountered severe production problems in the 1980s.[58]

Increased agricultural productivity is the critical issue for *ujamaa*. By comparison with other Africa states, Tanzanian productivity since the drought has been good, and the country is back on track toward food self-sufficiency.[59]

**Self-reliant Industry**

The small manufacturing and industrial sector has been expanded under the direction of the state and in cooperation with external private and state enterprises.

The model of socialism is the mixed economy of Northern Europe, rather than the total state enterprise of Eastern Europe or China under Mao. Nyerere admired the Chinese achievement, and the concept of self-reliance is derived directly from Mao's philosophy of rejection of foreign domination. However, the mixed economy of parastatals, private enterprise, and *ujamaa* villages is closer to Fabian socialism than Mao's Marxism. Post-Mao China as it develops a private sector may well be a case of the teacher learning from the pupil.

Following the Arusha Declaration of 1967, the National Development Corporation (NDC) became the central agency of development as the private sector waned in importance. Thus, by the end of 1967 industry and finance were under direct government control. Land, forests, mineral resources, electricity, postal service, and telecommunications, radio, and the railways were all government-owned or controlled. Through the NDC and other government boards, the state participates in or controls many other enterprises.

The achievements have been considerable in certain sectors and industries. The financial reforms have enabled the country to minimize profit-transfer pricing and other means of profit flight abroad, and helped the state to utilize capital internally. New industries have begun in textiles and motor vehicles. Under the leadership of the NDC, the industrial sector has grown faster than foreign enterprise, though the private sector has also expanded. A conscious spread of industry outside of Dar es Salaam has broadened urban employment and eased the pressures of shanty-town slums in the major seaport.

The notion that control has slipped from Tanzania into the hands of multinationals is curious, given the minor role that foreign private investment has played since 1967. The major initiative has been in the hands of parastatals, which are financed by various government banks and central agencies. The number of parastatals grew from 78 in 1969 to 139 in 1974.[60] The Tanzania Industrial Bank (TIB) has been the primary internal financier, while the World Bank has been the major external source. Private industry has been required to work within the framework of government restrictions, and when they have varied from basic government policy, they have been nationalized with minimum compensation, as in the case of the British multinational, Lonhroes.

The declining productivity of the industrial sector has been sharply criticized by Zaki Ergas, who attributes it not only to increased fuel costs (Tanzania has no oil), but to bureaucratic harassment of the managerial group and the inefficiency of the entire system. In support of his case he quotes a Chama Cha Mapinduzi White Paper which points out that income from NDC sales in 1967–1975 was up 401.4 percent but was exceeded by costs by 484 percent and the deficits were financed by the government.[61] These are short-term problems and gaps which do not offset the gains from central government initiative.

However, Cranford Pratt's conclusion about the first decade of socialism—that Tanzania has successfully established a new model for socialist development in Africa—is too optimistic.[62] Okwudiba Nnoli reaches a more restrained but also hopeful conclusion about the direction of the power struggle within the ruling elites. He believes the "progressive" petite bourgeoisie has gained the upper hand:

> The power struggle has been broadened to involve more than the narrow ruling groups. As a result, the growing power of opponents of Socialism is now countered by the growing strength of pro-Socialist forces, an alliance of the revolutionary elite and the politically-conscious workers and peasants.[63]

Nnoli concludes that self-reliance is the only alternative to the "slavish dependence advocated by the right wing" or the "dignified martyrdom" which would inevitably follow the left-wing program.[64]

The question still remains: Can it succeed? The mix of external aid is a crucial factor in the launching of self-reliance.

## External Aid

Tanzania has had more external economic assistance per capita than any other African country, primarily from multilateral sources following the principle of diversification of aid. The Tanzanians have retained the option of rejecting assistance if it placed compromising demands upon them. In the 1960s, Nyerere turned to China for military assistance. When the United States and Great Britain pressured him to drop his China ties, President Nyerere strongly resented the intrusion. This strengthened his resolve to free Tanzania from the consequences of superpower rivalry. After the Chinese completed the TAZARA railway in 1975, one year ahead of schedule, they began to phase out their extensive aid programs and were soon replaced by the Scandinavians who provided new sources of technical assistance and financial aid. Sweden in particular became a primary donor, and the U.N. Development Program instituted numerous projects, amounting to millions of dollars worth of assistance.[65]

## War in Southern Africa

There are military dimensions to the prospects for self-reliance. Tanzania has found close relations with Zambia, Zimbabwe, and Mozambique an alternative to security dependence on the superpowers. While the Tanzanian forces are small, and until 1981 were tied down in the occupation of Uganda, the considerable guerrilla armies now transformed into national forces in Mozambique and Zimbabwe are available to protect "African security." Zimbabwe, in particular, has a sophisticated air force capable of rapid intervention. Tanzania has a small air force equipped with Canadian and Chinese fighters. It also has defensive surface-to-air missiles protecting the major ports. The army has been seasoned in Uganda, where it demonstrated the results of Chinese training in the gradual defeat of the well-equipped Ugandans and Libyans. According to L. L. Matthews:

The TPDF has been standardizing on Chinese equipment, or such Warsaw Pact equipment that conforms to it. The tank battalion consists of two companies of the Chinese T-59 medium tank and one company of Chinese Type-60 light tanks. . . . The air force has a squadron composed of eight of the Chinese versions of the MiG-19 and twelve Soviet MiG-17s supplied by China; there is also a transport squadron of assorted light transport aircraft.[66]

However, the major source of supply since China's reduction in aid between 1975 and 1979 has been the Soviet Union.[67] This could accelerate if the situation in southern Africa deteriorates.

The greatest danger arises from a possible clash with South Africa—as the result of an escalation in the Namibian conflict, for example—in which South Africa takes retaliatory action, as she has done in Angola and Mozambique. Nyerere has given training bases to both the ANC and the South African PAC which has regrouped under D. K. Laballo (who served a term on Robben Island). South African strikes are likely to be limited to punishment rather than all-out war—much like the attack on the Angolan base of Cuamato in early January 1981; the raid into Mozambique at Matola, January 15, 1981; and the attacks on Botswana, Zambia, and Zimbabwe in June 1986.

African leaders like Mwinyi, Mugabe, and Chissano are cautious about giving too much away to the U.S.S.R. in the process. However, the direct attacks on their countries have forced them to reconsider their own security. Their response may be to react in favor of tributary protection from the Soviet side. They will move in that direction in order to survive, if they are not protected against South Africa by the West. Tanzania is in a less vulnerable position; but conflicts of this kind escalate quickly. If South African pressures continue, Zimbabwe, Zambia, and Tanzania could overnight opt to place Soviet-supplied "defensive units" on their soil, similar to what Kenya and Somalia have done in providing bases for U.S. planes, ships, and personnel. Such actions would further alarm South Africa and the United States, and perhaps even lead to more South African "preemptive" strikes.

Continuing escalation of the arms race in East Africa will end Tanzania's chances to move fully into a self-reliance pattern. The conflicts with Kenya are apt to increase as the *matajiri* try to hold onto Western support and their own political power. The two East African countries are moving along separate tracks, and if Tanzania and other Frontline States become active bases for antiapartheid arms and support, the superpower rivalry could become as fierce as in the Gulf and the Middle East. It would be most unfortunate for all concerned if Western power is deployed more directly in support of South Africa, and the fear of Soviet supply of armed liberation struggles is the defining line of the conflict. Aid to Savimbi in Angola has aligned the United States with South Africa. This direction will continue if the United States and the West fail to back Tanzanian self-reliance and the Frontline States against an increasingly aggressive South Africa. To divide Africa further by introducing the arms race directly into East

Africa and siding with South Africa against African self-reliance would be folly and a violation of the right to peace now specifically recognized in the Indian Ocean Zone of Peace.

## NOTES

1. See Samir Amin, *Unequal Development, An Essay on the Social Formation of Peripheral Capitalism*, (New York: Monthly Review Press, 1976); Terrence K. Hopkins, Immanual Wallerstein, et al., *World Systems Analysis, Theory and Methodology* (Beverly Hills, Calif.: Sage Publications, 1982); and Andre Gunder Frank, "The Development of Underdevelopment," *Monthly Review* 18, no. 4 (1966).

2. The author's first use of the tributary state concept was in "Demilitarization Proposals for the Indian Ocean," in *The Indian Ocean in Global Politics*, ed. Larry W. Bowman and Ian Clark (Boulder, Colo.: Westview, 1980).

3. Carl G. Rosberg, Jr. and John Nottingham, *The Myth of Mau Mau: Nationalism in Kenya* (Stanford, Calif.: Hoover Institution Publications, 1966), pp. 320–48.

4. Steven Langdon, *Multi-National Corporations in the Political Economy of Kenya* (New York: St. Martin's Press, 1981), pp. 41–43.

5. Alan B. Amey and David K. Leonard, "Public Policy, Class Inequality in Kenya and Tanzania," *Africa Today*, 26, no. 4 (1979).

6. Vincent Khapoya, "Kenya Under Moi: Continuity or Change?" *Africa Today* 27, no. 1 (1980).

7. See Amey and Leonard, "Public Policy," for a discussion of the pattern of growing repression (p. 16).

8. "Kenya Coup Violence Abates," *Africa News*, August 9, 1982.

9. Colin Leys, *Underdevelopment in Kenya* (Berkeley and Los Angeles: University of California Press, 1974).

10. Ibid., p. 27.

11. Langdon, *Multi-National Corporations*, pp. 32–34.

12. Ibid., pp. 41–42.

13. Ahmed Mohiddin, *African Socialism in Two Countries* (Totowa, N.J.: Barnes and Noble Books, 1981), p. 33.

14. Ibid., pp. 105–7.

15. Kes Hillman and Edmond Bradley Martin, "Countdown for Kenya's Rhino," *Africana* 6, no. 12 (1979).

16. International Labor Organization, *Employment, Incomes, and Equality; A Strategy for Increasing Productive Employment in Kenya* (Washington, D.C.: World Bank, 1972).

17. "Terms of Trade," *Accelerated Development in Sub-Saharan Africa* (Washington, D.C.: World Bank, 1981).

18. Colin Legum, ed., *Africa Contemporary Record: Survey and Documents 1981–1982* (New York: Africana Publishing Co., 1982), pp. B187–8.

19. Ibid., p. B203.

20. "Kenya: The End of an Illusion," *Race and Class*, Winter 1983, p. 237.

21. *Africa Contemporary Record*, p. B202.

22. L. L. Matthews, "Kenya," in *World Armies*, ed. John Keegan (New York: Facts on File, 1979), p. 403.

23. "The Image Cracks," *South*, August 1982.

24. *Africa News*, February 1982 and August 9, 1982.

25. Kate Currie and Larry Ray, "State and Class in Kenya—Notes on the Cohesion of the Ruling Class," *Journal of Modern African Studies* 22, no. 4 (1985), pp. 559-595.

26. See J. F. Rweyemmamu, Introduction to *Industrialization and Income Distribution in Africa* (Westport, Conn: Lawrence Hill, 1981).

27. Roy Preiswerk has defined the self-reliance strategy as more than nineteenth-century capitalist ideas. See Introduction to *Self-Reliance: A Strategy for Development*, ed. Johan Galtung and Peter O'Brien (Geneva: Institute for Development Studies, L'Ouverture Publications, Ltd., 1980), p. 12.

28. See Julius K. Nyerere, *Freedom and Socialism* (New York: Oxford University Press, 1970).

29. Issa Shivji, *Class Struggles in Tanzania* (New York: Monthly Review Press, 1976); and A. M. Babu, *African Socialism or Socialist Africa* (London: Zed Press, Ltd., 1981).

30. Howard Stein, "Theories of the State in Tanzania: A Critical Assessment," *Journal of Modern African Studies* 23, no. 1 (1985), pp. 105-25.

31. Okwudiba Nnoli, *Self-Reliance and Foreign Policy in Tanzania* (New York: NOK Publishers, 1978), p. 205.

32. Ibid., pp. 298-99.

33. Julius K. Nyerere, "Freedom and Development," reprinted in *The Nationalist* (Dar es Salaam), October 18, 1968.

34. Julius K. Nyerere, "South-South Options," *Third World Quarterly* 4, no. 5 (July 1982).

35. Julius K. Nyerere, *Freedom and Unity* (New York: Oxford University Press, 1967), p. 208.

36. *Africa Contemporary Record*, p. B284.

37. United States Arms Control and Disarmament Agency, *World Military Expenditures and Arms Transfers, 1970-79* (Washington, D.C.: U.S. ACDA, 1985), table iii, p. 132.

38. Ibid. China is the second largest supplier next to the U.S.S.R.

39. *Africa Contemporary Record*, p. B272.

40. Ibid., p. B273.

41. Ibid.

42. *Africa News*, December 7, 1979. Reginald Green, in "Sparring with the IMF," *Africa Report* 30, no. 5 (September/October, 1984), argues that despite inept negotiations Tanzania resisted IMF pressures.

43. UNDP, *Country Programme for United Republic of Tanzania, 1978-81*, DPGC/URT/R-2, Dar es Salaam (October 9, 1978).

44. Thomas Biersteker, "Self-Reliance in Theory and Practice in Tanzanian Trade Relations," *International Organization* 34, no. 2 (1980).

45. See Goran Hyden, in *Beyond Ujamaa in Tanzania: Underdevelopment and an Uncaptured Peasantry* (Berkeley and Los Angeles: University of California Press, 1980); and Crawford Young, *Ideology and Development in Africa* (New Haven, Conn: Yale University Press, 1983).

46. Robert S. Jaster, *A Regional Security Role for Africa's Front Line States: Experience and Prospects*, Adelphi Papers, no. 180 (London: I.I.S.S., 1983), pp. 11-12.

47. Ibid., p. 11.

48. David Coetzee, "Commonwealth in Crisis," *Africa Asia*, no. 33 (September 1986), p. 14.

49. See, for example, Zaki Ergas, "Why Did the Ujamaa Village Fail?" *Journal of Modern African Studies* 18, no. 3 (1980).

50. Thomas M. Callaghy, "The Difficulties of Implementing Socialist Strategies in Africa," in *Socialism in Sub-Sahara Africa*, ed. Carl Rosberg and Ian Callaghy (Berkeley, Calif.: Institute of International Studies, 1978).

51. Dean McHenry, "The Struggle for Rural Socialism in Tanzania," in *Socialism in Sub-Sahara Africa*.

52. Roger Yeaker, *Tanzania: An African Experiment* (Boulder, Colo.: Westview, 1982), p. 83.

53. See Amey and Leonard, "Public Policy."

54. Ergas, "Ujamaa Village."

55. David J. Vail, *Technology for Ujamaa, Village Development in Tanzania*, Foreign and Comparative Studies, African Series vol. 18 (Syracuse: Syracuse University Press, 1979).

56. Zaki Ergas, *The Tanzania Economy: What Went Wrong?* (Jerusalem: Truman Research Institute, Hebrew University of Jerusalem, 1981). See also, Charles Lofchie, "Agrarian Crisis and Economic Liberalisation in Tanzania," *Journal of Modern Africa Studies* 16, no. 3 (1978).

57. Colin Legum, "Socialist Tanzania May Be Climbing Out of Its Economic Hole," *Christian Science Monitor*, December 4, 1984.

58. The Lappe-Moore Comparison is a theoretical value-based study. An applied study of Louise Fortman should be noted: "Peasants, Officials, and Participation in Rural Tanzania's Experience with Villagization and Decentralization," (Ithaca: Cornell University, Center for International Studies, 1980). Also, the study by a Scandinavian team is critical but notes the progress made in the villages. See Jannik Boesen, Brigit Storgard Madsen, and Tony Moore, *Ujamaa—Socialism From Above* (Uppsala: Scandinavian Institute of African Studies, 1977).

59. *African Emergency*, no. 6 (January-February 1986). These reports are issued by the U.N. Status Report on the Emergency Situation in Africa. S. S. Mushi reaches this conclusion in "Tanzania Foreign Relations and the Policies of Non-Alignment, Socialism, and Self-Reliance" (University of Dar es Salaam, 1979).

60. Mohiddin, *African Socialism*, p. 145.

61. Ergas, *The Tanzania Economy*, p. 8.

62. Cranford Pratt, *Critical Phase in Tanzania, 1945–68: Nyerere and the Emergence of a Socialist Strategy* (Cambridge: Cambridge University Press, 1976).

63. Nnoli, *Self-Reliance*, p. 324.

64. Ibid.

65. UNDP, *Country Programme*. The total amount of dozens of projects came to $29,290,205 in 1979.

66. Matthews, "Kenya," p. 699.

67. *World Military Expenditures*, p. 132.

# 5

# Collective Self-reliance: The Indian Ocean Zone of Peace

*Tzu Li Keng Sheng* (Regeneration through Our Own Efforts)

—Mao Tse-tung, 1945

Third World countries appear more vulnerable than ever to the interventions and dominance of the superpowers after the invasion of Grenada in October 1983 and the continued occupation of Afghanistan by a reinforced Soviet army. In varying degrees, the fate of these small states reflects the vulnerability of most Third World states who have entered into military and economic linkages that have made them the tributaries of superpowers who profess to protect them.[1] However, small states and progressive liberation movements, in their search for an alternative to the tributary status, have given increasing attention to the concept of collective self-reliance.

## COLLECTIVE SELF-RELIANCE AS DEVELOPMENT

Various political theories explaining the concept of collective self-reliance have been put forward by activists such as Julius Nyerere in Tanzania[2] and the leadership of the Sandinistas in Nicaragua.[3] A number of collective self-reliance institutions have been established, notably, the Indian Ocean Zone of Peace (IOZP) and the Southern African Development Coordination Conference (SADCC). Many theorists have contributed to the development of the self-reliance concepts, including Samir Amin,[4] Okwudiba Nnoli, Johan Galtung, Thomas Biersteker, and Ashok Partjasratji.[5]

### The Liberation Consciousness

The search for an alternative to continued warfare in the Third World has created a new liberation leadership, aware of the growing cost in human lives of their subjection. The failure to develop—in fact, their tendency toward underdevelopment—has awakened this consciousness. This tendency has been no less marked among the tributaries of the Soviet Union than the United States, though for somewhat different reasons. The chronic symptoms of this underdevelopment are: the continuing single crop or mineral export on which most of their economies depend, such as copper for Zambia and coffee for Ethiopia; the deteriorating balance of payments; inflation; capital flight abroad; dependence on foreign technicians; military coups; and oppressively costly arms agreements. In all the economies of the Indian Ocean littoral states, the quality of life for the vast majority of their citizens has declined in an absolute sense, while their ruling elites have prospered.[6]

Out of this conflict and exploitation has emerged a progressive liberation movement that is the basis of a widespread demand for an alternative that can provide a goal of hope for the billions consigned to absolute poverty and chronic fear. This way calls for a major break with the methods and values of the past. Self-reliance is the culmination of the emergence of colonial peoples from the domination of the industrial revolution centered in the West. As Johan Galtung expressed it: "The politics of self-reliance is an important part of contemporary history—an effort to undo five centuries of dependency on the West."[7] The underlying principles are both political and economic: the fulfillment of human rights and the radical reorganization of the division of labor.

Among several African and Indian Ocean countries, self-reliance has become a strategy for breaking out of the economic dependency and the security manipulation of the tributary system.

Nyerere and Cabral have argued that a rejection of Western measures of development success is primary, whether capitalist or Marxist, because both are predicated on the capitalist concepts of production and consumption. Development cannot be assessed in terms of increased per capita income or higher consumption. Western standards are both too individualistic and materialistic. As President Nyerere put it when he received the second annual Third World Prize in New Delhi in 1982, the task is "not to try to catch up with the industrialized North." Instead, he urged the Third World to stress "people-oriented" development that would provide shelter and basic health to the populations of the poor countries. The standard he called for was "'not going to the moon but feeding ourselves.'"[8]

This view of development standards has been attacked as vigorously by African as by non-African critics. It is held to be a simplistic way to rationalize poverty. But Nyerere has replied that the Western way provides the good life for a few and misery for the vast majority.

The key to Nyerere's approach is the emphasis on equity and welfare as opposed to productivity. The gap between the rich and the poor cannot be very wide in a self-reliant society, though obviously it remains considerable, even in Tanzania. And, in addition, all members of the community must be supplied with the human necessities of food, shelter, education, and health care. The ability of the state to assist people in gaining these rights is the essence of development. Therefore, a self-reliant society will not judge itself in competition with industrial societies in production and trade. But the critics ask: How can you have services, if you don't have production and trade? The self-reliance response is that production is encouraged, but as a source for human services for all rather than as high consumption for the few while millions starve.

## Objectives of Self-reliance

If these standards of self-reliance are applied to the question of development, an entirely different result is reached than with the neoclassical model which has led to the tributary system. North-South dependence has not only been self-destructive, it has also been a false standard. Self-reliance stems from a different paradigm, with radically new objectives.

The application of this system has been limited but is important among African and Indian Ocean states, in terms of several basic policies:

1. Rejection of the dominance and security tributary linkages
2. Redistribution through human services and rural integration
3. Diversification of production
4. Majority participation
5. Increased growth of regional association and South-South cooperation

The initiative to break existing linkages has come from the Third World states, as in the case of the Iranian revolution in the late 1970s which forced the Carter administration to disengage. Intervention to preempt such a change is a constant counterrevolutionary threat to all self-reliance movements. The examples of preemptive intervention in Chile and Afghanistan which prevented a break must be put alongside those of Zimbabwe and Mozambique, who continue to resist the intrusion of the Western core into their liberation struggles. The initial acceptance of independence in Africa was turned into indirect attempts to dominate through South African subimperialism. In most cases, the change has been from one pattern of tribute to another. But in the struggle, several states have begun to develop elements of self-reliance.[9] Not all the linkages have been severed at the same time, and the process of transition is a complex of external negotiation combined with internal political balancing and a readjustment of associations with external powers.[10] Whether the steps are taken in concert with others on a regional basis or in direct negotiation, it is clear that the process does not begin until the tributary class has been internally defeated through major political action. In most cases, this has involved armed struggle of an internal or external type. Any new government that challenged its patron protector and was naïve enough to believe it did not need an alternative security system to defend its borders has failed to survive for long in the jungle of international politics. Similar self-preservation is needed against internal counterrevolutionary groups who resort to violence. However, force alone, as the major precipitant of change, has never initiated self-reliant development. A conscious will to liberation must exist first.[11]

Redistribution and rural generation are the initial self-reliance steps in societies with populations that remain 90 percent peasants. The breach between rural and urban interests can be bridged by redistribution. Under self-reliance, the vast majority have human rights that cannot be sacrificed to the privileged urban groups. This has been the theoretical underpinning of the major self-reliance advocates, from Gandhi to Mao and Cabral. The alienated peasantry, they have argued, can be brought back into the center of society through production and participation. The essence of indigenous culture is preserved and traditional democratic institutions protected from the modernizing bulldozers.[12] Communalism, with its social democratic values, is encouraged against the depersonalization of corporate farming (private or state). And the farmers are motivated to grow their own food and feed the nation, rather than concentrate exclusively on production for export, while depending on foreign imports of food.

Redistribution is not delayed until increased production takes place because it is seen as a condition of growth. Through health and education services, agriculture is improved. Scientific and technological benefits supplied by the government are spread by "villagization" and the extension of social services. Through public services, rural reintegration is facilitated and other underprivileged groups are assisted. Equity expands the productivity of workers, and thereby the entire society benefits.

Diversification of production and control is an additional goal. Increased production, self-reliance economists maintain, is best achieved through the control of the market by the state, rather than vice versa. Thus private and government external investment and technical-managerial skills are employed together for development. This assures that surpluses are reinvested and resources fully developed through indigenous industry as well as foreign enterprise. The way such controls are applied can vary enormously and there is no single formula. Clearly, some have been more successful than others, as several surveys have shown.[13] Colin Kirkpatrick and Frederick Nixson observed: "In general, however, it is only recently that attention has been focused on the complex relationships that exist between foreign interests and domestic classes or groups within African economies, and the manner in which these connections both determine and are determined by the activities of foreign capital within these countries."[14]

Under self-reliance, the shift is from external control of the financial and trading decisions to internal control, which allows the economy to grow in the interests of the small state. Too frequently this has been the point of failure because of dependence on foreign finance. Diversification of production and finance is one clear indicator of progress. Growth in production is often a misleading measure because it may conceal the continued unequal trade and the failure to redistribute within the tribute system.

Therefore, in attempting to assess development of self-reliance among the Third World states, we have to introduce human quality of change measures. Rajni Kothari and Johan Galtung for the World Order Models Project and Dennis Goulet for the Overseas Development Council were among the first to set forth specific indicators on the quality of life, such as minimal literacy, adequate food production and consumption, pure water, life expectancy, hospital beds, and employment. Human rights advocates consider political prisoners and newspaper censorship to be important. Self-reliance analysis uses a variety of these quality of life measures. Considered to be minimal are the basic human needs criteria adopted by the World Bank and first proposed by the International Labor Organization (ILO).[15] Since redistribution before growth has become the self-reliance development alternative, priority is given to social services such as education and health. The exact reverse takes place under the tributary relationship with growth in military costs and bureaucracy at the expense of essential human needs. This redistribution before significant growth is contrary to most neoclassical economic assumptions. But it is this kind of radical new economics that is advocated by self-reliance economists.[16] Food for home consumption has priority over export crops and this points up the conflict with traditional views of comparative advantage for African economies.[17]

Self-reliance development also includes specific measures for political human rights, as identified in the Charter of Human and People's Rights, adopted by the Organization of African Unity in Nairobi in 1982. These include the group rights of self-determination and peace as well as political expression and freedom from racial discrimination. The tributary class tends to repress the freedom of the opposition in the name of security and in the interest of the superpower, while at the same time professing development.[18]

Self-reliance promotes democratic participation as the initial step in the people's liberation from their colonial tributary mentality, and advocates popular progressive control of the state which in turn governs the new redistribution and production process. A full consideration of the economy of collective self-reliance is beyond the limits of this book, but an assessment of disengagement and South-South cooperation as alternatives to superpower tributary dominance is in order here.[19]

## Disengagement, Diversification, and Collective Security in the Zone of Peace

The first step in any sustained, collective self-reliant development involves disengagement from dependence upon a single superpower for military supplies and training. In short, this means stepping out of the arms race and war system through diversification. Fouad Ajami noted the centrality of the war system in the denial of Third World human rights and in its perpetuation of dominance.[20] Not only the enormous and growing cost of protection that a Third World tributary pays but also the control and subordination of its development to the national interests of the superpower necessitates the break. The use of a Third World country's own military as a counterrevolutionary device of the tributary class has been shown to be a widely prevalent means of indirect imperialism. All of these interventions—borne out by numerous instances among Indian Ocean states—have led to a growing realization by the progressive class that military disengagement and a shift to alternative means of defense have to be undertaken very early in the strategy of self-reliance.

There are many different strategies for such disengagement. The first is diversification of arms supply and training among several core powers and across the East-West divide. This has been a pattern advocated by nonalignment theorists and has been more easily suggested than implemented. Not only is it costly, but it also creates difficulties of weapons logistics and supply. Despite the difficulties, a number of Third World states have begun to diversify and develop alternative sources of supply and training for their own armed forces. Prominent among these in this study are the two leading advocates of self-reliance and nonalignment—Tanzania and India. India has recently begun to move away from dependence on the U.S.S.R. with licensing agreements from the West for the manufacture of her own sophisticated fighters and missiles (the Soviets refuse such concessions). Internal technological advances have made this possible. The Iranians and Iraqis have both moved into diversification as a result of the changes in their relations with major patrons. But the war between them has imposed new dependence in their search for arms, and Iraq has turned to the West through Saudi Arabia, while Iran is increasingly beholden to China and Syria and less to Libya. The increased role of China as an alternative source for certain countries such as Pakistan and Tanzania should be noted. Newly liberated areas of southern Africa have provided the major trend in this direction. After 1980 Zimbabwe began diversification, as have both Angola and Mozambique, following their revolutions. Counterrevolutionary attacks by South Africa have accelerated, not prevented, this process because of the threat to African self-determination.

Diversification is a very limited indicator of disengagement and needs to be carefully considered in relation to other steps in the delinkage process. The development of internal or regional sources of training and support are of even greater importance. The refusal to grant bases and renew prior agreements are secret, as provisions for overflight rights, military landings, and repair facilities are seldom made public. There are very few examples of countries that have succeeded in disengagement except as a result of revolution. Individual cases need to be very carefully examined in order to understand the pattern of changes made. As we have seen, Ethiopia has switched from one superpower to the other. The phenomenon cannot be understood in terms of the overall gross figures of arms transfers or agreements on bases throughout the region often used to describe policy. These show sharp increases in total amounts and in single sources of supply. Third World nations have signed agreements in the last decade for over $250 billion worth of arms. The United States sold $4.8 billion worth to the developing world in 1984, and the Soviet Union's exports were $8.6 billion.[21] Yet self-reliance diversification has been growing. Several countries among the nonaligned states, including India, Zimbabwe, Tanzania, Tunisia, and Nigeria have raised a serious challenge to the superpower dominance of the arms sale system as they have sought alternative sources of supply and means of self-defense.[22]

One of the most fully developed collective self-reliance systems is that of the Seychelles, Mauritius, and Tanzania. These three have a mutual assistance pact that enables the armed forces of each country to be available for the defense of the others. Among small states with few defense forces, this collective feature has proven very important. In each of these states, there is a popular determination to limit the presence of the superpowers according to the principles of the Indian Ocean Zone of Peace Agreement. As these small powers have discovered, their real security problem is not the threat of direct attack from one or the other of the superpowers or any of the core powers, but stems from regional third-party aggressors, who act either on their own or as a subimperial force in the interest of superpower hegemony. It is very rare for a direct attack to take place, such as that of Idi Amin of Uganda against Tanzania in 1978. There may have been some indirect Soviet influence in the harassment of Nyerere because of his association with China, but Tanzania's self-reliance policy did not leave it weak or unprepared, as within a period of six months it had toppled Amin.

Delinkage is the first step away from subimperialism, in which the protection framework of the superpower is abandoned in favor of nonalignment. A nonalignment of substance rather than rhetoric is attempted, though it is costly, as many states such as Tanzania, Zimbabwe, and Iran have discovered.

The attempt to diversify arms and training is an initial phase in delinkage, such as Zimbabwe's decision to use North Korean officers for training to reduce the number of British officers.[23] The use of Cuban troops in Mozambique and Ethiopia was also an attempt by African states to reduce their security dependence directly on one superpower.[24] Tanzania's resort, initially to China, and then to other small powers such as Canada and Scandinavia for training and supplies is the major example of divestment from military dependence. Somalia's switch from the Soviet Union to the United States simply retained the basic tributary relationship. Iraq attempted to diversify, especially after the break with the U.S.S.R., through her contract with France for weapons supply and nuclear power production. But Hussein's attack on Iran destroyed all prospects for nonaligned diversification.

Counterpressure against subimperialism is illustrated by the African, Arab, and Asian arms and trade embargo on South Africa; the arms embargo was made official for all member states by the U.N. in 1963.[25] On occasion, Third World countries such as Jordan and Indonesia have broken the embargo to sell arms to South Africa. The major offender has been Israel, herself the subject of a widespread embargo among Third World countries. This isolation of South Africa is a key part of African and Asian strategy against South Africa, which has become a source of counterrevolution and the nexus for U.S. and NATO intrusion into the Indian Ocean region.[26] Through persistent opposition to U.S. dominance, the African states, especially the Frontline group, have exposed subimperialism and created a climate of opinion that resists all U.S. attempts to build legitimacy for South African policies in Namibia and other southern African states.

Alternative security systems to protection by the superpowers have been organized with limited success. The idea of the people's militia has been implemented by Tanzania, Mozambique, and Angola. This is predicated on the assumption that the mobilization of people limits the amount of influence external powers can generate and is therefore a deterrent to any prospective aggressor, whether a neighbor state or a superpower. Angola's difficulties with South African aggression demonstrate the importance of determined popular resistance to sophisticated weaponry.[27] Following the initial attack by Iraq, Iran successfully resisted a better-equipped force with a people's militia. Obviously, even popular resistance cannot prevent superpower occupation, as Afghanistan has demonstrated; but it has served as a deterrent to the employment of armed might. U.S. hesitancy to use force against Iran after the fall of the Shah demonstrated that the superpowers take this into account.[28]

An insecure government, however, cannot arm its own people for fear of civil war. Thus this defensive technique is limited to popular regimes, and when employed, forces governments to initiate other forms of redistribution of power.

### Collective Self-reliant Security

Collective self-reliance has been initiated most successfully by one of the smallest of the Indian Ocean states, the Seychelles, against the hegemonic pressures on it by South Africa. After its withdrawal from the security system of Great Britain and the United States, President René's new government created a self-reliance system and people's militia, and turned to other regional states for protection, particularly Mauritius and Tanzania.

Mauritius was also a former British territory with substantial French interests. These two islands are the center of a major superpower rivalry because they have excellent harbor and communications facilities that the military of both sides have been able to only partially exploit. In addition, they straddle the oil trade route and offer great potential for the exploration and development of seabed minerals. Their politics are volatile and nonaligned, with militant antagonists on the left and right. Therefore, the zone of peace approach of their governments is a projection of their internal balance as well as of their delicate and dangerous international vulnerability.

Although the United States had a communication base on Mahé (established with the British in 1966), the port of Victoria was frequently visited by naval ships from all the major powers. President René called for the initiation of the zone of peace principles to reduce the presence of the superpowers.[29] He did not give in to Soviet pressures to grant them base facilities on another island.[30] Though the president did threaten to cancel the U.S. base if the United States expanded into the Indian Ocean, this was not carried out as he renewed the agreement in 1981.

The major threat to small states like the Seychelles and Mauritius is not superpower attack (Grenada was an exception), but an indirect superpower-sponsored, third-party intervention. Private interests, such as the deposed ruling class—the "grand blancs"—have been used for such purposes, as well as mercenary units from abroad. In 1978 a successful invasion by mercenaries from a neighboring island in the Comoro chain was led by the French soldier of fortune, Robert Denard. In November 1981 the attempt at an invasion of the Seychelles led by Michael Hoare from South Africa was defeated by the alert Seychellois militia themselves.[31] Tanzanian forces were also called in, and the invaders were quickly surrounded. Defeated, they seized an Air India plane and fled to South Africa. The incident revealed first, the importance of a local, alert militia, backed by allies, and second, the network of international intrigue. Over half the invading force were members of the South African armed forces reserves. Originally charged only with kidnapping, the group was later charged with hijacking under the Civil Aviation Offenses Act (for "terrorist act"), a much more serious offense, and finally convicted in South African courts.[32]

Several possible interests contributed to the abortive attack. Wealthy individuals interested in the tourist trade, such as the son of the former Shah of Iran, Prince Pahlevi, and the Saudi arms merchant, Adnan Khashoggi, have a keen desire to replace the socialist "pro-Soviet" government of René. Former president James Mancham was based in Kenya at the time and in touch with Kenyan government supporters. The South African government, although denying its implication, was engaged in an early stage of *swaardmag*. At his trial, Michael Hoare admitted that the South African cabinet and security forces supported the coup and that the CIA had some knowledge of the scheme.[33] Several later coup attempts have been reported, the most recent of which took place in September 1986. René has survived them all with his alert Seychellois and collective security arrangement, which included the presence of Tanzanian troops on nearby islands. A new issue—the use of the Seychelles in the communications system for Star Wars (SDI)—was reported by *Africa Confidential* to be a motive for the 1986 coup attempt in the Seychelles.[34] Involved were some of the right-wing groups in Washington, D.C., such as the Heritage Foundation, together with South African mercenaries.

The search for island bases by the United States and the Soviet Union has affected the politics of self-reliance in the zone of peace. Establishment of the Diego Garcia base by the United States and Great Britain in 1966 brought superpower rivalry into the center of concern for rival political factions in the island states. The dispersion of the inhabitants of Diego Garcia to other islands, especially Mauritius where three to four thousand were resettled, became a major issue. Opposition to this base has been a key issue for the Mauritian Militant Movement (MMM) which became the largest party in 1976 and later formed the government in 1982. Both the MMM and the Seychelles People's United Party have protested this dispossession of the simple fishing and farming people of the islands who have remained largely unemployed and impoverished.[35] Although in 1980 Great Britain offered compensation, no compensation was initially given. The former prime minister of Mauritius, Sir Seewoosagur Ramgoolam claimed the 1966 agreement between the United States and Great Britain was a violation of understandings regarding self-determination for the islands, and filed a case with the World Court.[36] Great Britain had created the British Indian Ocean Territory in 1965 out of islands from the Seychelles and Chagos Archipelago without warning representatives of the inhabitants that it intended to build a base, and before independence was granted to the Seychelles and Mauritius. Strategic considerations clearly prevailed, as shortly thereafter the agreement with the United States was made, although the terms were not made public for several years.[37]

In the 1970s, Diego Garcia became a major point of criticism of U.S. expansionism among a wide crosssection of Indian Ocean states led by India.

## THE INDIAN OCEAN ZONE OF PEACE

The idea for a zone of peace in the Indian Ocean grew out of the attempts by Third World nations to restrict the impact of superpower rivalry and to create alternative collective self-reliance systems. The proposals for nuclear-free zones and blocs of nonaligned nations, such as the OAU, had their origins in the same basic survival urge in the face of the extension of the cold war into their midst.

However, for many Third World tributary states associated with these proposals, there has always been the problem of "running with the hares while hunting with the hounds." They want to be seen as supporting the objectives of nonalignment while receiving the benefits of tribute. This contradiction is not always apparent in the speeches of Third World statesmen.

The 1971 U.N. General Assembly resolution served as the charter for the Indian Ocean Zone of Peace (IOZP).[38] The creation of an Ad Hoc Committee on the Indian Ocean by the General Assembly in 1972 provided the basis for a continuing discussion of the objectives of these nations.[39] Despite the charter's generalities, the objectives are clear: to end superpower intervention; to create a basis for the peaceful use of the zone for the development of *littoral* (maritime) and *hinterland* peoples and states; and to open the seas to peaceful maritime commerce. The achievement of an agreement on how to do this is another matter. Yet, from the beginning, the creation of arms control and limitation agreements in a zone of peace was a major goal.[40]

In July 1979, a conference was held of the littoral and hinterland nations to further define these goals, particularly with regard to the superpower arms race, permanent naval presence, and the growing threat of nuclear weapons. This New York conference reiterated the goals of the Declaration of the Indian Ocean Zone of Peace with only Australia dissenting.[41] It was a way of trying to bypass the Cold War II impasse between the superpowers. But the objective of translating this aspiration for the military withdrawal of the superpowers into reality remained very distant.

The membership of the IOZP had originally been open to those states that border on the Indian Ocean and its natural extensions, plus the permanent members of the Security Council, who did not join. It was obvious that the committee would not achieve much unless the superpowers as well as other major maritime powers accepted its resolutions. Countries such as Australia had been members from the start, and the Soviet Union joined in the first session of 1980. The United States finally decided to accept membership in the second session of 1980. But this was a mixed blessing, since it brought the central issues of the cold war directly into the debates. The atmosphere in the post-Afghanistan period was very acrimonious, and the basic position of the United States was that little could be done until the Soviets withdrew from Afghanistan. The Soviet response was to try to restrict the hinterland states from consideration and to focus on the American bases in the Indian Ocean, especially Diego Garcia.

Since 1979, the Ad Hoc Committee has spent most of its time debating the agenda and the terms for convening a conference on the Indian Ocean to be held in Sri Lanka. Originally the date was 1981, but the committee has been unable to agree on an agenda and the conference has therefore been repeatedly postponed. The U.S. position is that no conference can be useful unless some prior understanding is achieved on the substance of the agreements, especially concerning Afghanistan.

Since 1981 the United States, with the help of its supporters, which include Great Britain, West Germany, and, to a lesser extent, Australia and Canada, has used the Afghanistan issue to effectively block the conference, but it is doubtful that the Reagan administration was ever really interested in any of the possible outcomes of such a conference. The United States preferred to move ahead with the strengthening of such regional arrangements as ANZUS (now defunct), which was primarily concerned with the Pacific.[42] It also wanted to establish Diego Garcia and the CENTCOM in the zone before agreeing to a conference that might undermine U.S. negotiations for this dominance policy.

There is wide agreement (with the exception of India) that the hinterland states should be included in the discussions and that issues that effect them, such as Afghanistan, should not be excluded.[43] Most do not agree with the Soviet view that only "coastal" topics can be discussed and propose to take up all security issues at the conference. Resolutions and treaties are to be the methods of implementation for the zone of peace.

There has been considerable concern expressed by the maritime powers that an Indian Ocean zone of peace agreement might undermine the principle of freedom of the seas. They object particularly to being described as external powers, and claim rights of innocent passage through the Gulf of Aden and the Straits of Hormuz and Malacca, as well as freedom of the seas for their warships.[44] The general view of the littoral and hinterland states is that the maritime powers are indeed full members, and all shipping has rights of passage and trade, but that they cannot use the freedom of the seas to threaten the states of the IOZP.[45]

In general, the Indian Ocean states are opposed to the permanent deployment of major naval battle groups, and particularly nuclear weapons, by what they consider to be "extraregional states," which is the term used by Sri Lanka. "Sri Lanka believes the reduction and eventual elimination of extraregional military presence in the Indian Ocean arc will help create a climate conducive to resolving political, economic and social problems."[46]

The question of bases and facilities on the territory of littoral and hinterland nations is obviously the most difficult. Any agreement among the IOZP states on this matter is not apt to be specific in regard to particular bases, but would be couched in terms that would urge member nations to reduce and eliminate the bases and facilities that have been provided extraregional states and not to compromise their own sovereignty and the peace of the region by providing new facilities. The U.S.S.R. seems far more amenable to this kind of agreement than the United States because the Americans have been trying to find states willing to base their rapid deployment force. The Russians, however, would be reluctant to concede that they have any permanent bases, even in Afghanistan. Countries such as India and Tanzania have been the most outspoken against all foreign power bases. However, all might agree to reduce rather than expand these facilities within the framework of a superpower general arms reduction agreement.

A nuclear-weapon-free zone (NWFZ) and the adoption of the Nonproliferation Treaty (NPT) by all is another objective that has general agreement, with some opposition from the superpowers, depending on its definition. A few of the IOZP nations also oppose it. The idea of a NWFZ is generally accepted by most states as it is aimed at extraregional states. The U.S.S.R. favors such a zone for naval forces, but the United States does not accept a total exclusion of all nuclear weapons. In May 1983, the U.S. delegate to the Ad hoc Committee pointed out that the principle of opposition to the spread of nuclear weapons was covered in the NPT, as well as in the Geneva strategic arms reduction talks (START) and negotiations on intermediate nuclear forces (INF). "We believe such real nuclear arms reduction can lead to an atmosphere that will enhance the political and security climate of all areas in the world including the Indian Ocean region." It was felt that the principles of U.N. Document A/AC 159/L.44 were the bases for discussion and that these included "appropriately formulated nuclear weapon free zones in the region." This appeared to leave the door open for consideration of some form of nuclear weapons exclusion in addition to ratification of the NPT.[47]

On the question of nuclear weapons in the IOZP, India has a position which is complicated and, in general, not shared by the majority. As a nuclear power, India has long urged a global nuclear-weapon-free zone, in which all nuclear weapons in the world should be banned. The Indians say the superpowers cannot be left free to enter nuclear-free zones and threaten regional nations who have voluntarily disarmed. K. Subrahmanyam has argued that regional NWFZs are dated because of the covert development of nuclear capability by countries such as Israel, South Africa, and Pakistan. Verification has become impossible. Therefore, he is skeptical that proposals for an Indian Ocean NWFZ are part of a scheme by the dominant nuclear powers to keep their monopoly. The Latin American case of a NWFZ is not comparable in his view because they "have a shared perception of the security threat."[48] India has made similar arguments against ratification of the NPT.

Most Indian Ocean states disagree and have urged a NWFZ for the Indian Ocean because the major powers are escalating their nuclear deployment there. If it could be cut back or eliminated entirely, the nuclear threshold would be lowered. They also want to prevent the proliferation of nuclear weapons among the littoral and hinterland nations. A number have therefore signed the NPT. The Bangladesh statement is typical: "The nuclear weapons states should not establish nuclear bases in the Indian Ocean and should also refrain from conducting nuclear test activities in the Indian Ocean."[49]

India dissents because of the unequal treatment the superpowers give to Third World countries and her fear that China could use nuclear weapons. Such regional hostilities they believe are a major hindrance to the acceptance of any significant nuclear arms control treaty.

South Africa is not a member of the U.N. Committee on the Indian Ocean or the zone of peace, and its development of nuclear weapons is one of the most dangerous threats to peace. In the view of many specialists, there is no question they have "the bomb."[50] Once an accord is reached on a NWFZ, it will be easier to bring pressure on South Africa and other noncomplying states not to deploy these weapons.

While many of the differences among the littoral and hinterland states are the result of traditional rivalries, as in the case of Somalia and Ethiopia, the failure of the U.N. Committee on the Indian Ocean Zone of Peace is directly attributable to the interventionary activities of the superpowers. They do not tell their tributaries how to vote. These Indian Ocean states simply reflect the obvious implication of policies, and covertly support the increased presence of one superpower to offset what they fear from the other. As long as this is the case, they will be unable to establish an Indian Ocean collective system of self-reliance of their own.

## SOUTH-SOUTH REGIONAL COOPERATION

Samir Amin was one of the first theoreticians to call for North-South delinkage in order to free the southern states for development.[51] These ideas have aroused increased interest among Third World leaders but with limited results. Third World conditions deteriorated during the world recession of the 1970s, and have continued to do so into the 1980s due to falling commodity prices, the high cost of finance, and the loss of trade from spreading northern protectionism. Pleas for the acceptance of some of the demands of the developing countries, such as those made by the Group of 77, have been disregarded by the United States and other core powers at conferences (notably Cancun in 1982 and Williamsburg in 1983) as "global welfarism," and President Reagan has defended the old system of increasing debt dependence and expanding northern exports.

Prime Minister Zhao Ziyang, at the opening of the first of the triannual South-South conferences of Third World nations in Beijing in April 1983, stated that "strengthened South-South cooperation will help the Third World countries enhance their economic capability, strengthen their position in North-South negotiations, and play a great strategic role in breaking up the old international economic order and establish a new one."[52]

There has been a great deal of talk about the advantages of South self-reliance through increased trade among themselves. This is not easy to accomplish, not only because of the enormous and growing financial dependence of many leading tributaries on the industrial investment and technology of the North, but also because their own tributary class has a heavy investment in the existing system. Therefore, it is very difficult in large conferences of one hundred or more to agree upon anything but generalities of condemnation of the North and broad programs which never become implemented. Proposals for reform of the international lending agencies, as much as they are merited, may not be implemented by the dominant core powers for many years.

The Indian Ocean states have therefore turned increasingly to the implementation of South-South measures among themselves and regional agreements that may give concrete reality to their aspirations. There are certain trends that benefit them, despite the overall relative declining position of Third World countries. An increased proportion of world trade is taking place between the southern states and a new set of semiindustrialized nations, known as newly industrialized countries (NICs), who are in a position to provide manufacturing components in return for raw materials. If the NICs can provide the finance and banking for such trade, some economists see much to be gained in terms of economies of scale and Third World technology.[53]

In several regions of the Indian Ocean, NICs have begun to provide leadership within groups of nations that shows promise for a new regionalism that breaks out of the old subimperialism controlled by the hegemonic powers. This is the economic base for collective self-reliance that is becoming a counterforce to the old dominance reflected in the preferential trading zones of Africa, the Caribbean, and Pacific (ACP) and the Economic Organization of West African States (ECOWAS) which have been tied to the Western core. The subimperial states have dominated regionalism, New International Economic Order (NIEO) has been little more than a slogan. Now the NIEO has begun to be replaced by the serious gradual implementation of ideas of delinkage and South-South trade. Such programs are regarded with skepticism by the leaders of the OECD as "the pooling of poverty" and even written off by COMECON as "reformist capitalism"; but South-South cooperation is growing, despite the skeptics.

## Regional Agreements and South-South Cooperation

In southern Africa, the SADCC has undertaken joint planning to break linkages with South Africa, despite increased South African subimperial pressure. And in the Gulf, Arab and Islamic states have begun to find increased agreement in the Gulf Council of Cooperation (GCC) which has become an instrument for deflecting superpower intrusions. Also, a South Asian regional agreement between India and other South Asian countries has been established on the subcontinent.

Collective self-reliance within a regional context cannot be based simply on economic agreements—but political and economic policies are two sides of the same coin.

## India and South Asia

India's industrial leaders, who are a progressive comprador class, are eager to undertake the leadership of South Asian regional trade as indicated by the six-nation Federation of Indian Export Organizations. Heavy debt to the north and protectionist policies have made the South Asian countries open to regional trade. India's economy has industrialized in the past two decades and moved away from import substitution, so that its industrial capacities and technologies can be exported. While Pakistan's industry is more competitive, it is estimated that Indo-Pakistan trade alone could reach 5 billion rupees.[54] There are problems in the finance and trade policies of Nepal and Sri Lanka. As with Pakistan, these can only be met in the political realm as the demand for collective self-reliance grows.

Political interest has grown in India in creating a South Asian regional group that would include Pakistan.[55] This possibility was described by members of the Institute for Defense Studies and Analysis in New Delhi.[56] While it was clear that Indira Gandhi's government was regarded with deep suspicion in Bangladesh and Bhutan, as well as in Pakistan, the Rajiv government, formed in 1984, has overcome many of the past hostilities.

A major obstacle to India's role of regional leadership has been New Delhi's equivocation over the Soviet occupation of Afghanistan. Since 1984 it has backed a UN-sponsored Soviet withdrawal of troops and offered assistance for the huge refugee burden Pakistan has carried almost alone. Since the Soviets want a face-saving way out, the Indian leaders have put themselves in the position of providing good offices, thereby gaining leverage against either the dismembering or the rearming of Pakistan and the possibility of a regional association from

Bhutan to Iran, based upon self-reliance through the removal of superpower intervention.

A break with the Soviet alignment is seen by Bharat Waviarwala, associate director of the Institute of Defense Studies and Analysis (IDSA), as justified in the interests of regionalism. "The Soviet armed takeover of Afghanistan calls for serious reappraisal of our Soviet connection. If our goal is a cooperative subcontinent, free of excessive influence of external powers, then we must ask whether our security links with an extraregional power, the Soviet Union, serves our regional goal."[57]

Proposals for defusing the India-Pakistan conflict might become a reality, provided not only a break with the U.S.S.R. alignment is made but also a detente between China and India is found. There is good reason for India and China to seek this. China wants to isolate the U.S.S.R., and India is anxious to end the impact of the U.S.-China rearmament of Pakistan.[58] While the pro-Moscow lobby in New Delhi opposes this move, it is definitely in India's interest to seek it, in a way that does not arouse the encirclement fears of the U.S.S.R. There are also groups in Pakistan not anxious to be the sacrificial lambs to U.S.-China anti-Soviet activity. African leaders like Nyerere and Chissano, with excellent connections to the People's Republic of China, have urged India to find a new basis for working with the Asian giant that, by the end of the century, could be a superpower with rival interests in the Indian Ocean to both the United States and the Soviet Union.

## SADCC

Another important association for South-South cooperation among the Indian Ocean states is the Southern African Development Coordination Conference (SADCC), formed in Lusaka in 1980, shortly after the independence of Zimbabwe, by nine African states. The conference is the first major organization aimed at the long-held goal of creating an alternative to South African subimperial dominance of the region. This self-reliance objective was veiled in functional language about communications and trade development, yet the Frontline States knew they must build an alternative to economic dependence and military vulnerability to South Africa.[59] This is very difficult to do because South Africa is the economic hub of the region, supported by U.S. dominance. Their transportation, trade, and finance, as well as corporate structures, are all controlled by South Africa, either directly or indirectly. South Africa's campaign of economic manipulation and military-political expansionism has been very effective.[60] Zimbabwe and Zambia might become the semiindustrial leaders a self-reliant region needs, but their economies are in turn subordinated to South African and Western core manipulation. Eventually, it is likely that the U.S. core power penetration of southern Africa will support the SADCC's break with South Africa through sanctions to force a regime change in South Africa.

All nine southern African economies are closely tied to South African trade.

Lesotho, Botswana, and Swaziland are highly dependent on South Africa for trade and labor markets. Half the work force of Lesotho resides in South Africa, and their trade is completely controlled by joint customs arrangements. South Africa has become the transportation hub of the mining and manufacturing industries of the Frontline States. With the breakdown of alternative routes of export through Luanda and Maputo for Zimbabwe and Zambia, they have become 90 percent dependent upon trade routes through South Africa. South African corporations such as DeBeers and Rio Tinto Zinc own and control the private sectors of the economies of these two major opponents of apartheid. Botswana and Malawi have provided alternative routes for South African Airways in the expansion of air communication, even after Commonwealth sanctions were declared.

The South African campaign to gain hegemonic domination through its controlling position in transportation is closely linked to its military expansionist policy of *swaardmag*. By the support of insurgencies in Angola and Mozambique (i.e., UNITA and MNR), Botha has cut off the use of rail lines from Zambia through Angola and from Zimbabwe to Maputo. They have virtually strangled the economy of Mozambique and have seriously challenged the rule of FRELIMO. Greatly weakened, Zambia, Angola, and Zimbabwe have fought back. Tanzania is less affected, but the TAZARA railway from Lusaka to Dar es Salaam has been sabotaged and has badly deteriorated since 1982.

As the conflict over sanctions against South Africa has escalated since early 1986, the South African economic and military *swaardmag* program has had a devastating impact. Mozambique has suffered the most. Its revenues from ports and rails are down to 16.1 percent of 1973 levels. Its labor force inside South Africa was cut by 60,000. Zimbabwe has been forced to keep an army of between 10,000–14,000 in the Beira Corridor to keep open the rail line, and Zambia has been cut off from vital oil supplies, causing high inflation.[61]

In this struggle, the Frontline States have had to establish unified countermeasures of collective self-reliance. The external core power has slowly and painfully begun to support the African alternative to South African hegemony. Great Britain has been ahead of the United States in its supply of military training and assistance against the South African-backed MNR.[62] The United States has continued to back the nonindigenous insurgencies, especially UNITA. However, by the end of 1986, congressional pressures had forced a review of this policy. A policy of sanctions against South Africa without backing SADCC and the Frontline States clearly made no sense.

SADCC at first appeared headed for the same fate as other African regional integration attempts. But the trial by fire in the struggle with South Africa was forcing the desperate measures of economic cooperation, joint defense, and external core power assistance which initially had failed to emerge.[63] SADCC had a long way to go in a bitter struggle, but the elements of a successful collective self-reliance system had emerged.

The difference between these new South-South associations of the 1980s and their numerous predecessors is the difference between dominance and independence. In the opinion of an increasing number of critics, the former associations, especially the Lomé Convention, were essentially neocolonialist and perpetuated the exploitation of raw materials producers.[64] The building of alternative South-South trade, aid, and development links that will enable these regions to participate on the basis of greater equality in the world economy is underway. It will take decades of determined change to produce significant results, but the tributary system is breaking down and a new leadership determined to achieve greater independence has emerged in many countries of the Indian Ocean Zone of Peace.

## NOTES

1. Samir Amin, "The Class Structure of the Contemporary Imperialist System," *Monthly Review*, 31, no. 8 (1980).

2. Julius Nyerere was one of the early formulators. See Julius K. Nyerere, *Freedom and Unity* (New York: Oxford University Press, 1967).

3. Stephen Kinzer, "Nicaragua: The Beleaguered Revolution," *New York Times Magazine*, August 28, 1983.

4. Samir Amin, "Self-Reliance and the New International Economic Order," *Monthly Review*, 29, no. 3 (July/August 1977).

5. Okwudiba Nnoli, *Self-Reliance and Foreign Policy in Tanzania* (New York: NOK Publishers, 1978); Johan Galtung, *The True Worlds: A Transnational Perspective* (New York: Free Press, 1980); Thomas Biersteker, "Self-Reliance in Theory and Practice in Tanzanian Trade Relations," *International Organization*, 34, no. 2 (1980). Ashok Partjasratji, "Self-Reliance as Alternative Strategy for Development," *Alternatives* 2, no. 3 (September 1976).

6. Andre Gunder Frank, *Crisis in the Third World* (New York: Holmes and Mier, 1981), pp. 60–61.

7. Johan Galtung, "The Politics of Self-Reliance," in *From Dependency to Development*, ed. Heraldo Munoz (Boulder, Colo.: Westview, 1981), p. 173.

8. Julius K. Nyerere, "South-South Options," *Third World Quarterly* 4, no 5 (July 1982).

9. This view of a step-by-step transition to self-reliance is applied to the Southern African Development Coordination Conference (SADCC). See Carol B. Thompson, "SADCC: Toward the Liberation of Southern Africa," (paper presented at African Studies Association Annual Meeting, Los Angeles, October 1981).

10. Biersteker, "Self-Reliance in Theory and Practice."

11. Amilcar Cabral, *Return to the Source: Selected Speeches of Amilcar Cabral*, ed. Africa Information Service (New York: Monthly Review Press, 1973), pp. 42–43.

12. Ibid.

13. Iquacy Sachs, "Gandhi and Development: A European View," in *Self-Reliance: A Strategy for Development*, ed. Johan Galtung, Peter O'Brien, and Roy Preiswerk (Geneva: Institute for Development Studies, 1980), p. 47.

14. Colin Kirkpatrick and Frederick Nixson, "Transnational Corporations and Economic Development," *Journal of Modern African Studies* 19, no. 3 (1981), p. 368.

15. International Labor Organization, *Employment, Growth, and Basic Needs: A One-World Problem* (New York: Praeger, 1977).

16. Robert Browne and Robert Cummings, eds., *The Lagos Plan of Action vs. The Berg Report* (Lawrenceville, Va: Brunswick Pub. Co., 1985), pp. 29–32.

17. Ibid., pp. 52–54.

18. See George W. Shepherd, Jr., "The Power System and Basic Human Rights: From Tribute to Self-Reliance," in *Human Rights and Third World Development*, ed. George W. Shepherd, Jr. and Ved P. Nanda (Westport, Conn.: Greenwood Press, 1985), pp. 13–17.

19. Works that do consider the economy of self-reliance are: Paulo Freire, *Pedagogy of the Oppressed* (New York: The Seabury Press, 1970); J. F. Rweyemau, *Underdevelopment and Industrialization in Tanzania* (New York: Oxford University Press, 1973); Morris D. Morris, *Measuring the Condition of the World's Poor: The Physical Quality of Life Index*, Pergamon Studies, no. 42 (New York: Pergamon Press, 1979); A. K. Sen, *Choice, Welfare, and Measurement* (Cambridge: MIT Press, 1983); Francis Stewart and Paul Streeten, "New Strategies for Development: Poverty, Income Distribution and Growth," *Oxford Economic Papers* 28 (1978); Margaret E. Graham, ed., *Human Rights and Basic Needs in the Americas* (Washington, D.C.: Georgetown University Press, 1982).

20. Fouad Ajami, "Human Rights and World Order," in *Toward a Just World Order*, ed. Richard Falk, Samuel Kim, and Saul Mendlovitz, vol. 1 (Boulder, Colo.: Westview, 1982), p. 393.

21. *World Military Expenditures and Arms Transfers*, (Washington, D.C.: U.S. Arms Control and Disarmament Agency, 1985), table A, p. 42.

22. Ibid., table iii, pp. 133–134.

23. Robert S. Jaster discusses this in *A Regional Security Role for Africa's Front Line States*, Alelphi Papers, no. 180 (London: IISS, 1983).

24. Ibid.

25. The role of African states in the arms ban against South Africa is discussed in George W. Shepherd, Jr., *Anti-Apartheid*, (Westport, Conn.: Greenwood Press, 1977), pp. 105–108.

26. "Destabilization in Southern Africa," *The Economist*, July 16, 1983.

27. Southern Angola has been under virtual occupation by South African forces, who have assisted UNITA to form a rival government. However, popular support, plus the Cuban presence, has frustrated South African objectives. For an excellent discussion of these issues, see "Destructive Engagement," *Washington Notes on Africa*, Winter 1982.

28. Jack Anderson reported that President Carter rejected the National Security Council proposal to invade Iran in October 1980 partly because it would cause an enormous loss of life. "Crisis in Iran Almost Ignited Armegeddon," *Rocky Mountain News*, June 30, 1983.

29. *Africa News*, May 14, 1981.

30. René had stated in Paris in 1978 that he would not consider bases for either superpower. See J. P. Anand, "The Seychelles Group: A Profile," *IDSA Journal* (New Delhi) 11, no. 3 (January-March 1979), p. 299.

31. Alan Cowell, *New York Times*, December 3, 1981.

32. *New York Times*, December 3, 1981.

33. Richard Leonard, *South Africa at War* (Westport, Conn: Lawrence Hill & Co., 1983), p. 92.

34. *Africa Confidential* 27, no. 20 (October 1, 1986).
35. J. P. Anand, "Mauritius," *IDSA Journal* (New Delhi) 10, no. 2 (1978), p. 169.
36. The Court has not, as yet, heard the case.
37. U.S. Congress, House Subcommittee on the Near East and South Asia, *Hearings on the Proposed Expansion of U.S. Military Facilities in the Indian Ocean*, 93rd Cong., 1st sess., February 21, March 6, 13, 14, and 20, 1974.
38. United Nations, General Assembly Resolution No. 2832 (XXVI).
39. Ibid. Also, United Nations, General Assembly Resolution No. 2992 (XXVII) December 15, 1972, consisting of fifteen members originally: Australia, China, India, Indonesia, Iran, Iraq, Japan, Madagascar, Malaysia, Mauritius, Pakistan, Sri Lanka, United Republic of Tanzania, Yemen, and Zambia.
40. Later, on May 3, 1974, the Declaration of the Indian Ocean as a Zone of Peace was adopted by the General Assembly (A/AC/159/1).
41. United Nations, General Assembly, *Report of the Ad Hoc Committee on the Indian Ocean*, 35th sess., Suppl. 29 (A/35/29), 1979, p. 5.
42. In a letter dated July 22, 1978 the United States and Australia submitted the text of a communique on the ANZUS Council meeting of July 1978, which had been the first held since 1951. United Nations, General Assembly, *Report of the Ad Hoc Committee on the Indian Ocean* (A/AC 159/L58).
43. Ethiopia included the hinterland states in its definition of geographic limits. United Nations, General Assembly, Ad Hoc Committee on the Indian Ocean, A/AC 159/L55 May 23, 1983, p. 8.
44. The United States insists on "the right to peaceful use, transit and overflight of the world's oceans and seas by all nations as fundamental." Ibid., p. 29.
45. Ibid., p. 31.
46. Ibid., p. 40.
47. United Nations, General Assembly, Ad Hoc Committee on the Indian Ocean, A/AC 159/L55, Addendum 5.
48. K. Subrahamanyam, *Indian Security in Perspective* (New Delhi: ABC Publishing House, 1979), pp. 43–44.
49. United Nations, General Assembly, Ad Hoc Committee on the Indian Ocean, A/AC 159/L55, Addendum 1, India 6, July 1983.
50. United Nations Special Committee Against Apartheid, "The Development of South Africa's Nuclear Capability," (A/AC 115/L) October 25, 1983.
51. Samir Amin outlines conditions for this achievement in "Self-Reliance and the New International Economic Order."
52. "Third World Soul Searching," *South*, June 1983, p. 40.
53. Francis Stewart, "Paying Our Own Way," *South*, August 1983, p. 37.
54. Givigesh Pant, "A Regional Role for India's Growing Economy," *South*, August 1983.
55. Bharat Warianwalla, "Timid Search for Status," *Seminar* (New Delhi), December 1980.
56. Interviews with the staff of the Institute of Defense Studies and Analysis (IDSA) and others, New Delhi, February–March 1981.
57. Warianwalla, "Timid Search."
58. Note also that negotiations took place in 1982 between India and Pakistan for a "nonaggression pact," though differences prevented its conclusion. *New York Times*, February 2, 1982.

59. Carol Thompson, *Challenge to Imperialism: The Frontline States in the Liberation of Zimbabwe* (Harare: Zimbabwe Publishing House, 1985), pp. 258–94.

60. "Destabilization," *Economist*.

61. South African Research and Documentation Centre, *South Africa Imposes Sanctions Against Neighbours* (Harare: Zimbabwe Publishing House, 1986).

62. Michael Evans, "The Front-Line States, South Africa, and Southern African Security," *Zambezia* (University of Zimbabwe) 12 (1984–1985).

63. "Zimbabwe Sanctions Complicate Relations," *Africa News*, July 21, 1986.

64. Lynn Mytelka, "The Lomé Convention and a New International Division of Labour," *Journal of European Integration*, September 1977.

# 6

# Liberation from Dominance

> And finally, the god that the state preaches to us is not the God of the Bible. It is an idol. It is the god of the gun, the god of oppression.
>
> —Kairos Theologians, 1985

Dominance in the Third World, which has claimed so many lives, destroyed the independence hopes of new states, protected apartheid, and wrecked economies, throwing millions of refugees on the mercy of the humanitarian system, has paradoxically led to a growing liberation consciousness determined to build an alternative system capable of providing security and peace. In the new states, this has produced a class and cultural struggle for self-reliance, and in the dominant powers a supportive grass-roots movement has emerged to challenge in different ways the self-destructive policies of the superpowers.

In the Third World, these movements have struggled to break the dominance of Western intervention, from Nicaragua to South Africa and Afghanistan. As Samir Amin predicted: "The deadlock will continue until new social forces appear, open to the future, rather than dominated by the past, and capable of conceiving a strategy for liberation that goes beyond the narrow horizons of minor ex-colonial civil servants."[1] Some have been crushed; but others have succeeded despite intervention. And the weakening of the central hegemonic powers has given greater impetus to their prospects.

## NONDOMINANCE

Within the dominant centers of power, there has emerged in the Cold War II era a human rights movement opposed to the costly consequences and dangers of an unending arms race that militarizes society and threatens world atomic destruction. Michael Schultheis has correctly termed this turning point "a crisis of the human spirit, a crisis which has cultural and religious roots."[2]

There are significant differences in the two centers of dominance in the world system; but in both the United States and Soviet Union a right to peace exists and has begun to assert its challenge to the dangerous and deteriorating leadership of the state capitalist and state socialist ruling classes.[3] This movement has begun to make major inroads in both powers, especially in developing divisions within their alliances. The growing cost of the arms race, disagreement over new weapons systems such as the MX missile and "Star Wars" (SDI), and the expense of supporting new security zones have introduced serious political tensions. The guns or butter issue underlies much of the political unrest in Poland and the two Germanys. And in the United States, the tide began to turn against the increases in the military budget in 1985, because of the staggering deficit that the financial world fears will crush the economy, spread unemployment, stimulate inflation, and intensify the unrest of minorities and the poor. These new conditions have created the basis for a renewed challenge by the human spirit to "the national security state."

As superpower dominance has waned, the strength of self-reliant social forces has grown. Enormous difficulties and upheaval remain, and no easy transition lies ahead in any part of the globe. But despite the failure of earlier expectations, there are clear signs of cracks in the system of superpower dominance. As the Africans say, "The leopard does not change his spots," but he does grow old. Contradictions have set in and have begun to create the conditions for revolt and change toward a more just world. Not only the Marxists, like Samir Amin, have seen this shift in world history; but also liberation theologians, like Allan Boesak in South Africa, have predicted it as well: "The God of the Bible is the God of liberation, rather than oppression, a God of justice rather than injustice."[4] After centuries of suffering for the black man of South Africa, and elsewhere, these petitions appear to have been heard.

The self-reliance struggle in the Third World has found solidarity and support among a new nondominance coalition in the northern centers of power. This coalition represents both moral and materialist interests and is at the center of a historic struggle for the control of production and state redistributive power. In the Soviet Union, this change is led by the new technocrats who propose to improve technology and farm production at the expense of the arms export industry. And in the United States, new directions from the churches, peace movement, community groups, and farm protests have sprung up, both within established groups and in opposition to them. More like a renaissance of the human spirit than a political movement, it may take significant political form as the crisis matures.

In the United States, political adjustment to these new realities has been regressive at times. The managerial class thrives on anticommunist scare tactics, and vested interests in the arms race periodically use patriotism and false hopes to defeat disarmament proposals, adopt the next phase of weapons in the arms race, and reassert outmoded economic doctrines. Spy plane incidents and fears of "imperialist attack" have stoked the flames of fear and the war party in the Soviet Union. The militarization of the system, as Michael Randle has pointed out, has grown. While providing for the basic needs of the people, the Soviet economy has offered few luxuries and has expended an increasingly high percentage of its scarce resources on the arms race.[5]

In the United States a strong counterforce to social justice has strengthened militarization, threatening to plunge the world into new wars for control of the tributary states and embracing nuclear war as "Armaggedon." For a decade, the Moral Majority has incited millions of middle-class Americans to political action—to man the ramparts against "Godless communism" which is said to be undermining the family and the schools as well as threatening the Third World. The capacity of the powerful to manipulate opinion and control decisions cannot be underestimated in either superpower, though the ability of dissenters to directly influence established policy is obviously much weaker in the Soviet Union. The jingoistic impact of a Grenada, Afghanistan, or Falkland Islands war on reinforcing the status quo should not be overlooked.

However, as powerful as the international capitalist and military-industrial complex is, it is not determinative of the world system. It is being undercut by prevailing political economic trends, as Piven and Cloward have pointed out, in terms of the expansion of welfare democracy in America where a minimum floor for the poor, unemployed, and disabled has been established, despite all the Reagan cuts which have been only marginal. The next step, they suggest, is to prevent capital's flight abroad and to rebuild industries at home.[6] This, together with other trends such as the oil glut and the Third World debtors crisis, has split the international capitalist thrust and blunted the power of the military expansionists. And even in the Soviet bureaucracy there are those who have lost faith in nuclear deterrence and who genuinely seek weapons cuts and disarmament because they are more concerned with better corn production than new weapons systems.[7]

It is characteristic of historical change that Western dominance should have created the basis of its own demise. There is a pattern of social justice in the nature of things which some call "divine intent" that awakens new consciousness as a particular power system spreads and results in popular movements of the poor and deprived to demand human rights.[8] This forces sections of the ruling class to recognize the human rights of the weak and a crisis arises. At this time, a new order can be built in the world. Rather than simply compounding threats to annihilate the enemy and expanding violence to dominate, an opportunity for the world to find new policies has emerged. In the centers of power as well in the Third World, liberation has broken out. This is what theologians have called "the kairos," and political movements the "revolutionary moment." As the Kairos Document stated:

The time has come, the moment of truth has arrived. South Africa has been plunged into a crisis that is shaking the foundations and there is every indication that the crisis has only just begun and that it will deepen and become even more threatening in the months to come. It is the KAIROS or moment of truth not only for apartheid but also the Church.[9]

Thus, the world system is in crisis. The centers of power are fracturing within and the subimperial states and tributaries are in increasing revolt. The transformation of dominance into plural power centers and self-reliant development has begun and precipitated vast upheaval.[10] Out of this conflict, it is possible to see a new world order emerging that can begin the shift to a more equitable relationship between the superpowers and the smaller states, as well as a new understanding between the two major powers. Within this emerging new world system, the prospects for implementation of agreements like the Indian Ocean Zone of Peace become more meaningful.

## DEMILITARIZATION AND ARMS CONTROL IN THE INDIAN OCEAN ZONE OF PEACE

One of the first areas of the Third World where the nondominance policy has become applicable is the Indian Ocean Zone of Peace (IOZP). This is because the superpowers have reached a point in the global arms race where they have more to gain by an agreement to stabilize their relationship through arms control, including the reduction of forces and bases in the zone. Such regional agreements would reflect wider global arms control negotiations and agreements that are now mandatory in this crisis. A return to the pre–1980 period of negotiation and agreement between the Soviet Union and the United States and their allies with respect to nuclear weapons is now possible and, many argue, a necessity to preserve existing economic systems and avoid a self-destructive war which could quickly become a global nightmare. Nuclear deterrence through mutual fear is no longer—if it ever was—a reliable restraint. Therefore, global agreements that have a regional application are being imposed upon even the more bellicose leaders in the North and the South. One of the best possibilities for the reduction of nuclear weapons exists in the Indian Ocean zone because of the widespread Third World opposition to their deployment by the superpowers and their development by the littoral and hinterland nations.

In addition to the weapons-reduction incentive, the United States and the Soviet Union both have economic and political interests that are increasingly undercut by the costs and liabilities of the confrontations from the Gulf to the Cape. Today, arms sales to increasingly bankrupt Third World countries are less profitable sources of revenue for either power. Protracted conflicts, such as the Iran-Iraq war, have led to uncertainties and crises. Some leaders in the West have learned that investments and resource supply are not really preserved over the long run by an arms race that provides up- and downstream support for rival liberation and revolutionary movements. The war in the Gulf has demonstrated how such crises threaten oil flows, and the conflict in southern Africa between the Afrikaners and the Frontline States has created great economic uncertainty and moral outrage, as well as a threat to end all Western influence. These changes have initiated powerful popular protests that demand new policies. Of course, the momentum of the existing ideologies and structures of power is not easily changed, and it is within this continuing tension that we have to view the possibilities for new policies.

### Early Naval Arms Limitation Talks

The possibilities for arms limitations in the IOZP were given serious consideration in U.S. and Soviet policy in the 1977–1978 talks which followed President Carter's initiative in his 1977 U.N. speech. There had been repeated requests by the U.S.S.R. for agreements that would limit the escalation. Leonid Brezhnev had stated in 1971:

We have never thought and do not think now that it is an ideal situation when the navies of great powers are sailing for a long time at the other end of the world (the Indian Ocean) away from their native coasts. We are ready to solve this problem but to make an equal bargain.[11]

In the mid–1970s, both superpowers were prepared for such steps since this seemed to be a natural outgrowth of the SALT II negotiations that were underway and in the new spirit of demilitarization of conflict areas that the Carter administration had proposed. Among the littoral and hinterland nations of the Indian Ocean, the demand for an Indian Ocean Zone of Peace became well established with the formation of the U.N. Ad Hoc Committee on the Indian Ocean in 1972. The superpowers were not members of the Ad Hoc Committee then, and both had reservations about the objectives of this IOZP, but they were under some pressure to consider the views of the Indian Ocean states since bases were being built there and arms sold amounting to billions of dollars.

Demilitarization of the Indian Ocean region was interpreted by the Carter administration and the Soviet government as a "stabilization" or an arms-limitation policy. It was not an ill-considered action but reflected changes in circumstances and the attempt to deal with these through a rational agreement to end the competition of the arms race and an attempt to reduce conflict through diplomatic and economic measures rather than through escalation of force.[12] The realpolitik school of thought, reflected most directly in the Committee on the Present Danger, rejected out of hand such an approach. It was also reflected in the vested interests of certain services, especially the U.S. Navy which went all the way to the National Security Council with its objections. It was reported that the Soviet admirals were also unhappy. The American opponents of arms control in the Indian Ocean argued that this would basically be an advantage to the Soviet Union, not the United States, because the United States was a maritime power and the Soviet Union was a land-based power.[13] This view was rejected within the Carter administration because it reflected a geopolitical Mahan view that made little sense in a world of international ballistic missiles and nuclear warheads. Moreover, it did not take into account the strategic implications of Trident submarine development and other technologies that made bases and facilities in the Indian Ocean far less significant in global strategy.[14]

Advocates of arms control in the Carter administration and the Congress had pointed out that gunboat diplomacy and the concentration of new-force capability were not the ways to resolve the problems of the Indian Ocean region or to foster and protect U.S. interests in resources and supply lines there. These views were particularly maintained by Secretary of State Cyrus Vance and Paul Warnke, then head of the Arms Control and Disarmament Agency, and by Leslie H. Gelb, director, Politico-Military Affairs of the State Department. In the early days of the Carter administration, the opponents of this view, such as the director of the National Security Council, Zbigniew Brzezinski, either held their peace or bided their time.[15]

The practical approach of the arms control advocates was based on the rising costs and dangers of the increased arms transfers to the Indian Ocean states.[16] They had the support of the president and the secretary of state, as well as major leaders in Congress. There were also advocates of an arms control approach in the security field, such as Adam Yarmolensky.[17]

A group favoring arms control had formed and in the U.S. Senate, a substantial number of senators favored the limitation of U.S. forces in the Indian Ocean. In 1974, two years before the election of President Carter, Senator Kennedy, with Senators Cranston, Chase, Humphrey, Stevenson, and Tunney, introduced a concurrent resolution "expressing the sense of Congress that negotiations be sought with the Union of Soviet Socialist Republics relative to naval and military strength in the Indian Ocean and littoral states."[18] These senators were originally opposed to the acquisition of Diego Garcia but by 1974 were persuaded to accept a limited and periodic presence of the United States in the Indian Ocean. However, they were opposed to any unilateral buildup as an incitement to an arms race with the Soviet Union. The State Department and the CIA also attempted, during the 1970s, to offset the demands for a permanent force and, in particular, a fifth fleet. Joseph Sisco, assistant secretary, Bureau of Near Eastern and South Asian Affairs, stated it cogently in 1972: "The sub-continent is very far away." And Ronald Spiers, former director of the State Department's Bureau of Politico-Military Affairs, could see "no requirement at this time for us to feel impelled to control or even decisively influence, any part of the Indian Ocean or its littoral."[19]

This position stemmed not only from the Vietnam War, in which a policy of force escalation had obviously failed, but also from the increasing opposition in the country to the costs of military deployment. The navy's desire to launch a fifth fleet in the Indian Ocean was repeatedly rejected, and the early stages of negotiation for a new base at Diego Garcia were reviewed with considerable skepticism. Senator Gary Hart (D., Colorado) sought to limit naval costs through the building of smaller aircraft carriers. Later, Hart became a leading opponent of the use of military force in the Gulf "to secure access to needed resources." In a letter to his constituents, he argued in 1984 that "There are inherent logistical limitations on U.S. force projection capabilities in the region... We must all recognize the danger of escalation should U.S. ground forces be overwhelmed."[20]

## Naval Arms Limitation Talks

The details of the 1978 series of meetings with the Russians, in which the American side was chaired by Paul Warnke, have remained classified information, but from public testimony to Congress and statements by members of the Carter administration, it is possible to piece together the main theme of the proposed settlement.[21] The two superpowers were to end their expansion of bases and facilities in the Indian Ocean. While they never did agree on precisely where the Indian Ocean lay, and whether or not the hinterland states were to be included, the general agreement was to cover the area from the Straits of Malacca to the Bay of Bengal, the Persian Gulf, the Red Sea and the Mozambique Channel, and the Cape Route. The Soviets, of course, sought the direct exchange of bases and the withdrawal of the United States from all similar facilities from the Northwest Cape of Australia to Bahrain. However, the United States was interested in an agreement that stabilized the status quo. It is apparent that the United States was willing not to expand the Diego Garcia base into a major servicing and repair facility in return for a phase-down of Berbera. But the Soviet "expulsion" from Somalia in 1977 made this a moot point.

The United States was especially eager to limit the Soviet navy's access to the Indian Ocean and sought an agreement, it is thought, which limited the number of ship days there. The response of the Soviet negotiators was to try to limit navies on the basis of tonnage of ships. Since the U.S. Navy is much larger and heavier, this was obviously unacceptable to the U.S. side. Despite technical differences on this point, the two sides appeared to have a viable Naval Arms Limitation Talks (NALT) agreement. As William Stivers summarized it: "Each side would agree not to increase its naval strength in the Indian Ocean nor to alter significantly previous patterns of military deployments in the area."[22]

The draft agreement included limitations on the size and frequency of superpower task forces in the area and on permanent forces and facilities.[23] The Soviets were also eager to exclude nuclear missiles from at least the northern quadrants of the Indian Ocean. The United States, which had never admitted to any consistent deployment in that region, found this a very difficult proposal because at that time it was seen as a part of the global deterrent and even counterforce strategy. However, the United States did agree to limit facilities at Diego Garcia for B-52 aircraft. It is doubtful that the superpowers ever discussed seriously the requests of the Indian Ocean Zone of Peace countries for a complete withdrawal of all nuclear weapons and an end to the deployment of support facilities that both powers had placed on the territory of the littoral and hinterland states.

Several IOZP countries suggested that a cessation of the U.S. Poseidon "periodic deployment" might become part of an extended Strategic Arms Limitation Talks (SALT) II agreement. None of this materialized, though, because of increased U.S.-Soviet tensions.

Considerable opposition to these talks remained, chiefly in the U.S. National Security Council and the Joint Chiefs of Staff, based on a range of conservative views that only greater force and facilities would deter the Soviets. This view especially objected to limitations of U.S. sea power, since such forces provided the primary U.S. interventionary force in regions thousands of miles from home bases. The crises of the Gulf region, the defense of Israel, and the protection of Western interests in Africa could only be managed with a permanent, stronger U.S. force. The opponents to arms control, recovering from their defeat in Vietnam, argued again that force limitation in the Indian Ocean reflected the "central wooly-headed" weakness of liberalism.

Events played into the hands of the proponents of force and expansion.[24] The revolutions in Angola and Ethiopia were backed by Soviet and Cuban force. Expansionists were able to focus public attention on these events rather than on the history of how NATO support for prolonged Portuguese colonialism in Africa led to revolution and how U.S. backing of Haile Selassie sustained feudalism in Ethiopia until it collapsed. A similar revolt led to the overthrow of the U.S.-supported government in Iran in 1979 and the seizure of American hostages. Thus, extreme anti-Americanism gave emotional impetus to those who opposed the agreements.

The talks were suspended in early 1978 by the United States, and the agreement was not accepted by either side. By October 1979, President Carter had ended his commitment to the idea, even prior to the seizure of the hostages in Iran. The U.S.S.R. continued to call for the resumption of these talks, despite the U.S. buildup of facilities at Diego Garcia and the presence of the rapid deployment force. The Reagan administration, elected in 1980, rejected further talks, obviously determined to increase U.S. force in the Indian Ocean region. In the U.N. Ad Hoc Committee on the Indian Ocean, the United States had made it clear that it believed any discussion of arms limitation was dependent on a Soviet withdrawal from Afghanistan and commitment not to resort to the expansion of its forces in the Indian Ocean. There is little evidence that the Reagan administration has had any interest in bilateral talks with the Soviets on issues of arms limitation covering points of conflict in the Indian Ocean. Outside the Administration, support for the revival of these arms-limitation talks with the U.S.S.R., and within the U.N., has begun to generate political interest again in the United States because of the failures of the expanded-force policy and the increased cost of the Indian Ocean arms race. These concerns, as found in the Washington-based Center for Defense Information, are related to the basic issue of global arms control between the superpowers, for which there is increased urgency. As stated by Senator Hart, the inability of a force-based strategy to assure U.S. access to the resources of the region, or to influence the sound development of the economies of these new states, added to the danger of nuclear escalation and required a new policy.

**Deficit and Disengagement**

The widespread Western-based demand for nuclear arms limitation has provided the political force for reviving arms control agreements that no U.S. government can ignore. The reactivation of U.S.-Soviet arms control discussions in Geneva is but one aspect of this new trend. U.S.-Soviet maneuvering over the Geneva talks concerning the future of SALT II, new medium missile limits, and SDI research are preliminaries to a new phase of arms control that cannot be limited to European powers but must include such potentially explosive regions as Africa and the Indian Ocean. All of this affects the prospect of a return to NALT and other proposals for arms reduction such as the IOZP.

It is therefore conceivable that the Indian Ocean talks could be revived in American policy in the not-too-distant future, either through a political change or a crisis that reveals the underlying pressures toward stabilization. The reasons are both economic and strategic. The economic pressure in the United States is the national deficit, which is in large part a product of escalating military requests ($2.6 trillion for 1982–1989), while taxes have been reduced! The cost of the new CENTCOM is estimated to be $44.9 billion per annum by 1988.[25] Should there be another emergency leading to extensive deployment of naval task forces, it could go much higher.[26] Technological changes that produce new weapons systems are affecting strategy. The new Trident II submarines which are already in use and will be fully deployed by the 1990s have SLBMs capable of hitting all the industrial and the military targets in the U.S.S.R. from the Atlantic and the Pacific. The deployment of the Polaris in the Arabian Sea is therefore a case of overkill. The argument for the Polaris remaining in the Indian Ocean is as a "counterforce reserve," enabling the United States to either follow up on a first strike or to free the Trident for initial targeting. However, this is redundant, since the Trident, with its greater accuracy and range, is an invulnerable force in the Triad at the present level of technology.[27]

There is no real advantage to either side in deploying either Polaris nuclear SLBMs or cruise missiles (SLCMs) in the Indian Ocean or its extensions. There would, in fact, be an advantage to the United States on a global scale to have an agreement not to deploy SLCMs, because its coastline is longer and more populous than the Soviet Union's. The Soviet incentive would be a reduction in the complexity of U.S. nuclear capability in a region like the Indian Ocean. Thus, the advance in technology of certain weapons does facilitate agreement.[28]

**Superpower Agreements: NALT II**

The changing political climate and technological developments of the late 1980s may well provide a propitious opportunity for the reestablishment of talks between the two superpowers over arms control in the Indian Ocean and this, in turn, can create the prospect for a realistic IOZP policy. The cost of a continued arms race in this zone and the creation of yet another major theater of operations for superpower rivalry is exerting enormous internal political pressure on both superpowers to find some alternative. The increased insecurity of littoral and hinterland states has arisen from the arms race. And the escalating level of arms transfers has strengthened the desire for an Indian Ocean zone of peace. Therefore, during the 1980s and 1990s if a permanent cap can be put on the superpower rivalry, the opportunity may well present itself to make a number of agreements that will establish a framework for real disarmament.[29]

The two superpowers will need first to create a new atmosphere by reaching an accord themselves in a number of areas. The most important is the possibility of a mutual withdrawal of forces from the South Asian region where the Soviet Union has occupied Afghanistan and the United States has deployed a Poseidon SLBM capability and, since 1980, one to three battle groups. The mutual withdrawal of Soviet land forces and U.S. naval units would provide greater security for the superpowers as well as the littoral and hinterland states. The Soviet position in Afghanistan threatens Pakistan and has been used by the United States to justify an initial $3.2 billion, followed by a $4.2 billion, program of arms aid and training from 1986 to 1990. Soviet bases in Afghanistan make it possible for the Russians to attack shipping in the Gulf and the Red Sea more directly. And the U.S. presence in Pakistan provides foes of the U.S.S.R. with a close-in position on the subcontinent from which to pressure or attack the Soviets by the southern invasion route through Iran. A U.N. plan for Soviet withdrawal in return for recognition of a new representative government in Kabul has been given serious scrutiny by the superpowers and their tributaries. The U.S.S.R. will doubtless continue to play a major role in Kabul, and a compromise can be made with the insurgent factions over the nature of the regime if the U.N. proposals are supported by the West and the conservative Islamic states. Pakistan would welcome the end of the conflict that has sent over three million refugees into her territory and created domestic instability. The opposition in Pakistan, especially the Pakistan People's Party, is against the extensive CIA intervention in Afghanistan. In order to assure a negotiated Soviet withdrawal, the United States might well agree to a phase-out of its permanent naval units in the Arabian Sea.[30] The removal of the U.S. fleet would reduce the threat of an SLBM deployment, and the withdrawal of the Soviets from Afghanistan would limit their capacity or need to expand southward either into Pakistan or Iran.

The Diego Garcia base should be phased out in return for similar reductions by the Soviets at Socotra and Dahlak. The argument that Diego Garcia is useful for support action against Soviet-sponsored coups and intrusion around the littoral is based on the assumption of further Soviet expansion. If arms reduction agreements are reached for South Asia and the Gulf, the major reasons for CENTCOM and U.S. bases are removed.

The protection of the oil supply has been a major U.S. concern. These supplies

# Liberation from Dominance 151

are neither as threatened or as crucial to West European economies as they appeared to be in the past. The Soviets have little reason to try to acquire the Gulf oil supplies. Revolution threatens the Gulf states, but the presence of the U.S. fleet is an incitement to such movements rather than a deterrent. Withdrawal would do more to promote reform and regional self-reliance which is the best basis for peace.

The French, with their base at Djibouti, have a more than adequate force to deal with any closure of the Straits of Hormuz by Iran or an attempt to throttle shipping in the Gulf or through the Red Sea. The Soviet Union is not about to try to close off trade around the Cape Route. And the Straits of Malacca are protected both by the British and by the Seventh Fleet at Subic Bay, not to mention the Australians. Moreover, most of the IOZP states are opposed to these bases and would prefer to see them terminated. The Indians have said that Diego Garcia should be returned to its original inhabitants, who were never fully compensated and whose plight has become an international issue. If such action is made a part of a wider arms control agreement by the superpowers, this step would not weaken the U.S. position but in fact would be withdrawal from a vulnerable and expensive position in return for the withdrawal of the U.S.S.R. from a commanding position in the Gulf of Aden.[31]

A second subject for prospective agreement is a revival of NALT to limit each superpower to certain numbers of task forces and lengths of time (ship days) in the Indian Ocean. A return of superpower presence to pre–1980 levels should be the goal. Such limitation could start from the reality of the lower level of superpower force needed for the protection of shipping in the Indian Ocean after reductions in Southwest Asia and the Arabian Sea. The continuous presence of battle groups and squadrons would become unnecessary through the presence of an international force. The stability of small powers could be achieved. Littoral naval powers such as India and Australia have the capability to protect all straits against regional action. The French force, based at Djibouti, might also be added to an international peacekeeping naval task force. These countries are interested in ending the arms race and rivalry which threaten the security of the entire IOZP.[32]

An agreement of this kind would be in the interest of the United States because it would be based on the principle that regional powers provide the major costs of their own defense. The cost of the U.S. CENTCOM rapid deployment force, as projected into the 1980s, will be increasingly criticized. Even national security zones will be scrupulously reviewed in the interest of reducing the national deficit. As a third major theater of operations, CENTCOM will be hard to justify once its costs are known, especially as it is a political and military liability. Therefore, the practical step is to end the rivalry that is leading to these escalating expenditures and dangerous confrontations.

The Soviets would be interested in a NALT II because it would reduce the U.S. nuclear threat from the Indian Ocean and it would also limit some of the additional pressure from Pakistan and China on them. Their fears regarding

China's introduction of nuclear capability into the Indian Ocean are great. The cost of maintaining naval forces is also a burden to their economy.

A NALT II should also initially, and then in consultation with the IOZP states, establish a NWFZ for the Indian Ocean. The deployment of nuclear weapons of both the SLBM and the newer SLCM types is now negotiable for the United States. The original agreement now lapsed under SALT II to prohibit their deployment should be renewed.

To seriously consider introducing Tomahawk nuclear weapons in a landward interventionary action among the littoral and hinterland states is unwise. Any power that attempted such a strategy would immediately be severely criticized by the states and people of the Indian Ocean region. These weapons should be banned from this arena, and an agreement not to deploy them would not only be in the best interest of both the Soviet Union and the United States but would be a step toward the elimination of all types of nuclear weapons which is sought by the IOZP countries.

Verification of an agreement, as the Indians and Americans have said, is necessary, especially for the small SLCMs. However, Soviet objection to on-site inspection has changed. Detection of submarines is difficult in the Indian Ocean, especially in remote areas; but satellite technology is promising. Prohibition of nuclear weapons in many Indian Ocean ports could be standard practice. Verification systems are improving, and a major research effort would speed this program.

Superpower agreements can then be made with the IOZP discussions at the U.N. There are several agreements that would become possible, and the U.N. Ad Hoc Committee on the Indian Ocean is the best forum in which to develop such a zone of peace. These agreements are not simply regional concerns. As this analysis has shown, there is a global and regional interrelationship that cannot be separated. The failure of the Ad Hoc Committee in its first decade was due primarily to the arms race and dominance rivalry between the major powers. Since 1980 they have joined the committee, and provided they can reach broad agreements among themselves about arms limitation, the work of the committee can combine both the global and the regional interests of all states. It is very important for lasting agreements that the interests of the littoral and hinterland nations themselves not be neglected. The concerns of even the smallest of these states, regarding such issues as the exploitation of the seabed, that countries like the Seychelles and Mauritius have raised, need to be collectively resolved. The U.N. IOZP forum is an excellent one in which to give full hearing and to draft agreement. This could reactivate the disarmament conference system at the U.N. and find application to other regions where global strategic considerations intersect.

The initiative for collective self-reliance measures has come from the Indian Ocean states themselves. But under the tributary system they have not been able to carry out these aspirations. Several of these states have begun to build independent polices and self-reliance systems despite superpower intervention.

## PEOPLE'S RIGHTS: THE END OF DOMINANCE

The present U.S. system stands under judgment, and the age of our innocence or illusion is over, if it ever existed. The future is not with us, it is with all those peoples who are struggling for their human identity and dignity. Their demands are going to increase and not diminish and all the means we use to try to defeat this are doomed to failure.[33]

Liberation movements are undermining the powerful Western dominance system, but far more slowly than the original optimistic liberal estimates of the post–World War II world. These movements exist across national lines in the North and the South. They form the core of the opposition to systems of repression and apartheid and the militarization of the state and society in defense of the privileges of the rich against the poor. It may take well into the twenty-first century to end the dominance system, but the trend is clear.

### People's Rights

At the center of this resistance is an acceptance of the concept of the right of all people to peace, development, and justice.

The right to peace means the right to establish collective self-reliance systems, of zones of peace which exclude the superpower nuclear and conventional rivalry.[34] The refusal by the superpowers to honor this right is similar to the colonial mentality of the past century that assumed the right of stronger people to colonize the weak. Metropolitan powers created a world system of dominance which ignored these rights. Today, liberation recognizes clearly for the first time this right and places into the hands of people and states the means of winning back from the powerful what has been taken from them. It may be some time before the powerful states are prepared to accept these claims, but the world will be conflicted by revolution until they recognize at least a portion of this right. One of the reasons for the demise of support for the United Nations in the West has been the symbolic way that so many issues have come to reflect the claims of the weak against the powerful. Such recognition in no way justifies all the violence and even terrorism by which certain groups have tried to maintain this claim, but it does put into perspective the way in which the West has lost the moral leadership of the world. Since the struggle against Nazism gave way to the renewed attempt to impose the peace of the powerful on the poor and weak, the new superpowers have lost whatever mandate they had from humanity.

The right to development is closely related to the issue of peace.[35] New and weak states cannot develop even a minimal standard of living as long as their territories are the subject of continuous economic and military rivalries for resources, trade, and military bases. The two objectives of security and development become hopelessly entangled in superpower rivalry. And the only way small states and weaker peoples can hope to undertake a program of genuine human development is to break out of their economic dependence. This cannot happen without different forms of collective South-South self-reliance. As yet, the acceptance of this idea in the imperialistic economic systems of COMECON and OECD has not happened. The growing debt crisis of Third World countries is only one example among many. The widespread underdevelopment pattern is as much the responsibility of the dominant powers as the result of failures on the part of the comprador leadership. A shift to a nondominance economic world system can come only with new classes who recognize the injustice of the present relationship and are committed to move toward a more equitable world. The liberation movement is the source of the recognition of this claim again in the North as well as the South. The struggle over disinvestment from apartheid, as much as the rights of Third World nations to the resources of the seabed, are an integral part of this confrontation.

Revolutionary movements in Third World states to establish the claims of the poor are a widespread indication of the power of resistance, although not all acts of violence are justifiable or appropriate. But to expect the poor to accept their subjection peacefully is to deny them the dignity of resisting evil.

**A Just Social Order**

The dream of a new, just social order is not something people get from the state, which in general has been programmed to socialize and assimilate dissent, even in its more enlightened social forms. But justice, as the liberation theologians have shown us, is the product of the human conscience in all of us. Resistance to injustice may take the form of peaceful protest and possibly the acceptance of imprisonment, torture, and death. It may also lead to class and armed struggle. Ruling states and classes are usually unwilling to listen to the demands for justice in countries like South Africa before it is too late to prevent enormous conflict and bloodshed. This is a sad condition which has not changed much in the power politics of the superpowers. The alternative of enlightened reform does not come generally until it is too late. The alternatives are either to accept the rule of the unjust or to resist that evil in order to improve the prospects of future generations. It is obvious that the liberation movement has chosen resistance and the dream of a better future. Most of us in the privileged world have the opportunity for a choice—whether to support them or injustice. But the poor have no choice. They are the victims, the trampled ones, until the new age gives a meaning to their suffering.

**Transnational Communities**

Awareness of these conditions should not lead to despair, but to the hope that the world can be changed from one of inequality and injustice to a global community. We find our alienated identity, as Christian Bay has envisioned, as much through transnational communities as through the state:

> I shall argue that the way toward a communitarian and free world must begin from where we are today, within our liberal corporate societies, with a rejection of national loyalties, and with a continuing struggle to strengthen the bonds that will build mutual trust and social responsibility within our natural communities and at the same time facilitate a sense of transnational solidarity with all human communities.[36]

These are voluntary associations of interest and solidarity created out of the growing communications between peoples around this planet. People of faith and common working interests have shown how they can unite in the mutual belief in nondiscrimination in racially conflicted societies like the United States and South Africa. Political killings and torture are also repugnant to most thinking persons made aware of such conditions both in the East and West. Bay believes we cannot allow corporate or state power to dictate our values and choices but must find ways of creating these democratically, locally, and transnationally. "Small is beautiful," and the place to begin to build transnational solidarity is in our own local communities. We have more in common with the resisting blacks in South Africa and the antinuclear weapons people of New Zealand than some of our own citizens. Human interest in peace and justice transcends national narcissism and requires the end of dominance in our world.

Such powerful associations have an impact on state policy and erode the base of the superpowers. The United States cannot ignore the international law of human rights against the growing tide of world opinion. The two superpowers are constrained to end an arms race that threatens the world with extinction and their economies with bankruptcy. And in regions of the Third World such as Africa and the Indian Ocean, the comprador leaders that act as pawns in this rivalry cannot survive the liberation movements. The Shah of Iran, Botha of South Africa, and Marcos of the Philippines have all been overwhelmed by this popular movement.

The State is not our salvation. The fact that ruling classes have abused power and used the State to justify their repression cannot stop the growth of the people's consciousness and the building of transnational communities.

In finding and building solidarity with people across the barriers of dominance and imperialism, we gradually create the foundations of a new world the iron-heeled dictators cannot control.

## NOTES

1. Samir Amin, *Neo-Colonialism in West Africa* (New York: Monthly Review Press, 1972), p. 226.
2. Michael Schultheis, "Refugees: The Structure of a Global Justice Issue," *Studies in the International Apostolate of Jesuits* 8, no. 1 (June 1984), p. 29.
3. In one of the best studies of this phenomenon, David Holloway shows how a

military-political class controls the Soviet economy; see "War, Militarism, and the Soviet State," *Alternatives* 6 (1980).

4. Allan Boesak, *Farewell to Innocence* (Maryknoll, N.Y.: Orbis, 1977), p. 10.

5. Michael Randle, "Militarism and Repression," *Alternatives* 7 (1981). See also George W. Shepherd, Jr., "Non-Dominance: The Material and Moral Basis of a New Politics," Colorado Consortium on International Policy, Occasional Papers, no. 1 (University of Denver, 1984); and Fritjof Capra and Charlene Spretnak, *Green Politics: The Global Promise* (New York: E.P. Dutton, Inc., 1984).

6. Frances Fox Piven and Richard Cloward, *The New Class War: Reagan's Attack on the Welfare State and Its Consequences* (New York: Pantheon Books, 1982), p. 12.

7. Albert Szymanski, "The Socialist World System," in *Socialist States in the World System*, ed. Chase Dunn (Beverly Hills, Calif.: Sage Publications, 1982).

8. Alan Wolf has elucidated this long-term rectification view most recently in *America's Impasse* (Boston: South End Press, 1981); and "Why Is There No Green Party in the United States?" *World Policy* 1, no. 1 (Fall 1983).

9. Kairos Theologians, "Challenge to the Church: The Kairos Document," Braamfontain, S. Afr., September 25, 1985, p. 1.

10. Johan Galtung has outlined a theory of this transformation in *The True Worlds: A Transnational Perspective* (New York: Free Press, 1980).

11. Quoted in Duck Broder, "Brezhnev Asks Talks on Navies: Indian Ocean, Mediterranean Limits Urged," *Washington Post*, June 12, 1971.

12. A good summary of these objectives is found in William Stivers, "Doves, Hawks, and Detente," *Foreign Policy*, on. 45 (Winter/Spring 1981/82).

13. See Richard A. Best, "Indian Ocean Arms Control," *Proceedings*, February 1980, p. 45.

14. Ibid.

15. Stivers, "Doves,"

16. U.S. Congress, House Committee on Armed Services, *Hearings on Indian Ocean Arms Limitations and Multilateral Cooperation on Restraining Conventional Arms Transfers*, 96th Cong., 2nd sess., October 3, 10, 1978, p. 10.

17. See the statement of Dr. Gelb to the House Committee on Armed Services, Ibid., pp. 16–17.

18. Reproduced in *The Defense Monitor* 3, no. 3 (April 1974), p. 12.

19. Ibid.

20. Senator Gary Hart, "Letter on Iran-Iraq War," correspondence item no. 647, Washington, D.C., July 2, 1984.

21. U.S. Congress, House Committee on Armed Services, *Hearings on Indian Ocean Forces Limitations and Conventional Arms Transfer Limitation*, January 16, 1978.

22. Stivers, "Doves," p. 127.

23. Richard Haas, "Naval Arms Limitation in the Indian Ocean," *Survival* 20, no. 2 (March/April 1978). See also congressional *Hearings* and the testimony of Warnke and Gelb.

24. Stivers, in "Doves, Hawks, and Detente," describes well this historical progression.

25. Congressional Budget Office, *Rapid Deployment Forces: Policy and Budgetry Implications* (Washington, D.C.: CBO February 1983), p. 11.

26. One scenario is a U.S. naval escort for oil tankers in the Gulf. See Jack Anderson's column in *Rocky Mountain News*, August 27, 1984.

27. Alva M. Bowen, "Navy Nuclear Armed Tomahawk Cruise Missile," Library of Congress, Foreign Affairs and National Defense Division, issue brief no. 1B84101 (updated) (Washington, D.C.: Congressional Research Service, May 18, 1984).

28. Alva M. Bowen, *Nuclear Armed Sea-Launched Cruise Missiles*, (Washington, D.C.: Arms Control and Foreign Policy Caucus, U.S. Congress, May 12, 1984), pp.14–16.

29. George Shepherd, Jr., "Collective Self-Reliance in the Indian Ocean Zone of Peace," *IDSA Journal* (New Delhi), Summer 1982.

30. Selig Harrison has outlined this proposal in several articles, including "Cut a Regional Deal," *Foreign Policy*, no. 62 (Spring 1986).

31. An alternative national budget for the United States estimated that $13.7 billion a year could be saved if CENTCOM was removed from the military budget. This is part of the proposal to save $79.8 billion in the defense budget. Jobs With Peace Campaign, Boston, March 1986, p. 2.

32. The author first outlined these proposals at the December 1984 meeting in New Delhi of the Indo-American Task Force on the Indian Ocean, convened by the Institute for Defense Studies and Analysis and the Carnegie Endowment for International Peace. The discussions were published as *India, The United States, and the Indian Ocean* (Washington, D.C.: Carnegie Endowment for International Peace, 1985).

33. Paul Albrecht, "U.S. Christians and the World Struggle," *Christianity and Crisis*, August 16, 1976, p. 188.

34. Baffour Agyeman-Duah, "Nuclear Weapons Free Zones and Disarmament," *Africa Today*, 32, nos. 1 and 2 (1985), p. 77.

35. Ved P. Nanda, "Development and Human Rights: The Role of International Law and Organizations," in *Human Rights and Third World Development*, ed. George W. Shepherd and Ved Nanda (Westport, Conn.: Greenwood Press, 1985), pp. 290–91.

36. Christian Bay, *Strategies of Political Emancipation* (Notre Dame, Ind.: University of Notre Dame Press, 1981), p. 171.

# Bibliography

The sources are vast for this Africa and Indian Ocean regional coverage. For comparative economic data, World Bank reports and special studies, such as "Accelerated Development in Sub-Saharan Africa: An Agenda for Action" (1981), are basic. Additional material has been derived from *Africa Contemporary Record*, published in New York. The London-based monthly *South* also has up-to-date economic information. And *The Indian Ocean Newsletter* (Paris) is a general source. Government documents such as annual economic reports have been used extensively. Special studies by groups of experts, such as those by the ILO, IMF, OAU, and the Commonwealth of Nations, have been most useful. *The Country Reports of Human Rights Practices* by the U.S. State Department and the *World Military Expenditures and Arms Transfers* of the Arms Control and Disarmament Agency have provided useful data. Important hearings before House and Senate subcommittees have been consulted.

United Nations documents and records are used throughout, especially the annual reports of the Ad Hoc Committee on the Indian Ocean. Supplemental reports of this committee are available at Documentation Centers. The U.N. Center on Apartheid has a Notes and Documents Series.

In addition to the *New York Times* and *Manchester Guardian*, numerous newsletters by independent observers were consulted, including *Africa Today*, *Africa Confidential*, and *Africa News*, as were publications by parties and liberation movements, including *Sechaba* (London: ANC), *Zimbabwe Review* (Lusaka: ZAPU), *Namibia News* (SWAPO, Council for Namibia, UN), and "Creating a Popular Economic, Political, and Military Base" (New York: EPLF, irregular mimeo). For details on the documents of the liberation movements, see *The African Liberation Reader*, vols. 1–3, ed. Aguino de Branca and Immanuel Wallerstein (London: Zed Press, Ltd., 1982).

The publications of research agencies and institutes were also used. The Institute for Defense Studies and Analysis in New Delhi publishes reports, studies, and *IDSA Journal*. The International Institute for Strategic Studies in London (IISS) publishes statistics in the Adelphi Papers and *The Military Balance*, and the Stockholm International Peace

Research Institute (SIPRI) in Uppsala publishes annual reports and studies. In Washington, D.C., the Center on Defense Information has published studies of the Indian Ocean security problems in *The Defense Monitor*. Studies published by independent research institutes in South Africa such as the Bradlow Series by the South African Institute of International Affairs at Braamfontein and *Race Relations News* by the South African Institute of Race Relations in Johannesburg, have also been used. The publications of the Institute for Black Research and materials from the various political groups from the UDF to the Conservative party are available.

Western institutes with a special interest in the regions and topics of this study are numerous. They include the African Studies centers at UCLA, Berkeley, Michigan State, Denver, Boston, SAIS, and Georgetown in Washington, D.C. Scholars from these centers have contributed heavily, as indicated in the list of journal articles and books below. African and Asian universities have a growing number of first-rate specialists, from Jawarlal Nehru University in New Delhi to the University of Zimbabwe, and dozens of scholars have contributed research supplementing the long-standing centers of scholarship in the universities of London, Paris, and Uppsala.

Most useful have been the numerous reports and newsletters of activist organizations known as INGOs, such as the International Defense and Aid Fund in London and the Anti-Apartheid Movement with various branches in Europe. The Washington Office on Africa's *Notes*, the American Committee on Africa's *Action News*, and the African-American Institute's *African Report* supplied articles and reports especially relevant to U.S. policy. Other groups based in the United States, such as Trans Africa, Free South Africa, and the Eritrean Relief Committee, as well as Amnesty International in London and New York, were invaluable. Churches have begun regular newsletters on African political and economic subjects, such as the Episcopal Churchmen for South Africa in New York and the United Church of Christ which publishes *Peace and Justice*. The World Council of Churches Programme to Combat Racism in Geneva has pioneered in several areas of research and has issued a series of studies used in this book.

The following is a list of some of the most useful journal articles and books through 1986 on these subjects.

Adam, Heribert. *Modernizing Racial Domination*. Berkeley and Los Angeles: University of California Press, 1971.

———. "Minority Monopoly in Transition: Recent Policy Shifts of the South African State." *Journal of Modern African Studies* 18, no. 4 (1986).

Adam, Heribert, and Moodley, Kosila. *South Africa Without Apartheid: Dismantling Racial Domination*. Berkeley and Los Angeles: University of California Press, 1986.

Africa Fund. "U.S. Business in South Africa: Voice for Withdrawal." New York, 1980.

Aganafar, Fantu. "The Independence of Djibouti." Ph.D. dissertation, University of Denver, 1980.

Agyeman-Duah, Baffour. "Nuclear Weapons Free Zones and Disarmament." *Africa Today* 32, nos. 1 and 2 (1985).

Ahmed, Iqbal. "Iran and the West: A Century of Subjugation." In *Tell the American People: Perspectives on the Iranian Revolution*. Philadelphia: Movement for a New Society, 1980.

Ajami, Fouad. *Human Rights and World Order*. New York: World Order Model Project (WOMP), Institute of World Order, 1978.

Ake, Claude. *Revolutionary Pressures in Africa*. London: Zed Press, Ltd., 1978.
Albright, David E. "Soviet Policy in Southern Africa." *African Index*. Nov. 3, 1980.
Allen, Philip M. "Super Powers Draw Back." In *Africa Contemporary Record*. Edited by Colin Legum. New York: Africana Publishing Co., 1981–82.
Amey, Alan B., and Leonard, David K. "Public Policy, Class Inequality in Kenya and Tanzania." *Africa Today* 26, no. 4 (1979).
Amin, Samir. *Neo-Colonialism in West Africa*. New York: Monthly Review Press, 1972.
———. *Unequal Development, An Essay on the Social Formation of Peripheral Capitalism*. New York: Monthly Review Press, 1976.
———. "Self-Reliance and the New International Economic Order." *Monthly Review* 29, no. 3 (1977).
———. "The Class Structure of the Contemporary Imperialist System." *Monthly Review* 31, no. 8 (1980).
Anand, J. P. "Mauritius." *IDSA Journal* (New Delhi) 10, no. 2 (1978).
———. "The Seychelles Group: A Profile." *IDSA Journal* (New Delhi) 11, no. 3 (1979).
Anglin, Douglas G. "Economic Liberation and Regional Cooperation in Southern Africa: SADCC and PTA." *International Organization* 37, no. 4 (1983).
Babu, A. M. *African Socialism or Socialist Africa*. London: Zed Press, Ltd., 1981.
Bailey, Martin, and Rivers, Bernard. "Oil Sanctions Against South Africa." In *Notes and Documents* 12. New York: United Nations Center against Apartheid, June 1978.
Barclay, Glen St. T. "In Defense of South Africa." *Strategic Review* 10 (1982).
Bay, Christian. *Strategies of Political Emancipation*. Notre Dame, Ind.: University of Notre Dame Press, 1981.
Beazley, Kim C., and Clark, Ian. *Politics of Intrusion: The Super Powers and the Indian Ocean*. Sydney: Alternative Publishing, 1979.
Bender, Gerald J. "Angola, Left, Right, and Wrong." *Foreign Policy*, no. 43 (1981).
Benson, Mary. *Nelson Mandela: The Man and the Movement*. New York: W. W. Norton, 1985.
Best, Richard A. "Indian Ocean Arms Control." *Proceedings*, February 1980.
Betts, Richard K. "A Diplomatic Bomb for South Africa." *International Security* 4, no. 2 (1979).
Biermann, Werner. "U.S. Policy Towards Southern Africa in the Framework of Global Empire." *Review of African Political Economy* 17 (1980).
Biersteker, Thomas. "Self-Reliance in Theory and Practice in Tanzanian Trade Relations." *International Organization* 34, no. 2 (1980).
Bigo, Pierre. *The Church and the Third World*. Maryknoll, N.Y.: Orbis, 1983.
Biko, Steve. *I Write What I Like*. New York: Harper and Row, 1986.
Bissel, Richard E., and Crocker, Chester, eds. *Africa into the 1980s*. Boulder, Colo.: Westview, 1980.
Boesak, Allan A. *Farewell to Innocence*. Maryknoll, N.Y.: Orbis, 1977.
Boesan, Jannik; Storgard Madsen, Brigit; and Moore, Tony. *Ujamaa—Socialism From Above*. Uppsala: Scandinavian Institute of African Studies, 1977.
Bowman, Larry, and Clark, Ian. *The Indian Ocean in Global Politics*. Boulder, Colo.: Westview, 1980.
———. "The Strategic Importance of South Africa to the United States: An Appraisal and Policy Analysis." *African Affairs* 81, no. 3 (1982).

Boyer, Sandy. "Divesting From Apartheid: A Summary of State and Municipal Legislative Action in South Africa." New York: Africa Fund, 1983.
Browne, Robert, and Cummings, Robert, eds. *The Lagos Plan of Action vs. the Berg Report.* Lawrenceville, Va.: Brunswick Pub. Co., 1985.
Burchett, Wilfred. *Southern Africa Stands Up.* New York: Urizen Books, 1979.
Cabral, Amical. *Return to the Source: Selected Speeches of Amilcar Cabral.* Edited by African Information Service. New York: Monthly Review Press, 1973.
Callaghy, Thomas M. "The Difficulties of Implementing Socialist Strategies in Africa." In *Socialism in Sub-Sahara Africa.* Edited by Carl Rosberg and Ian Callaghy. Berkeley, Calif.: Institute of International Studies, 1978.
Campbell, Kurt M. *Soviet Policy Towards South Africa.* New York: St. Martin's Press, 1986.
Carter, Gwendolyn M., and O'Meara, Patrick, eds. *Southern Africa: The Continuing Crisis.* Bloomington: Indiana University Press, 1979.
Chege, Michael. "Revolution Betrayed, Ethiopia 1974–79." *Journal of Modern African Studies* 17, no. 3 (1979).
Clarke, D. G. "Policy Issues and Economic Sanctions on South Africa," no. 1. Geneva: International University Exchange Fund, 1980.
Clough, Michael. "Beyond Constructive Engagement." *Foreign Policy* (Winter 1985/86).
Cockroft, James D.; Gunder Frank, Andre; and Johnson, Dale L., eds. *Dependence and Underdevelopment.* New York: Doubleday, 1972.
Coetzee, David. "Commonwealth in Crisis." *Africa Asia*, no. 33 (September 1986).
Coker, Christopher. "Collective Bargaining as an Internal Sanction: The Role of U.S. Corporations in South Africa." *The Journal of Modern African Studies* 19, no. 4 (1981).
———. *The United States and South Africa 1968–1985: Constructive Engagement and Its Critics.* Durham, N.C.: Duke University Press, 1986.
Commonwealth Group of Eminent Persons. "Mission to South Africa: The Commonwealth Report." New York: Viking Penguin, Inc., 1986.
Copson, Raymond W. *South Africa: Reform Proposals/U.S. Policy.* Report no. 83–132F. Washington, D.C.: Congressional Research Service, 1983.
Crocker, Chester. "South Africa, Strategy for Change." *Foreign Affairs* 59, nos. 2–3 (Winter 1980).
———. *South Africa's Defense Posture: Coping with Vulnerability.* Washington Papers, no. 84. Beverly Hills: Sage Publications, 1981.
Currie, Kate, and Ray, Larry. "State and Class in Kenya—Notes on the Cohesion of the Ruling Class." *Journal of Modern African Studies* 22, no. 4 (1985).
Danahar, Kevin. *In Whose Interest? A Guide to U.S.–South African Relations.* Washington, D.C.: Institute for Policy Studies, 1984.
———. *The Political Economy of U.S. Policy Toward South Africa.* Boulder, Colo.: Westview, 1985.
Davies, Robert; O'Meara, Don; and Dlamini, Sipho. *The Struggle for South Africa*, 2 vols. London: Zed Press, Ltd., 1984.
Davis, Jennifer, et al. "Economic Disengagement and South Africa: The Effectiveness and Feasibility of Implementing Sanctions and Divestment." *Law and Policy in International Business* 15, no. 12 (1983).

# Bibliography

"Destabilization in Southern Africa." *The Economist*, July 16, 1983.
Dowdy, William L., and Trood, Russel B. *The Indian Ocean Perspectives on a Strategic Arena.* Durham, N.C.: Duke University Press, 1985.
Dugard, John. "Commentary," *Race Relations News*, no. 1. Johannesburg: South African Institute of Race Relations, 1977.
Dumont, René. *False Start in Africa.* New York: Praeger, 1969.
———. *Stranglehold on Africa.* London: Andre Deutsch, 1983.
Edgar, David. "Reagan's Hidden Agenda: Racism and the New American Right." *Race and Class* 22 (1981).
Emerson, Rupert. *From Empire to Nation: The Rise of Self-Assertion of Asian and African Peoples.* Cambridge: Harvard University Press, 1960.
Ergas, Zaki. "Why Did the Ujamaa Village Fail?" *Journal of Modern African Studies* 18, no. 3 (1980).
———. *The Tanzania Economy: What Went Wrong?* Jerusalem: Truman Research Institute, Hebrew University of Jerusalem, 1981.
Evans, Michael. "The Front-Line States, South Africa, and Southern African Security." *Zambezia* (University of Zimbabwe) 12 (1984–1985).
Falk, Richard. "Human Rights." *Commentary*, November 1981.
Farer, Tom S. *War Clouds on the Horn of Africa: A Crisis for Detente.* New York: Carnegie Endowment for International Peace, 1976.
Fatton, Robert, Jr. *Black Consciousness in South Africa: The Dialectics of Ideological Resistance to White Supremacy.* Ithaca: State University of New York Press, 1986.
Ferguson, Clyde, and Cotter, William R. "South Africa: What Is to Be Done?" *Foreign Affairs*, October 1978.
Firebrace, James, and Stuart, Holland. *Never Kneel Down: Drought, Development, and Liberation in Eritrea.* Trenton, N.J.: The Red Sea Press, 1985.
Foltz, William. *Elite Opinion on U.S. Policy Toward Africa.* New York: Council on Foreign Relations, 1979.
Galtung, Johan. "A Structural Theory of Imperialism." *Journal of Peace Research* 2 (1971).
———. *The True Worlds: A Transnational Perspective.* New York: Free Press, 1980.
———. "The Politics of Self-Reliance." In *From Dependency to Development: Strategies to Overcome Underdevelopment and Inequality.* Edited by Heraldo Munoz. Boulder, Colo.: Westview, 1981.
Galtung, Johan, and O'Brien, Peter, eds. *Self-Reliance: A Strategy for Development.* Geneva: Institute for Development Studies. L'Ouverture Publications, Ltd., 1980.
Geldenhuys, Deon. *The Diplomacy of Isolation: South African Foreign Policy Making.* New York: St. Martin's Press, 1984.
Gerhart, Gail M. *Black Power in South Africa.* Berkeley and Los Angeles: University of California Press, 1978.
Goulbourne, H. *Politics and the State in the Third World.* London: Macmillan & Co., 1979.
Gran, Guy. *Development by People.* New York: Praeger, 1983.
Green, R. H. *Manpower Estimates and Development Implications for Namibia.* Lusaka: United Nations Institute for Namibia, 1978.

Grundy, Kenneth W. *The Militarization of South African Politics*. Bloomington: Indiana University Press, 1986.
Gunder Frank, Andre. "The Development of Underdevelopment," *Monthly Review* 18, no. 4 (1966).
———. *Crisis in the Third World*. New York: Holmes and Mier, 1981.
Gupta, Bhabani Sen. "Scrambled Strategic View." *India Today*, November 15, 1982.
Gutierrez, Gustavo. *A Theology of Liberation*. Maryknoll, N.Y.: Orbis, 1972.
Gutteridge, William. "South Africa: Strategy for Survival." *Conflict Studies*, June 1981.
Haas, Richard. "Naval Arms Limitation in the Indian Ocean." *Survival* 20, no. 2 (1978).
Hall, Judith Vidal. "Crisis of Conscience." *South*, no. 31 (May 1983).
Halliday, Fred. *Iran: Dictatorship and Development*. New York: Penguin, 1978.
———. *Soviet Policy in the Arc of Crisis*. Washington, D.C.: Institute for Policy Studies, 1981.
———. *The Making of the Second Cold War*. London: Verso, 1983.
Halliday, Fred, with Molyneux, Maxine. *The Ethiopian Revolution*. London: Verso, 1982.
Hanks, Robert J. "The Indian Ocean Negotiations: Rocks and Shoals." *Strategic Review* 6 (1978).
Hansen, William, and Shultz, Brigette. "Dependency Theory, Social Class and Development." *Africa Today* 28, no. 3 (1981).
Hardin, Blaine. *Anti-Apartheid: Transnational Conflict and Western Policy in the Liberation of South Africa*. Westport, Conn.: Greenwood Press, 1977.
Harrington, Michael. *The Vast Majority: A Journey to the World's Poor*. New York: Simon and Schuster, 1977.
Harrison, Selig. *In Afghanistan's Shadow: Baluch Nationalism and Soviet Temptations*. New York: Carnegie Endowment for International Peace, 1981.
———. *The United States and the Indian Ocean*. Washington, D.C.: Carnegie Endowment for International Peace, 1985.
———. "Cut a Regional Deal." *Foreign Policy*, no. 62 (Spring 1986).
Hauf, Theodore. "Report on Urban Blacks and Whites." Berlin: Arnold Bergstraesser Institute for Socio-Political Research, 1980.
Henderson, K. *Sudan Republic*. New York: Praeger, 1965.
Hermasi, Elbaki. *The Comparative Study of Revolutions: The Third World Reassessed*. Berkeley and Los Angeles: University of California Press, 1980.
Hiwet, Addis. "Analysing the Ethiopian Revolution." *Review of African Political Economy*, November 30, 1984.
Holt, P. M. *A Modern History of the Sudan*. London: Weidenfield and Nicolson, 1961.
Hopkins, Terrence K., Wallerstein, Immanual, et al. *World Systems Analysis, Theory and Methodology*. Beverly Hills, Calif.: Sage Publications, 1982.
Hyden, Goran. *Beyond Ujamaa in Tanzania: Underdevelopment and an Uncaptured Peasantry*. Berkeley and Los Angeles: University of California Press, 1980.
International Labor Organization. *Employment, Growth, and Basic Needs: A One-World Problem*. New York: Praeger, 1977.
Jackson, Henry F. *From the Congo to Soweto: U.S. Foreign Policy Toward Africa Since 1960*. New York: William Morrow and Co./Quill, 1984.
Jaster, Robert S. *South Africa's Narrowing Security Options*. Adelphi Papers, no. 159. London: International Institute for Strategic Studies (IISS), 1980.
———. *A Regional Security Role for Africa's Front Line States: Experience and Prospects*. Adelphi Papers, no. 180. London: IISS, 1983.

# Bibliography

Jones, Rodney W. "Ballistic Missile Submarines and Arms Control in the Indian Ocean." *Asian Survey*, March 20, 1980.
Kahoma, C. George; Maliyamkono, T. L.; and Wells, Stuart. *The Challenge for Tanzania's Economy*. Portsmouth, N.H.: Heineman Educational Books Inc., 1986.
Kairos Theologians. "Challenge to the Church: The Kairos Document." Braamfontain, S. Afr., September 25, 1985.
Kanu, James. "Holding Back the Facts of Famine." *South*, December 1984.
Kapur, Ashok. *The Indian Ocean Regional and International Power Politics*. New York: Praeger, 1983.
Karioki, James. *Tanzania's Human Revolution*. University Park: Pennsylvania State University Press, 1979.
Karis, Thomas G. "Revolution in the Making: Black Politics in South Africa." *Foreign Affairs* 62, no. 2 (Winter 1983/84).
Kirkpatrick, Colin, and Nixson, Frederick. "Transnational Corporations and Economic Development." *Journal of Modern African Studies* 19, no. 3 (1981).
Klare, Michael, and Arnson, Cynthia. "Gunboat Diplomacy, Lightening War and the Nixon Doctrine." *Race and Class* 17, (1976).
———. *Supplying Repression: U.S. Support for Authoritarian Regimes Abroad*. Washington, D.C.: Institute for Policy Studies, 1981.
Kopkind, Andrew. "Facing South Africa." *The Nation* 243, no. 1 (November 22, 1986).
Krasner, Stephen. *Structural Conflict: Third World Against Global Liberalism*. Berkeley and Los Angeles: University of California Press, 1985.
Lancaster, Carol, and Williamson, John, eds. *African Debt and Financing*. Institute for International Economics Special Report, May 5, 1986.
Landis, Elizabeth. *Namibian Liberation: Self-Determination, Law and Politics*. New York: Episcopal Churchmen for South Africa, 1982.
Langdon, Steven. *Multi-National Corporations in the Political Economy of Kenya*. New York: St. Martin's Press, 1981.
Laski, Harold. *The State in Theory and Practice*. London: George Allen and Unwin, Ltd., 1949.
Lawyers Committee for Human Rights. *Zimbabwe Wages War*. New York, 1986.
Lefort, René. *Ethiopia: An Heretical Revolution?* London: Zed Press, Ltd., 1983.
Legum, Colin, ed. *Ethiopia, The Fall of Haile Selassie's Empire*. New York: Africana Publishing Co., 1975.
———. *Africa Contemporary Record: Survey and Documents 1981–1982*. New York: Africana Publishing Co., 1982.
Leonard, Richard. *South Africa at War*. Westport, Conn.: Lawrence Hill & Co., 1983.
Lernoux, Penny. *Cry of the People*. New York: Penguin, 1982.
Leys, Colin. *Underdevelopment in Kenya*. Berkeley and Los Angeles: University of California Press, 1974.
———. "The 'Overdeveloped' Post-Colonial State: A Re-evaluation." *Review of African Political Economy* 5 (January–April 1976).
Lijphert, Arend. *Power Sharing in South Africa*. Berkeley: Institute for International Studies, University of California, 1985.
Lipton, Merle. *Capitalism and Apartheid*. Totowa, N.J.: Rawman and Allenheld, 1985.
Lofchie, Charles. "Agrarian Crisis and Economic Liberalisation in Tanzania." *Journal of Modern African Studies* 16, no. 3 (1978).

Love, Janice. *The United States Anti-Apartheid Movement: Local Activism in Global Politics*. New York: Praeger, 1985.
McGowan, Patrick, with Kordan, Bohdan. "Imperialism in World Systems Perspective: Britain, 1870–1914." *International Studies Quarterly*, March 1981.
McHenry, Dean. "The Struggle for Rural Socialism in Tanzania." In *Socialism in Sub-Sahara Africa*. Edited by Carl Rosberg and Ian Callaghy. Berkeley, Calif.: Institute of International Studies, 1978.
Magubane, Ben. *The Political Economy of Race and Class in South Africa*. New York: Monthly Review Press, 1979.
Mandela, Nelson. *No Easy Walk to Freedom: Articles, Speeches and Trial Addresses*. Edited by Ruth First. New York: Basic Books, 1965.
———. *The Struggle is My Life*. New York: Pathfinder Press, 1986.
Manning, Marble. "The Continuing Burden of Race." *Radical America* 15, nos. 1 and 2 (1981).
Mantel-Niecko, Joanna. *The Role of Land Tenure in System of Ethiopian Imperial Government in Modern Times*. Warsaw: University of Warsaw, 1980.
Markakis, John, and Nega, Ayele. *Class and Revolution in Ethiopia*. London: Spokesman, 1978.
Marks, Shula. *The Ambiguities of Dependence in South Africa: Class, Nationalism and the State in Twentieth-Century Natal*. Baltimore, Md.: Johns Hopkins University Press, 1986.
Martin, David, and Johnson, Phyllis, eds. *Destructive Engagement: Southern Africa at War*. Harare: Zimbabwe Publishing House, 1986.
Matthews, L. L. "Kenya." In *World Armies*. Edited by John Keegan. New York: Facts on File, 1979.
Minter, William. *King Solomon's Mines Revisited: Western Interests and the Burdened History of Southern Africa*. New York: Basic Books, 1986.
Misra, K. P. "The Indian Ocean as a Zone of Peace." *India Quarterly*, January–March 1977.
Mittelman, James H. "America's Investment in Apartheid." *The Nation*, June 9, 1979.
Mohiddin, Ahmed. *African Socialism in Two Countries*. Totowa, N.J.: Barnes and Noble Books, 1981.
Moorsom, Richard. *Walvis Bay, Namibia's Port*. London: International Defense and Aid Fund, 1984.
Munger, Edwin. *Notes on the Formation of South African Foreign Policy*. Pasadena, Calif.: Castle Press, 1965.
Munoz, Heraldo, ed. *From Dependency to Development: Strategies to Overcome Underdevelopment and Inequality*. Boulder, Colo.: Westview, 1981.
Mytelka, Lynn. "The Lomé Convention and a New International Division of Labour." *Journal of European Integration*, September 1977.
Nanda, Ved P. "Development and Human Rights: The Role of International Law and Organizations." In *Human Rights and Third World Development*. Edited by George W. Shepherd and Ved Nanda. Westport, Conn.: Greenwood Press, 1985.
Neuberger, Benyamin. *National Self-Determination in Post-Colonial Africa*. Boulder, Colo.: Lynne Rienner Publishers, Inc., 1986.
Niebuhr, Reinhold. *Moral Man and Immoral Society*. New York: Charles Scribner's Sons, 1932.

Nnoli, Okwudiba. *Self-Reliance and Foreign Policy in Tanzania*. New York: NOK Publishers, 1978.
Nyerere, Julius K. *Freedom and Unity: A Selection from Writings and Speeches 1952–1965*. New York: Oxford University Press, 1967.
———. "Freedom and Development." Reprinted in *The Nationalist* (Dar es Salaam), October 18, 1968.
———. *Freedom and Socialism: A Selection from Writings and Speeches 1965–1967*. New York: Oxford University Press, 1970.
———. "South-South Options." *Third World Quarterly* 4, no. 5 (1982).
Ottaway, Marina. *Soviet and American Influence in the Horn of Africa*. New York: Praeger, 1982.
Ottaway, Marina and David. *Ethiopia: Empire in Revolution*. New York: Africana Publishing Co., 1978.
Pant, Givigesh. "A Regional Role for India's Growing Economy." *South*, August 1983.
Partjasratji, Ashok. "Self-Reliance as Alternative Strategy for Development." *Alternatives* 2, no. 3 (1976).
Perham, Margery. *The Government of Ethiopia*. Evanston, Ill.: Northwestern University Press, 1979.
Piven, Frances Fox, and Cloward, Richard. *The New Class War, Reagan's Attack on the Welfare State and Its Consequences*. New York: Pantheon Books, 1982.
Pollack, Jonathan D. "Chinese Global Strategy and Soviet Power." *Problems of Communism*, January–February 1981.
Pratt, Cranford. *Critical Phase in Tanzania, 1945–68: Nyerere and the Emergence of a Socialist Strategy*. Cambridge: Cambridge University Press, 1976.
Rogers, Barbara, and Bolton, Brian. *Sanctions Against South Africa: Exploding the Myths*. Manchester, Eng.: Manchester Free Press, 1981.
Roherty, James. "Beyond Limpopo and Zambesi: South Africa's Strategic Horizons." Paper presented to the Conference on the Indian Ocean, Perth, University of Western Australia, August 1979.
Rosberg, Carl G., Jr., and Nottingham, John. *The Myth of Mau Mau: Nationalism in Kenya*. Stanford: Hoover Institution Publications, 1966.
Ross, Dennis. "The Soviet Union and the Persian Gulf." *Working Paper*. Philadelphia: Center for Foreign Policy Development, University of Pennsylvania, 1983.
Rweyemamu, J. F., ed. *Industrialization and Income Distribution in Africa*. Westport, Conn.: Lawrence Hill, 1981.
Samatar, Ahmed I. "Underdevelopment in Somalia: Dictatorship Without Hegemony." *Africa Today* 32, no. 3 (1985).
Samuels, Mitchell A. "White Paper on the Horn of Africa." *Washington Review of Strategic and International Studies*, 1978.
Sandbrook, Richard. *The State and Basic Needs*. Toronto: University of Toronto, 1982.
Saul, John S. *The State and Revolution in Eastern Africa*. New York: Monthly Review Press, 1979.
Saul, John S., and Gelb, Stephen. *The Crisis in South Africa*. New York: Monthly Review Press, 1986.
Schlemmer, Lawrence, and Webster, Eddie. *Change, Reform, Economic Growth in South Africa*. Johannesburg: Raven Press, 1978.
Schmidt, Elizabeth. "The Sullivan Principles: Decoding Corporate Camouflage." New York: United Nations, Center Against Apartheid, March, 1980.

———. "Impose Tough Sanctions on South Africa." *New York Times*, January 17, 1986.
———. "South Africa Sanctions Fact Sheet: Lessons From Rhodesia." New York: Episcopal People for a Free South Africa, 1986.
Seidman, Ann, and Seidman, Nova. *South Africa and U.S. Multinational Corporations*. Westport, Conn.: Lawrence Hill & Co., 1977.
Seiler, John. "South Africa in Namibia: Persistence, Misperception and Ultimate Failure." *Journal of Modern African Studies* (1983).
Selassie, Bereket Habte. *Conflict and Intervention on the Horn of Africa*. New York: Monthly Review Press, 1980.
———. "The Dergue's Dilemma: The Legacies of a Feudal Empire." *Monthly Review* (July-August 1980).
Shaw, Timothy, and Adedeji, Adebaya. *Economic Crisis in Africa*. Boulder, Colo.: Lynn Reimer Association, 1985.
Shepherd, George W., Jr. *Anti-Apartheid*. Westport, Conn.: Greenwood Press, 1977.
———. "Collective Self-Reliance in the Indian Ocean Zone of Peace." *IDSA Journal* (New Delhi) 15, (Summer 1982).
———. "The United States' South African Policy: The Failure of Constructive Engagement." *Africa Today* 31, no. 2 (1984).
———. "The Power System and Basic Human Rights." In *Human Rights and Third World Development*. Edited by George W. Shepherd, Jr. and Ved P. Nanda Westport, Conn.: Greenwood Press, 1985.
Sherman, Richard. *Eritrea: The Unfinished Revolution*. New York: Praeger, 1980.
Shivji, Issa. *Class Struggles in Tanzania*. New York: Monthly Review Press, 1976.
Sick, Gary. *All Fall Down: America's Tragic Encounter with Iran*. New York: Random House, 1985.
Singham, A. W. "The Non-Aligned at the United Nations." *Mainstream* (New Delhi), February 7, 1981.
Sjollema, Baldwin. *Isolating Apartheid*. Geneva: World Council of Churches, 1982.
Sklar, Richard L.; Bender, Gerald J.; and Coleman, James S., eds. *African Crisis Areas and U.S. Foreign Policy*. Berkeley and Los Angeles: University of California Press, 1985.
Smiley, Xan. "Misunderstanding Africa." *Atlantic Monthly*, September 1982.
"South Africa in Struggle." *Monthly Review* 32, no. 11 (1986).
South African Research and Documentation Centre. *South Africa Imposes Sanctions Against Neighbours*. Harare: Zimbabwe Publishing House, 1986.
Southall, Roger. "The Beneficiaries of the Transkeian Independence." *The Journal of Modern African Studies* 15, no. 1 (1977).
South-West Africa People's Organization. *To Be Born a Nation: The Liberation Struggle for Namibia*. London: SWAPO and Zed Press, 1982.
Spencer, John H. *Ethiopia, the Horn of Africa, and U.S. Policy*. Cambridge, Mass.: Institute for Foreign Policy Analysis, 1977.
———. *Ethiopia at Bay: A Personal Account of the Haile Selassie Years*. Edited by Anne Fredericks. Algonac, Mich.: Reference Publications, 1984.
Stadler, Alf. *The Political Economy of Apartheid*. New York: St. Martin's Press, 1986.
Stavrianos, L. S. *Global Rift, The Third World Comes of Age*. New York: William Morrow and Co./Quill, 1981.

Stein, Howard. "Theories of the State in Tanzania: A Critical Assessment." *Journal of Modern African Studies* 23, no. 1 (1985).
Stephenson, David J. "Enforcing Decree No. 1 in the Domestic Courts of the United States." *Africa Today* 30, nos. 1 and 2 (1982).
Stewart, Francis. "Paying Our Own Way." *South*, August 1983.
Stivers, William. "Doves, Hawks, and Detente." *Foreign Policy* no. 45, (Winter/Spring 1981/82).
Stockwell, John. *In Search of Enemies: A CIA Story*. New York: W. W. Norton & Co., Inc., 1978.
Streak, Barry. "Organizing the Struggle: Cyril Ramaphosa, Gen. Sec. of the National Union of Mineworkers." *Africa Report* 31, no. 2 (March–April 1986).
Subrahamanyam, K. *Indian Security in Perspective*. New Delhi: ABC Publishing House, 1979.
Suliman, Ali Ahmed. *Issues in the Economic Development of the Sudan*. Khartoum: Khartoum University Press, 1975.
Szymanski, Albert. "The Socialist World System." In *Socialist States in the World System*. Edited by Chase Dunn. Beverly Hills: Sage Publications, 1982.
Thomas, Clive. *Dependence and Transformation*. New York: Monthly Review Press, 1979.
Thomas, Franklin, ed. *South Africa: Time Running Out*. Rockefeller Commission Report. Berkeley and Los Angeles: University of California Press, 1981.
Thompson, Carol. *Challenge to Imperialism: The Frontline States in the Liberation of Zimbabwe*. Harare: Zimbabwe Publishing House, 1985.
———. "SADCC's Struggle for Economic Liberation." *Africa Report* 31, no. 4, (1986), pp. 59–64.
Thompson, W. Scott. "The Persian Gulf and the Correlation of Forces." *International Security* 7, no. 1 (1982).
Tullis, F. Leonard. *Politics and Social Change in Third World Countries*. New York: John Wiley and Sons, 1973.
Tutu, Desmond. "Black South African Perspective and the Reagan Administration." *TransAfrica Forum* 1, no. 1 (1982).
Ungar, Sanford, and Vale, Peter. "Why Constructive Engagement Failed." *Foreign Affairs*, Winter 1985/86.
Utley, Garrick. "Globalism or Regionalism? United States Policy Towards Southern Africa." London: International Institute for Strategic Studies, 1980.
Vail, David J. *Technology for Ujamaa, Village Development in Tanzania*. Foreign and Comparative Studies, African Series, vol. 18. Syracuse, N.Y.: Syracuse University Press, 1979.
Wai, Dunstan. "Revolution, Rhetoric, and Reality in the Sudan." *Journal of Modern African Studies*, 17, no. 1 (1979).
Wall, Patrick. *The Indian Ocean and the Threat to the West*. London: Stacey International, 1975.
Wallerstein, Immanuel. *The Modern World, Capitalist Agriculture and the Origins of the European World Economy in the 16th Century*. New York: Academic Press, 1974.
Wallerstein, Immanuel, and de Bragance, Aguino, eds. *The African Liberation Reader*, vols. 1–3. London: Zed Press, Ltd., 1982.

Walters, Ron. "Uranium Politics and U.S. Foreign Policy in Southern Africa." *Journal of Southern African Affairs* 4, no. 3 (July 1979).
Warianwalla, Bharat. "Timid Search for Status." *Seminar* (New Delhi), December 1980.
Williams, William Appleman. *Empire as a Way of Life*. New York: Oxford University Press, 1980.
Wirsing, Robert, and Roherty, James. "The United States and Pakistan." *International Affairs* 58 (1982).
Wolf, Alan. *America's Impasse*. Boston: South End Press, 1981.
―――. "Why Is There No Green Party in the United States?" *World Policy* 1, no. 1 (1983).
Wolfers, Michael. "Race and Class in Sudan." *Race and Class* 23 (1981).
Wright, Sanford. "Constructive Disengagement: U.S. Sanctions Against South Africa." *The Black Scholar*, November–December 1985.
Yahuda, Michael B. *China's Role in World Affairs*. New York: St. Martin's Press, 1978.
Yeaker, Roger. *Tanzania: An African Experiment*. Boulder, Colo.: Westview, 1982.
Young, Andrew. "The United States and Africa." *Foreign Affairs* 59, nos. 2–3 (1980).
Young, Crawford. *Ideology and Development in Africa*. New Haven, Conn.: Yale University Press, 1983.

# Index

ACP (African, Caribbean, and Pacific), trading zones, 132
Aden, 73
Afghanistan, 6, 13, 15, 28, 121, 126, 129–30, 133, 134, 143, 150
African National Congress (ANC), 27, 29, 30, 36–40, 52, 80, 115; infiltration into Frontline, 51; nonracial character of, 34; and transition to socialism, 54
Afrikaner Resistance Movement, 36, 54
Agency for International Development (AID): in Ethiopia, 71, 82; in the Sudan, 85; in Tanzania, 108
Agriculture: in Kenya, 101; in Mozambique, 112; in Namibia, 44; in Tanzania, 111–12
Ahmed, Abdullah Yusuf, 80
Ajami, Fouad, 124
AKTUR, 47–48
All-Ethiopian Socialist Movement (MEISON), 73, 75, 76
Aman, General, 75, 82
American Committee of Africa (ACOA), 52, 100
Amin, Idi, 94, 101, 125
ANC. *See* African National Congress
Andom, General Aman Michael, 74
Angola, 23, 26, 29, 43, 45, 48, 58, 110, 115, 135, 148

Antiapartheid, 41, 59
Anya Nya, 84, 85
ANZUS (Australia, New Zealand, and United States), 129
Apartheid, 25, 37, 58, 135, 154; in Namibia, 45. *See also* South Africa
Arab-Israel October War, 70, 72
Armaments Development and Production Corporation (ARMSCOR), 24
Arusha Declaration, 105, 110, 113
Asians, in East Africa, 98
Assab, 81, 82
Association of Concerned African Scholars, 52
Australia, and the IOZP, 129, 151
Azanian People's Organization, 34

Barre, General Said, 72, 78, 79, 80, 101
Bay, Christian, 155
Beira Corridor, 135
Berbera, Somalia, 78, 79, 147
Black People's Convention, 37
Black Sash, 35
Boesak, Allan, 14, 37, 142
Botha, Pieter, 34–35, 37, 42, 48, 110, 135
Botswana, 135
British Indian Ocean Territory, 128

Buthelezi, Chief M. Gatsha, 34, 35; behind Mandela in polls, 38; rivalry with ANC, 40; trade unions, 37

Cabral, Amilcar, 33, 120, 122; on "progressive petite bourgeoisie," 14, 37, 95
Canada, in relation to Tanzania, 109, 114, 125
Cape of Good Hope, 22, 23, 24, 45, 53
Carter administration, 24, 27, 32, 121, 145; approval of $140 million for military in the Sudan, 86; arms control advocates in, 146–47; failure to support Barre, 79; reduced complicity with South Africa, 52; support of negotiations of Nambia conflict, 45
Carter Doctrine, 9
Castro, Fidel, 48, 73
Center for Defense Information (CDI), 148
Central Command (CENTCOM), 9, 22, 86, 89, 101, 129, 149, 150; as political and military liability, 151
Central Intelligence Agency (CIA), 127; in Afghanistan, 150; covert support for UNITA, 46, 51
Chad, 68, 83, 90
Chama Cha Mapinduzi party (CCM), 105
China, 27, 29, 114, 124, 125, 151–52; communalization, 112; development of new socialism, 113; and India, 134; interests in Tanzania, 108; and the PAC, 39; reduction of aid to Tanzania, 115
Chissano, 115
Ciskei Report, 34
Civil Aviation Offenses Act, 127
Client state, 11
Cold War II, 7, 9, 22, 58, 129, 141
Collective self-reliance, 15, 126, 132, 133
Coloured, 36, 49
Comprador class, 11, 22, 29, 33, 74, 81, 85, 89, 94, 95, 96, 97, 99, 110, 111, 154–55; in India, 133
Congress of South African Trade Unions (COSATU), 37, 40
Conservative party (South Africa), 36
Constructive engagement, 25, 31, 50, 55

Contact Group of Five, 43, 46, 110
Core powers, 3–6, 8; indentity of whites with, 7; regional conflicts, 4; rivalry, 3; security interests of, 22
Council for Mutual Economic Assistance (COMECON), 7, 12, 133; imperialistic economic system, 154; in South Africa, 28; tributary relationships, 9
Councils in government for Coloured and Indian minorities, 34
Crocker, Chester, 25, 46; incorrect assessment of U.S. economic interests in Namibia, 44; on international law and Namibia Decree No. 1, 50
Cuba, 12, 13, 28, 43, 109; airlift by Soviets, 76; in Angola, 48–50, 148; cultural agreements with Tanzania, 108; in Eritrea, 82; offer to mediate in Somalia, 78, 79; troops in Mozambique and Ethiopia, 125

el Dahab, General Abdel Rhaman Siwar, 87
Dahlak Islands, Soviet facility, 73
DeBeers, 135
Democratic Turnhalle Alliance (DTA), 47
Derg, 73–82, 85
Diego Garcia, 22, 26, 71, 102, 127–29, 146, 147, 148, 150, 151
Dinka, 84, 85
Disinvestment, 59
Djibouti, 69, 151

East Africa, 94–115
Economic Organization of West African States (ECOWAS), 132
Eritrea, 68, 70, 73, 74, 76–77, 80–83
Eritrean Liberation Front (ELF), 75, 81, 82
Eritrean People's Liberation Front (EPLF), 72, 81, 82
Ethiopia, 13, 70, 71–82, 124, 125, 148
Ethiopian People's Revolutionary Party (EPRP), 75
European Economic Community (EEC), trade and investment in Tanzania, 109

Federation of Indian Export Organization, 133
Federation of United Workers of South Africa (UWSA), 37
Food and Agriculture Organization, 112
Friendship and Cooperation Treaty, 78
Front for the Liberation of Mozambique (FRELIMO), 135
Frontline States, 29, 31, 43, 47, 48, 49, 94, 107, 109, 110, 115, 126, 134, 135, 144; arms for Eastern Europe, 58; cost of sanctions, 52, 53, 56; South African attacks, 51

Galtung, Johan, 6, 7, 119, 120, 123
Gandhi, Indira, 133
Gandhi, Rajiv, 133
Garang, Colonel John, 82, 83, 85, 88
General and Allied Workers Union (GAWU), 37
Grand blancs, 127
Group Areas Act, 34, 35
Gulf Council of Cooperation (GCC), 133
Gulf states oil, 30

Haig, General Alexander, 24, 46
Haile Selassie, 70, 71, 74, 81, 148
Hart, Senator Gary, 146-48
Herero, 48
Heritage Foundation, 127
Herstigte National Party (HNP), 36, 47
Hoare, Michael, 127
Hobbes, Thomas, 8
Human rights, 5, 104, 155

India, 4, 28, 39, 131, 133, 151
Indian Ocean, 22, 26, 67, 101, 102, 107, 110, 144-53, 155; arms race, 94; littoral states, 120; U.S. deployment in, 102
*Indian Ocean Newsletter, The*, 159
Indian Ocean Zone of Peace (IOZP), 107, 119, 125-28, 130-31, 144-45, 147-50
Industry, in India and Pakistan, 133
Inkatha, 40
Institute of Defense Studies and Analysis (IDSA), 134

International Institute for Strategic Studies in London (IISS), report on Kenya, 100
International Labor Organization (ILO), 123
International Monetary Fund (IMF), loans to: South Africa, 41; the Sudan, 87; Tanzania, 108-9
Israel, 12, 13, 22, 70

Jackson, Jesse, 50

Kagnew, 70, 81
Kairos, 143
Kaunda, 110
Kennedy, Senator Edward, 50
Kenya, 11, 13; agriculture, 101; economic report, 100; militarization, 101-4; tributary bases for U.S., 115; as Western tributary state, 95
Kenya African Union (KAU), 96
Kenya African National Union (KANU), 97
Kenyatta, Jomo, 96-97, 99, 101
Kiambu, 96
Kissinger, Henry, 24, 27
Kulak class, 111

Landis, Elizabeth, 46, 50
Laski, Harold, 8
Lesotho, 135
Luo, as compradors, 97
Lusaka Conference, 38
Lutheran church, influence of in Namibia, 49
Lutheran World Federation, 48

al Mahdi, Sadig, 85, 88
Mandela, Nelson, 33, 36-39
Mandela, Winnie, 35
Mangobe, Chief Lucas, 34
Masai, 111
Matajiri, 96-98, 99-104, 105, 115
Mau Mau, 96
Mauritian Militant Movement (MMM), 128
MEISON. *See* All-Ethiopian Socialist Movement

Mengistu, Lt. Col., 73, 75, 76, 77, 82–83
Military Assistance Advisory Group (MAAG), 70
Mining, in Namibia, 43–45
Moi, President, 97, 100, 101, 103
Moslem Brothers, 87, 88
Mozambique, 26, 27, 29, 107, 112, 114, 115, 121, 125, 126, 135
Mozambique National Resistance (MNR), 31, 51, 58, 135
MPL. *See* Popular Movement for the Liberation of Angola
Mugabe, 36, 115
Multinationals, 30, 99, 111, 113
Muzorewa, Bishop, 110

Namibia, 42–51, 126; mining, 43–45; South Africa's policies in, 47–48; SWAPO, 48–49; Tanzania's role in, 110, 126; Western failure in, 45–47
Nasser, 78
National Development Corporation (NDC), 113
National Forum Committee (NFC), 34, 37
National Resistance Movement (NRM), 94
National Security Council (NSC), 46
National Union for the Total Independence of Angola (UNITA), 31, 43, 46, 135; attack on Gulf oil in Angola, 58; destabilizing pressure on Zimbabwe and Mozambique, 58
Naval Arms Limitation Talks (NALT), 151
New International Economic Order (NIEO), 132
Newly industrialized country (NIC), 132
Nigeria, 125
Nimeiri, 71, 72, 83–87
Njonjo, Charles, 96, 103
Nkomati Accord, American backing of, 51
Nnoli, Okwodiba, 106, 113–14
Non-Proliferation Treaty (NPT), 25
North Atlantic Treaty Organization (NATO), 7, 23, 24, 25, 126, 148; alienation of African leadership, 27; in Namibia, 45
North-South, dependence, 121, 131–32
Nubia, 84
Nuclear-weapon-free zone (NWFZ), 130–31, 152
Nyerere, Julius, 105–14, 119, 120

Obote, Milton, 94, 97, 102
O'Dowd thesis, 30, 32, 33
Ogaden, Somali invasion, 72, 73, 76, 80
Organization for Economic Cooperation and Development (OECD), 7, 11, 12, 30, 53, 109, 133, 154
Organization of African Unity (OAU), 39, 47, 49, 81, 107, 123
Ovambo, 48
Overseas Development Council, 123

Pakistan, 12, 22, 133, 150, 151
Pakistan People's Party, 150
Pan-Africanist Congress (PAC), 29, 38–39, 115
Parastatals, 113
Patriotic Front, 110
People's Liberation Army of Namibia (PLAN), 45–46, 48
Polaris, 149
Popular Movement for the Libertion of Angola (MPLA), 23, 26, 48
Poseidon, 148

Qaddafi, 68, 78, 83

Reagan administration, 129; against "global welfarism," 132; allied with South Africa, 26; beset with huge deficits, 89; brought South Africa from tributary to subimperial status, 31; "constructive engagement," 25; decline in support of Tanzania, 108; endorsed "total strategy" of South Africa, 43; enmity toward Tanzania, 108–9; failure of "constructive engagement," 55; forced to act by sanctions, 53; Kissinger policy, 27; linkage of Cuban troops to South African occupation of Namibia, 46; linking Cuban

withdrawal from Angola to South Africa, 43; military aid to Sudan, 86; rehabilitation of apartheid strategy, 32; secret transfers of missiles to South Africa, 52; supporting South African military power, 43; support of South Africa in Namibia, 45; support of UNITA, 43
Refugees, 5; in Somalia, 79; in Sudan, 87
René, President Albert, 102, 109, 126, 127
Rio Tinto Zinc, 135
Rivonia trial, 39
RPLF, 78

Sadat, 71, 72
Safire, William, 53
SALT II, 145, 148, 149
Sanctions, 42, 54–59, 135
Savimbi, Jonas, 46
Scandinavia, aid to Tanzania, 109, 114, 125
Schroeder, Congresswoman Pat, and Council for Namibia Decree No. 1, 50
Sea-launched cruise missile (SLCM), 152
Self-determination, Eritrea, 83
Self-reliance, 6, 13–16, 58, 127, 142, 144, 152–55; as development, 119–26; Eritrean claims to, 83; among Frontline States, 52; in Seychelles, 126; South, 132; states, 95; in Tanzania, 105–14
Seychelles, 102, 109, 125, 126, 127, 152
Sharpeville massacre, 30
Shermerke, Dr. Abdar-Rashid Ali, 77
Shilluk, 84, 85
Simonstown, 24, 25
Somalia, 68–73, 77, 147; bases for U.S., 115; invasion of Ogaden, 72; as key U.S. tributary, 79; military updating by Soviets, 78; refugee state, 79; as Soviet tributary, 72; strategic interests of Soviets in, 72
South Africa, 12, 13, 22–59, 115, 121, 124–27; counter-revolutionary attacks, 109; development of nuclear weapons, 131, 133, 134, 135, 154–55; economy, 41; liberation movement, 33; major investors, 30; as subimperial state, 50
South African Black Alliance (SABA), 34, 37
South African Congress of Trade Unions (SACTU), 37
South African Defense Force (SADF), 24–25, 31, 43
Southern African Development Coordination Conference (SADCC), 52, 109, 119, 133–35
South-South cooperation, 107, 121, 123, 132, 133, 134, 135; self-reliance, 154
South-West African People's Organization (SWAPO), 27, 39, 43, 46–49, 52–54, 110
Soweto, 30
Soweto Committee of Ten, 40
Sri Lanka, 129, 130, 133
Star Wars (SDI), 127, 142, 149
State capitalism, 7
State socialism, 7
Stockholm International Peace Research Institute (SIPRI), 52, 160
Subimperial state, 12–13, 21–23; embargo on South Africa, 125; as pawns, 58; South Africa as, 25, 31
Submarine-launched ballistic missile (SLBM), 77, 78, 101, 150, 152
Sudan, the, 68, 73, 83–90; balance of trade, 86; debt, 86; economic failures, 85; oil, 83; refugees, 87; sanctuary for Eritreans, 82
Sudanese People's Liberation Army (SPLA), 84
Sudanese People's Liberation Movement (SPLM), 84–85
Suez Canal, 101
Sullivan Principles, 32
Swaardmag, 31, 37, 127, 135
SWANU, 47
Swaziland, 135
Sweden: backer of ANC, 39; nonmilitary aid to SWAPO, 48

Tambo, Oliver, 38, 39, 40, 54–55
TANU, 110
Tanzania, 94, 99; economic report, 100;

self-reliance, 104–15; tributary status, 107, 124, 125, 126, 130, 135
Tanzania Industrial Bank (TIB), 113
TAZARA, 108, 114, 135
Thatcher, Prime Minister Margaret, 109
Thee, Marek, 10
Tomahawk nuclear weapons, 152
Tourism, in Kenya, 99–100
Trade unions, in South Africa, 35, 53
Transnational political class, 10–11, 44
Trans World Airlines, in Ethiopia, 70
Treurnicht, Andries, 35–36
Tributary, 3, 6–8, 13, 93, 143; cost of, 90; Ethiopia, 70; Horn of Africa, 68; Nimeiri and Sadat, 71; as pawns, 58; Russia and the United States, 71; Somalia, 71; state, 5; the Sudan as, 86; system, 5; Uganda as, 94
Tributary class, 4, 22, 45, 93, 96, 123, 152
Trident II, 149
Tutu, Bishop: on sanctions, 55

Uganda, as Soviet tributary, 94
Ujamaa, 105; as socialist, 106, 111
UNESCO, 16
Unilateral declaration of independence (UDI), 57, 96, 105
Union of Soviet Socialist Republics (USSR), 8–13, 72–74, 102, 108, 115, 124, 129, 130, 133, 142–44, 146; airlift of Cuban forces, 76; alignment with India, 139; arms to Tanzania, 108; arms to Third World, 125; bases in Eritrea and Aden, 101; communalism, 112; in Gulf of Aden, 151; and Horn of Africa, 67; navy, 147, 148; policy toward South Africa, 26–29; possible new accord on Horn, 89; ready to agree in South Africa, 58; in Somalia, 71; in the Sudan, 86; supporter of ANC, 39; tributary relationships on the Horn, 69
UNITA. *See* National Union for the Total Independence of Angola
United Democratic Front (UDF), 37
United Kingdom (U.K.), 102, 127–28; banking in Kenya, 99; British-trained army in Uganda, 94; colonial power, 84; Diego Garcia, 22; economic and military aid to Tanzania, 109
United Nations (U.N.), 145, 146, 152; arms ban, 24; ban on arms to South Africa, under Chapter 7, 57; Charter for IOZP, 128; Charter, Chap. 7, Article 41, 51; Committee on the IOZP, 131, 145, 146; demise of support in the West, 153; development program, 114; emergency relief program in Sudan, 87; Eritrea policy, 80; plan for Soviet withdrawal in Afghanistan, 150; Resolution 432, 50; Resolution 435, 51; sanctions, 56, 110
United States (U.S.), 8, 12, 35, 44, 86, 115; aid to Sudan, 86; arms sales, 11; arms to developing world, 125; bases in Kenya, 99; Berbera and Mombasa, 101; Cape, 25; corporations in South Africa, 41; disengagement, 53–59; economic interests on Horn, 68–70; Eritrea, 80; Ethiopia, 71; food to Ethiopia, 82; in Indian Ocean, 22–23; intrusion into Indian Ocean region, 126; Kenya as tributary of, 102–4; in Namibia, 46–52; NATO, 25; Navy, 147–51; OECD, 7; security, 9; in Seychelles, 126–30, 132, 142; in Somalia, 77–80; and South Africa, 13; veto of Ambassador Saim, 108
UWSA. *See* Federation of United Workers of South Africa

Verkrampte, 36, 53
Verligte, 34, 35
Vietnam War, 146, 148
Villagization, 122

Walvis Bay, 25, 45, 50
Warsaw Pact, 7
Western dominance, 1–3
Western Somalia Liberation Front (WSLF), 73, 75, 79
West Germany, aid to Tanzania, 109
Wiehahn Commission, 35
World Bank: in Sudan, 87; in Tanzania, 108, 112, 113

World Council of Churches, 39
World Court, 128
World War II, 8

Zambia, 135
Zimbabwe, 58, 121, 135; challenge to superpowers, 125; Soviet protection, 115; war in Southern Africa, 114
Zimbabwe African National Union (ZANU), 27
Zimbabwe African People's Union (ZAPU), 27

**About the Author**

GEORGE W. SHEPHERD, Jr., is Professor of International and African Studies at the University of Denver's Graduate School of International Studies, which he helped to establish. Among his book publications are *Anti-Apartheid: Transnational Conflict and Western Policy in the Liberation of South Africa* (Greenwood Press, 1977), *Global Human Rights*, and *Human Rights and Third World Development* (Greenwood Press, 1985). He is one of the founders of the American Committee on Africa and the African Studies Association.

www.ingramcontent.com/pod-product-compliance
Lightning Source LLC
Chambersburg PA
CBHW051100230426
43667CB00013B/2386